Amy Grant 238 Success Facts

Everything You Need To Know About /

MW01706759

Contents

House of Love (Amy Grant song) - Background

Following the huge triumph of her 1991 hit collection Heart in Motion|Heart In Motion, Amy Grant took a few time off as of transcriptioning and touring. She devised her 3rd kid in first 1992, and Sarah Cannon Chapman was born on October 11. That similar month, Grant's second Christmas collection, Home for Christmas (Amy Grant album)|Home For Christmas was disseminated, spawning 2 chief singles: Breath of Heaven (Mary's Song)|Breath Of Heaven and Grown Up Christmas List.

Grant consumed a lot of 1993 authoring tunes for her following collection, House of Love, however as well noticed time to record Songs as of the Loft, a commend and reverence collection for adolescents that gained the 1994 GMA Music Awards|GMA Music Award for Praise Worship Album of the Year. House of Love was shortly finished afterward, and the name trail, a duo with region vocalist Vince Gill, was released as its second sole.

Two adaptations of the tune remained recorded. One with maker Keith Thomas; one other with maker Michael Omartian. Only Thomas' was disseminated on the collection although Grant indicated she originally contemplated placing them either on the collection. A piece of Omartian's variant, with a somewhat further hip-hop cadence, may be perceived on the docudrama Building the House of Love, a audiovisual that recorded the creating of the collection. Omartian's variant has not ever been disseminated (the alternating adaptations on the Maxis remained remixes, not alternating recordings). Gill chanted on either adaptations.

The tune may as well be perceived over the ending acclaims of the Michael Keaton/ Geena Davis amorous farce Speechless (1994 film)|Speechless.

Every Heartbeat

Listen
|filename=Amy Grant - Every Heartbeat.ogg
|title=Amy Grant Every Heartbeat (1991)
|description=30 second tester as of Amy Grant's Every Heartbeat.
|format=Oggcol-begincol-2col-2col-end

Heart in Motion - Production

* Producers: Brown Bannister, Michael Omartian, Keith Thomas (producer)|Keith Thomas.
*** Executive Producer: Michael Blanton, Amy Grant.**
* Production Assistant: Jennifer Cooke, Todd Moore.
* Production Coordination: Richard Headen, Janet Hinde, Traci Sterling.
* Engineers: David Ahlert, Jeff Balding, Terry Christian, Gregg Jampol, Laura Livingston, Bill Whittington.
* Overdub Engineer: Steve Bishir, Terry Christian, Bill Deaton, Clark Germain, Rick Soldier Will.
* Assistant Engineers: Todd Culross, Bob Loftus, Pat McDougal, Todd Moore, Kelly Pribble.
* Mixed by: Jeff Balding, Terry Christian, Brian Malouf.
* Mixing assistant: Clif Norrell.
* Mastered by: Stephen Marcussen.
* Arranger: Keith Thomas.
* Horn Arrangements: Chris McDonald, Charlie Peacock.
* Design: Rowan Moore.
* Photography: Victoria Pearson-Cameron.

Dominic Sena - Videoography

*I Need You, Maurice White (1985)
*Say It, Say It, Elizabeth Daily|E.G. Daily (1986)
*No Easy Way Out, Robert Tepper (1986)
*Don't Walk Away, Robert Tepper (1986)
*Shake You Down, Gregory Abbott (1986)
***The Next Time I Fall, Peter Cetera Amy Grant (1986)**
*Top Gun Anthem, Harold Faltermeyer Steve Stevens (1986)
*I Wish You Were Here, Tease (1986)
*Big Mistake, Peter Cetera (1987)
*Let's Wait Awhile, Janet Jackson (1987)
*Listen to the Beat of a Heart, The Burns Sisters (1987)
*Flash in Japan, Eikichi Yazawa|Yazawa (1987)
*The Pleasure Principle (song)|The Pleasure Principle, Janet Jackson (1987)
*Should've Known Better (Richard Marx song)|Should've Known Better, Richard Marx (1987)
*They Dance Alone, Sting (musician)|Sting (1987)
*Little Lies, Fleetwood Mac (1987)
*Victim of Love, Bryan Adams (1987)
*Indian Summer, The Dream Academy (1987)
*Don't You Want Me (Jody Watley song)|Don't You Want Me, Jody Watley (1987)

*The Lover in Me, Sheena Easton (1988)
*Why'd You Lie?, Colin James (1988)
*Get to You, Dan Reed Network (1988)
*Don't Mean Nothing, Richard Marx (1989)
*Fragile (song)|Fragile, Sting (1988)
*Don't Say It's Love, Johnny Hates Jazz (1988)
*Don't Walk Away, Toni Childs (1988)
*Satisfied (Richard Marx song)|Satisfied, Richard Marx (1989)
*Miss You Much, Janet Jackson (1989)
*Rhythm Nation, Janet Jackson (1989)
*I Don't Wanna Lose You, Tina Turner (1989)
*Come Back to Me (Janet Jackson song)|Come Back to Me, Janet Jackson (1990)
*Headlights on the Parade, The Blue Nile (1990)
*I'll Be Your Shelter, Taylor Dayne (1990)
*More (The Sisters of Mercy song)|More, The Sisters of Mercy (1990)
*One Shot (Tin Machine song)|One Shot, Tin Machine (1991)
*Love Is a Wonderful Thing (Michael Bolton song)|Love Is a Wonderful Thing, Michael Bolton (1991)
*If (Janet Jackson song)|If, Janet Jackson (1993)

Honeymoon in Vegas - Track listing

#Viva Las Vegas (song)|Viva Las Vegas - Bruce Springsteen
#Hound Dog (song)|Hound Dog - (score) - Jeff Beck and Jed Leiber
#Are You Lonesome Tonight? - Bryan Ferry
#Heartbreak Hotel - Billy Joel
#Jailhouse Rock (song)|Jailhouse Rock - John Mellencamp
#Suspicious Minds - Dwight Yoakam
#Burning Love - Travis Tritt
#That's All Right - Vince Gill
#Love Me Tender - Amy Grant
#All Shook Up - Billy Joel
#Blue Hawaii - Willie Nelson
#(You're the) Devil in Disguise - Trisha Yearwood
#Wear My Ring Around Your Neck - Ricky Van Shelton
#Surrender - Elvis Presley
#Jailhouse Rock (song)|Jailhouse Rock - Elvis Presley
#That's All Right - Elvis Presley
#Can't Help Falling in Love - Bono
#It's Now either Never - Elvis Presley
#Can't Help Falling in Love - (score)
Le Donna e Mobile - Franco Bonisolli

#Hawaii Kua Uli - (score)
#Happy Talk - Peter Boyle
#Hilo March - (score)
#(Let Me) Be Your Teddy Bear - (score)
#Ka Lae O Makahonu - (score)
#Waikiki Beach - (score)
#Bali Hai - Peter Boyle

2012 Grammy Awards - Country

;Best Country Solo Performance
*'Mean (song)|Mean – Taylor Swift'
* Dirt Road Anthem – Jason Aldean
* I'm Gonna Love You Through It – Martina McBride
* Honey Bee (Blake Shelton song)|Honey Bee – Blake Shelton
* Mama's Song – Carrie Underwood

;Best Country Duo/Group Performance
*'Barton Hollow (song)|Barton Hollow – The Civil Wars'
* Don't You Wanna Stay – Jason Aldean Kelly Clarkson
* You and Tequila – Kenny Chesney presenting Grace Potter and the Nocturnals|Grace Potter
* Are You Gonna Kiss Me either Not – Thompson Square

;Best Country Song
*'Mean (song)|Mean'
*'Taylor Swift, composer (Taylor Swift)'
* Are You Gonna Kiss Me either Not
** Jim Collins (singer)|Jim Collins David Lee Murphy, songwriters (Thompson Square)
* God Gave Me You
** Dave Barnes, composer (Blake Shelton)
* Just Fishin'
** Casey Beathard, Monty Criswell Ed Hill, songwriters (Trace Adkins)
* Guitar Slinger (Vince Gill album)|Threaten Me with Heaven
**** Vince Gill, Amy Grant, Owsley (musician)|Will Owsley Dillon O'Brian, songwriters (Vince Gill)**
* You and Tequila
** Matraca Berg Deana Carter, songwriters (Kenny Chesney presenting Grace Potter and the Nocturnals|Grace Potter)

;Best Country Album

*'Own the Night – Lady Antebellum'
* My Kinda Party – Jason Aldean
* Chief (album)|Chief – Eric Church
* Red River Blue – Blake Shelton
* Here for a Good Time – George Strait
* Speak Now – Taylor Swift

Best-selling Christmas/Holiday albums in the United States - 1991–2012

Miracles: The Holiday Album / Kenny G ~ 7,277,000
Noël (Josh Groban album)|Noël / Josh Groban ~ 5,550,000
Merry Christmas (Mariah Carey album)|Merry Christmas / Mariah Carey ~ 5,261,000
These Are Special Times / Celine Dion ~ 5,257,000
Christmas in the Aire / Mannheim Steamroller ~ 3,735,000
A Fresh Aire Christmas / Mannheim Steamroller ~ 3,645,000
Christmas (Mannheim Steamroller album)|Mannheim Steamroller Christmas / Mannheim Steamroller ~ 3,493,000
Now That's What I Call Christmas! / different creators ~ 3,443,000
Christmas Eve and Other Stories / Trans-Siberian Orchestra ~ 3,347,000
A Charlie Brown Christmas (album)|A Charlie Brown Christmas / Vince Guaraldi|Vince Guaraldi Trio ~ 3,226,000
When My Heart Finds Christmas / Harry Connick, Jr. ~ 3,119,000
Christmas Extraordinaire / Mannheim Steamroller ~ 2,953,000
My Christmas / Andrea Bocelli ~ 2,901,000
Faith: A Holiday Album / Kenny G ~ 2,752,000
Christmas (Michael Bublé album)|Christmas / Michael Bublé ~ 2,749,000
Home for Christmas ('N Sync album)|Home for Christmas / *NSYNC ~ 2,713,000
Beyond the Season / Garth Brooks ~ 2,649,000
 # Home for Christmas (Amy Grant album)|Home for Christmas / Amy Grant ~ 2,542,000
The Magic of Christmas (Nat King Cole album)|The Christmas Song / Nat King Cole ~ 2,507,000
A Very Special Christmas (album)|A Very Special Christmas / different creators ~ 2,496,000
The Lost Christmas Eve / Trans-Siberian Orchestra ~ 2,261,000
A Very Special Christmas 2 / different creators ~ 2,191,000
The Gift (Susan Boyle album)|The Gift / Susan Boyle ~ 2,123,000
The Christmas Album / Neil Diamond ~ 1,911,000
Christmas Portrait / The Carpenters ~ 1,895,000
Merry Christmas (Bing Crosby album)|White Christmas / Bing Crosby ~ 1,887,000

December (George Winston album)|December / George Winston ~ 1,845,000
The Christmas Attic / Trans-Siberian Orchestra ~ 1,803,000
Let There Be Peace on Earth / Vince Gill ~ 1,787,000
Christmas Interpretations / Boyz II Men ~ 1,767,000

My Kind of Christmas - Reception

The collection gathered varied appraisals as of tunes journalism|music reviewers, a few of them condemned her voices. AllMusic corrector Stephen Thomas Erlewine authored that not one of the spic-and-span tunes are knockouts however it does propose that she might not be a meager one-album marvel. Chris Willman as of Entertainment Weekly considered that Aguilera oversings thus madly that there would not have been sufficient oxygen in the kiosk to endure one other existence shape. An corrector as of Rolling Stone condemned the collection like being chilly, enforced and exaggerate, when The Atlanta Journal-Constitution was not affected towards Aguilera's vocal capacity on the collection. On the optimistic evaluation, Andy Coleman authoring for the Evening Mail commended My Kind of Christmas as a fashionable and soulful gathering of customary Christmas carol|carols and spic-and-span matter.

My Kind of Christmas launched at numeral 38 on the Billboard 200|Billboard 200, and afterward climbed to numeral 28, its top. It finally reached its highest point on top the Billboard Holiday Albums. Due to its graph triumph, the Recording Industry Association of America (RIAA) endorsed the collection RIAA certification|platinum, experiencing traded further compared to 991,000 duplicates within the region. The Christmas Song grew to be Aguilera's 3rd top-twenty hit on the Billboard Hot 100, peaking at numeral 18 on the graph. It as well charted at numeral 22 in Canada. By the conclusion of 2000, My Kind of Christmas was the second finest vending break collection of the annum, creating Aguilera one of the 4 feminine creators to have the second finest vending break collection of a schedule annum, amid Amy Grant (1992), Mariah Carey (1994), and Jackie Evancho (2010). In November 2013, the collection accessed the International Albums graph in Gaon Chart|South Korea at numeral 37.

Hope Set High

'Hope Set High' is a 1991 sole by Contemporary Christian music|Christian tunes and pop tunes vocalist Amy Grant. It was disseminated like the second sole as of the Heart In Motion collection, and the foremost as of the collection

disseminated to Contemporary Christian music|Christian broadcast.

Hope Set High is a gloomy tune with weighty employ of drumming. Similar to a commend and reverence tune, the words in Hope Set High frequently admit God's goodness with the expression When it altogether appears down, if there is whatsoever high-quality that occurs in existence, it's as of Jesus. The song's rhythmical drill was generated utilizing a Korg Wavestation, a well-liked tool in the tunes business at the time.

Mosaic: Pieces of My Life So Far - Music

The publication is wrapped with an unique link that readers may admit in to their net browser to get back 2 gratis .mp3 downloads as of Grant's index. The gratis tunes are Sing Your Praise to the Lord as of 1982's Age to Age and Wise Up (Amy Grant song)|Wise Up as of 1985's Unguarded.

In whole, Mosaic holds words to 33 of Grant's self-penned tunes.

The Next Time I Fall

'The Next Time I Fall' is a 1986 Billboard Hot 100 No.1 tune authored by Bobby Caldwell and Paul Gordon, recorded as a duo by Peter Cetera and Amy Grant for Cetera's 1986 collection Solitude/Solitaire, and like a unaccompanied by Caldwell him self for his 1988 collection Heart of Mine. The sole extended No.1 on either the Hot Adult Contemporary|Adult Contemporary graph and the U.S. Billboard Hot 100|Billboard Hot 100 graph. It proceeded to No.1 in December 1986, still existing in that placing for one 7 days. It was proposed for a Grammy Award for Best Pop Performance by a Duo either Group with Vocals.

As a duo, the tune was Grant's foremost of 2 No.1 pop selects and her foremost raid in to the nonreligious tunes area (she had netted some No.1 selects in Contemporary Christian Music previously). Grant disseminated the tune on her Greatest Hits 1986–2004 collection and the tunes audiovisual on the comparable Greatest Hits 1986-2004 DVD.

Harpeth Hall School - Notable Students

Famous Harpeth Hall alumnus/a|alumnae include:

* Tracy Caulkins, 3-time gold-medal-winning Olympic Games|Olympic swimmer
* **Amy Grant, Grammy Dove Award conquering Singer and Songwriter**
* Reese Witherspoon, Academy Award conquering actress
* Minnie Pearl, region entertainer
* Mildred T. Stahlman, neonatology surgeon
*

Next Big Thing - Background vocalists

*Bekka Bramlett
*Jenny Gill
*Vince Gill
***Amy Grant**
*Emmylou Harris
*Kim Keyes
*Michael McDonald (singer)|Michael McDonald
*Leslie Satcher
*Dawn Sears
*Harry Stinson
*McBride the Ride|Billy Thomas
*Jeff White
*Lee Ann Womack
*Andrea Zonn

Saved by Love

'Saved by Love' is a 1988 sole by the Contemporary Christian music|Christian tunes vocalist Amy Grant. It was disseminated like the foremost sole as of her Lead Me On (Amy Grant album)|Lead Me On collection.

Chad Cromwell - Career

Cromwell commenced transcriptioning and touring with Joe Walsh in 1986,Gomez, Alex M. (November 27, 1987). Joe Walsh holding youthful, South Florida Sun-Sentinel, p. 22. Materializing on 2 collections, Got Any Gum? and Ordinary Average Guy.

In 1987, Cromwell started a cooperation with composer Neil Young. The opening meetings grew to be Neil Young The Bluenotes. Since then he has recorded and visited with Young on some times, and shows onto collections such like Freedom

(Neil Young album)|Freedom (1989), Prairie Wind (2005) Living with War (2006) and Chrome Dreams II (2007). He has as well emerged in Neil Young: Heart of Gold|Heart of Gold, a docudrama seizing the first public appearance of Neil Young's collection, Prairie Wind (along with different Young classics).Varga, George (February 23, 2006). The right chemistry: Demme, Young 'were on the similar page' for 'Neil Young: Heart of Gold', The San Diego Union-Tribune, p. ND. This was shot at the Ryman hall and directed by Jonathan Demme.

Cromwell is as well familiar for his donations to Mark Knopfler's unaccompanied collections Golden Heart (1996), Sailing to Philadelphia (2000), The Ragpicker's Dream (2002) and Shangri-La (2004). He was as well piece of Knopfler's group throughout the visits of his foremost unaccompanied collections.Morse, Steve (March 22, 1996). Mark Knopfler bears a Strait-country row on unaccompanied CD, The Boston Globe, p. 62.

Cromwell visited with Crosby, Stills, Nash Young in the summertime of 2006.[http://www.thrasherswheat.org/ritfw/nashville-august-2005.htm Neil Young evaluation, August, 2005]

He has as well operated with numerous different creators containing Dave Stewart, Vince Gill,(June 13, 2003). Pop music: Gill's going forceful, The Press-Enterprise (California)|The Press-Enterprise, p. AA3. Amy Grant, Lady Antebellum, Diana Krall, Willie Nelson,Danton, Eric R. (December 31, 2006). Rockin' at one point again: Big Al Anderson's spic-and-span collection proceeds back to his origins, The Hartford Courant, p. G1. Jackson Browne,Caudle, Todd (August 17, 1989). Browne allows tunes undertake the talking: More rock, fewer marshal this time, Colorado Springs Gazette-Telegraph, p. D5. Boz Scaggs, Wynonna, Trisha Yearwood, Miranda Lambert, Bonnie Raitt, Peter Frampton,Sandler, Adam (October 2003). Peter Frampton; Joe Bonamassa, Variety (magazine)|Variety Review Database. Allison Moorer,Novak, Ralph (September 11, 2000). The Hardest Part, People (magazine)|People '54' (11): 52. Chris Knight (musician)|Chris Knight,McGuinness, Jim (April 24, 1998). Dark aspect of Knight: A itty-bitty hard-luck tunes, The Record (Bergen County)|The Record, p. 36. Joss Stone, Rodney Crowell, Marty Stuart, and Stevie Nicks.

In the middle 2000s, Cromwell created the group Fortunate Sons alongside with Michael Rhodes, Gary Nicholson, Kenny Greenberg, and Reese Wynans. They disseminated a self-titled collection in 2004.Bumgardner, Ed (April 1, 2004). Fortunate Sons, Winston-Salem Journal, p. 9. He is as well a associate of the infrequent touring group, Big Al Anderson and The Balls, guided by erstwhile NRBQ guitar player Al Anderson.

In 2012, he emerged on The Beach Boys|The Beach Boys' workshop collection allowed That's Why God Made the Radio. In 2013, he was highlighted onto Bonnie Tyler|Bonnie Tyler's collection, Rocks and Honey.

Cromwell endorses Craviotto drums, Zildjian cymbals, DW Hardware, Vic Firth sticks, Universal Audio, Focusrite, and QuikLoc.

1991 MTV Video Music Awards - Best Female Video

'Janet Jackson — Love Will Never Do (Without You)'
* Paula Abdul — Rush Rush
* Neneh Cherry — I've Got You Under My Skin
* **Amy Grant — Baby Baby (Amy Grant song)|Baby Baby**
* Madonna (entertainer)|Madonna — Like a Virgin (song)|Like a Virgin (Truth either Dare version)

Let's Make Sure We Kiss Goodbye - Track listing

#One (Vince Gill) - 3:47
#Feels Like Love (Gill) - 4:15
#Let's Make Sure We Kiss Goodbye (song)|Let's Make Sure We Kiss Goodbye (Gill) - 4:04
#For the Last Time (Steve Diamond, Gill) - 3:52
#When I Look Into Your Heart (Gill, Amy Grant) - 3:07
#*duet with Amy Grant
#Shoot Straight as of Your Heart (Gill) - 3:52
#The Luckiest Guy in the World (Gill, Michael Omartian) - 3:34
#Little Things (Gill, Leslie Satcher) - 3:44
#Baby Please Don't Go (Gill) - 3:36
#Look What Love's Revealing (Gill, Grant) - 4:23
#That Friend of Mine (Gill, Reed Nielsen) - 4:37
#Hey God (Gill) - 3:20

1983 in music - Release Date Unknown

***Ageless Medley EP – Amy Grant**
*Ain't It Good to Be Free – Bo Diddley
*All Alone with Friends – Hank Marvin
*All the Best (Stiff Little Fingers album)|All the Best – Stiff Little Fingers
*Amore (The Hooters album)|Amore – The Hooters
*Angstlos – Nina Hagen

*Bad Influence (Robert Cray album)|Bad Influence – Robert Cray
*Bay of Kings – Steve Hackett
*Before Hollywood – The Go-Betweens
*Behind the Scenes – Reba McEntire
*The Belle Stars (album)|The Belle Stars – The Belle Stars (debut)
*The Blasting Concept – Various Artists
*Buzz either Howl Under the Influence of Heat – Minutemen (band)|Minutemen
*A Call to Us All – Teri Desario
*Catch as Catch Can (album)|Catch As Catch Can – Kim Wilde
***A Christmas Album – Amy Grant**
*Come Away with ESG – ESG (band)|ESG
*Crystal Logic – Manilla Road
*Dagger and Guitar – Sort Sol
*Dancing for Mental Health – Will Powers (actually Lynn Goldsmith)
*Desperate (Divinyls album)|Desperate – Divinyls
*Dressed for the Occasion – Cliff Richard and The London Philharmonic Orchestra (Live)
*Emergency Third Rail Power Trip – Rain Parade
*Escapade (album)|Escapade – Tim Finn
*Everywhere at Once – The Plimsouls
*Even the Strong Get Lonely – Tammy Wynette
*Fall In a Hole – The Fall (band)|The Fall
*Feeding the Flame – Sad Lovers and Giants
*Feel My Soul – Jennifer Holliday
*The First Four Years – Black Flag (band)|Black Flag
*Forged in Fire – Anvil (band)|Anvil
*Friends of Hell – Witchfinder General (band)|Witchfinder General
*Golden Shower of Hits – Circle Jerks
*Good Love Heartbreak – Tammy Wynette
*Heart to Heart – Merle Haggard
*Ich stop Zubird Dir – Die Flippers
*Imagination – Helen Reddy
*Into Glory Ride – Manowar
*Into the Unknown (Bad Religion album)|Into the Unknown – Bad Religion
*Introducing The Style Council – The Style Council
*Jonathan Sings! – Jonathan Richman
*Killer Dwarfs – Killer Dwarfs (Debut)
*Klass (album)|Klass – Bad Manners
*The Kitchen Tapes (The Raincoats album)|The Kitchen Tapes – The Raincoats
*Lesson Well Learned EP – Armored Saint
*Let's Start a War – The Exploited

*Love Is the Law (Toyah album)|Love Is the Law – Toyah (band)|Toyah

*Merry Twistmas – Conway Twitty
*Metal Magic – Pantera (Debut)
*Mommy's Little Monster – Social Distortion
*Music for the Hard of Thinking – Doug and the Slugs
*Night Dubbing – Imagination (band)|Imagination
*No Rest For The Wicked – Helix (band)|Helix
*Over the Edge – Wipers
*Passionfruit (album)|Passionfruit – Michael Franks (musician)|Michael Franks
*Platinum Blonde (album)|Platinum Blonde – Platinum Blonde (band)|Platinum Blonde (debut EP)
*Privilege (Ivor Cutler album)|Privilege – Ivor Cutler
*Prodigal Sons – The Dubliners
*The Real Macaw – Graham Parker
*Riding with the King – John Hiatt
*Secretos – José José
*Shine On (George Jones album)|Shine On – George Jones
*Shock Troops (album)|Shock Troops – Cock Sparrer
*Sleep in Safety – 45 Grave
*Song and Legend – Sex Gang Children
*Speeding Time – Carole King
*Stages (Elaine Paige album)|Stages – Elaine Paige
*Star People – Miles Davis
*Steeler (American album)|Steeler – Steeler (Yngwie Malmsteen Ron Keel's 1st group, This band's solely release)
*Strive to Survive Causing the Least Suffering Possible – Flux of Pink Indians
*Struggle For Pleasure - Wim Mertens
*Syncro System - King Sunny Ade and his African Beats
*Thank You for the Music: A Collection of Love Songs – ABBA – compilation
*That's the Way Love Goes (Merle Haggard album)|That's the Way Love Goes – Merle Haggard
*Travels (Pat Metheny Group album)|Travels – The Pat Metheny Group
*21 Years On – The Dubliners (live)
*A Walk Across the Rooftops – Blue Nile
*Water Sign (Chris Rea album)|Water Sign – Chris Rea
*We Are One – Maze (band)|Maze presenting Frankie Beverly
*Weeds Water – Riders in the Sky (band)|Riders in the Sky
*Words and Music (Tavares album)|Words and Music – Tavares (band)|Tavares
*XXV – The Shadows
*Yes Sir, I Will – Crass
*Yokan (Hunch) – Miyuki Nakajima
*You Ain't Seen Nothing Yet (album)|You Ain't Seen Nothing Yet – Bachman–Turner Overdrive – compilation
*Zeichnungen Des Patienten O. T. (Drawings of Patient O. T.) – Einstürzende Neu-

bauten

Top Christian Albums - Most number-one albums

*WOW series|WOW serials (19)
***Amy Grant (16)**
*Michael W. Smith (13)
*Steven Curtis Chapman (9)
*MercyMe (7)
*Carman (6)
*Casting Crowns (6)
*Kirk Franklin (6)
*Newsboys (6)
*P.O.D. (6)
*Third Day (6)
*Jeremy Camp (5)
*Hillsong United (band)|Hillsong United (5)
*Petra (5)
*Switchfoot (5)
*David Crowder Band (4)
*Jars of Clay (4)
*Lecrae (4)
*Mary Mary (4)
*Passion Conferences|Passion (4)
*Sandi Patti (4)
*Point Of Grace (4)
*Relient K (4)
*Chris Tomlin (4)

Op zoek naar Mary Poppins - Week three (20 December)

Angenita was the 4th Mary to be removed in the Results show on Sunday.

The show executions were:
*'Group performances:'
**Opening number: Sleigh Ride by The Ronettes
**Group numeral 1: Supercalifragilisticexpialidocious
**Group numeral 2: I Will Follow Him as of the feature Sister Act

*'Individual performances' (in direction of performance):

**Irene: Why Couldn't It Be Christmas Every Day? by Bianca Ryan
**Sophie: Wat is mijn stag by Marco Borsato
**Angenita: Santa Claus is Coming to Town by Mariah Carey
**Noortje: I Could Have Danced All Night|Kom Terug En Dans Met Mij (I Could Have Danced All Night) as of the melodic My Fair Lady
****Willemijn: Winter Wonderland by Amy Grant**
**Rosalie: Cheek to Cheek by Jane Monheit
**Carmen: A Change in Me|Dat zegt Het stag (A Change in Me) as of the melodic Beauty and the Beast (musical)|Beauty and the Beast
**Simone: All I Want for Christmas Is You (Mariah Carey song)|All I Want for Christmas Is You by Mariah Carey

*'Jury's most liked Mary Poppins:'
**Erwin van Lambaart: Simone
**Pia Douwes: Rosalie
**Thom Hoffman: Sophie

*'Sing-off:'
**Irene and Angenita remained in the Sing-Off. They chanted Nog een kans (by Vera Mann).
**Willem Nijholt selected to retain Irene and ballot Angenita off.

Target Stores - Holiday advertising

Promoting Christmas selling is a ensign of Target's marketing. Target has enlisted numerous crooning characters to advance its break selling. Amy Grant and Charlotte Church have been amid the spokespersons noticed over the annums. One specific Christmas drive highlighted LeAnn Rimes carrying out Holiday in your Heart with the Looney Tunes types (Bugs Bunny, etcetera.) row swaying alongside.

Peter Cetera - Solo career

Almost right away, Cetera sustained his vein of triumph. His foremost sole, Glory of Love (the subject to the film The Karate Kid, Part II), was a US No. 1 hit in 1986, and attained alike triumph all over the planet. It proceeded on to gain an ASCAP Award for Most Performed Songs as of Motion Pictures and a BMI Film TV Award for Most Performed Song as of a Film. It was as well proposed for either an Academy Award and a Golden Globe in the class of Best Original Song, as well like a Grammy Award for Best Pop Vocal Performance by a Male Artist.
His collection, Solitude/Solitaire, disseminated within 1986, was as well prosperous, vending over 1 million duplicates and making one other No. 1 hit sole,

The Next Time I Fall, a duo with Amy Grant, that was proposed for a Grammy Award for Best Pop Vocal Performance by a Duo either Group. Solitude/Solitaire outsold Chicago 18 (#35), the foremost Chicago (band)|Chicago collection short of him.

In 1988 he linked up with maker Patrick Leonard and disseminated his 3rd unaccompanied collection, One More Story, whoever held the No. 4 hit sole One Good Woman and Save Me, the first beginning subject for the TV show Baywatch. Leonard co-wrote 8 of 10 tunes, containing the name tune One More Story, and he as well played keyboard instrument and synthesizers on the collection. Save Me was co-written with David Foster, whoever as well co-wrote the foregoing hit Glory of Love.

The collection as well contained one other duo, Scheherazade, this time with Madonna (entertainer)|Madonna in appearance as 'Lulu Smith'. They remained accompanied alltogether by Patrick Leonard whoever had authored and created some of Madonna's strikes.

The tunes Body Language and You Never Listen To Me either characteristic David Gilmour of Pink Floyd on stringed instrument.

In 1989, Cetera recorded one other duo, this time with Cher, named After All (Cher song)|After All, that was contained on the sound recording of the film Chances Are (film)|Chances Are. It extended #6 on the US graphs..

In 1992, his ultimate collection on Warner Bros. Records, World Falling Down, was disseminated. It highlighted the Adult Contemporary #1 hit, Restless Heart (Peter Cetera song)|Restless Heart, as well like 2 additional prosperous singles: Even a Fool Can See and a duo with Chaka Khan, Feels Like Heaven.

In 1995, Cetera disseminated his foremost collection for River North Records, One Clear Voice, and highlighted the hit sole, (I Wanna Take) Forever Tonight, a duo with female actor Crystal Bernard. Following the discharge of the collection, Cetera started his foremost unaccompanied tour—accompanied by his River North labelmate, region vocalist Ronna Reeves – enduring in to 1996.

1997 accompanied You're the Inspiration: A Collection, a gathering of altogether his Duets as of over the annums, alongside with 3 re-recorded tunes he had authored when a associate of Chicago, and 2 brand spic-and-span recordings.

2001 saw the discharge of Another Perfect World.

In 2002, Cetera accomplished a potpourri of 4 of his tunes at The Concert for World

Children's Day, sponsored by David Foster and an ensemble at Arie Crown Theater in Chicago. Subsequently, this guided to his emergence, in 2003, with the Chicago Pops Orchestra on the Public Broadcasting Service|PBS tunes programme Soundstage (TV program)|Soundstage, that was transmitted all over the United States and disseminated on DVD.

From 2003 till summertime 2007, Cetera accomplished a real restricted numeral of musical performances every one annum with a 40 bit ensemble, performing re-arrangements of tunes as of all over his vocation, containing some as of his term as a associate of Chicago.

In 2004, Cetera disseminated a gathering of break epitomes, You Just Gotta Love Christmas, that highlighted context and duo voices by his oldest girl, Claire.

Cetera has sung Take Me Out to the Ball Game at Wrigley Field for a Chicago Cubs game at minimum 3 times: in 2003;[http://www.fogpog.com/showthread.php?t=4358 www.fogpog.com]. Retrieved March 21, 2010. On August 16, 2007, for a game that was broadcasted on WGN-TV; and once more on May 2, 2009 on Comcast Sports Net.

In December 2007, Cetera got on on the You Just Gotta Love Christmas journey of the United States. It pronounced his return to a customary rock group show, his foremost eversince 1996, highlighted tunes as of his 2004 Christmas collection and as of all over his vocation.

Shortly following Cetera was highlighted in the cover tale of the December 2007 subject of Bass Player (magazine)|Bass Player periodical he saw Mike Huckabee, erstwhile head of a state of Arkansas, performing deep-toned stringed instrument on TV. Cetera dispatched his praises, alongside with an autographed duplicate of the subject, to Huckabee, whoever was at that time a head of state confident in the Republican Party (United States) head of state primaries, 2008|2008 Republican primaries. Huckabee indicated, I was completely awestruck to get a letter as of Peter Cetera. ...having one of the largest deep-toned participants in my propagation offer myself a praise is like conquering New Hampshire primary|New Hampshire. Bedard, Paul (February 8, 2008). [http://www.usnews.com/blogs/washington-whispers/2008/02/28/chicago-endorses-bassist-mike-huckabee.html Chicago Endorses Bassist Mike Huckabee]. U.S. News and World Report. Retrieved March 24, 2010.

Cetera was alluded to in an ad for Heineken ale that foremost screened in summertime 2010. A youthful individual at an assisted-living home contains up a duplicate of the World Falling Down LP cover and queries one of the inhabitants wherefore he likes Cetera. The aged denizen answers that he does not like Cetera, however the women do, and if you like the women, additionally by preset, you like Cetera.

Cetera's tune Restless Heart (Peter Cetera song)|Restless Heart as of the World Falling Down collection is perceived performing in the context.

Tapestry Revisited: A Tribute to Carole King

'Tapestry Revisited: A Tribute to Carole King' is a 1995 accolade collection honoring American vocalist, composer, and Pianist Carole King. It attributes a varied lineup of creators containing Amy Grant, Celine Dion, Rod Stewart, Bee Gees and Aretha Franklin. The thought of this discharge was to re-create King's 1971 collection Tapestry (Carole King album)|Tapestry track-for-track utilizing additional creators.

The collection reached its highest point at numeral 53 on the Billboard 200[http://www.allmusic.com/album/tapestry-revisited-a-tribute-to-carole-king-r228770/charts-awards Billboard 200] and was endorsed gold in the United States.[http://www.riaa.com/goldandplatinumdata.php?content_selector=gold-platinum-searchable-database RIAA]

Mosaic: Pieces of My Life So Far - Background

Grant had been advanced toward by producers to pen a publication eversince the first phases of her vocation. Though she issued some publications for kids and relatives and a not so large break cohort publication to her 1992 tune, Breath of Heaven (Mary's Song), it was not till 2007 that Grant proclaimed that she ought to eventually issue a correct autobiography.

The book's issue was planned to concur with Grant's 30th annum in the tunes business. 2007 as well pronounced Grant's retreat as of her long-time Contemporary Christian Music record label, Word Records, and her spic-and-span transact with EMI's Sparrow Records. EMI re-released 17 of Grant's collections as digitally remastered out of the ordinary versions within the similar month as Mosaic, as well like a spic-and-span Greatest Hits (Amy Grant album)|Greatest Hits CD and DVD set, altogether of that remained cross-promoted with Mosaic in chief retail traders and on the web. Additionally, an on the web gathering of nearly all of Grant's tunes, allowed The Storytellers' Collection, and a digital ringtone store presenting different Amy Grant tunes, remained started at the similar time.

Prior to Mosaic, solely unconfirmed life stories of Grant's existence and voca-

tion had been issued. Bob Millard had written the unconfirmed Amy Grant in 1986, afterward reconsidered, upgraded, and reissued as Amy Grant: The Life of a Pop Star in 1994. Mosaic grew to be the foremost chief publication to Chronicle Grant's existence and vocation eversince her headline-making annulment as of spouse Gary Chapman (musician)|Gary Chapman in 1999, wedding to Vince Gill in 2000, introduction in to the Gospel Music Hall of Fame in 2002, return to pop tunes in 2003, and 6th Grammy gain in 2005.

Ageless Medley (EP)

'Ageless Medley' was a 1983 (see 1983 in music) expanded play|EP disseminated by Amy Grant's record label, Myrrh Records. It was disseminated within apart Compact acoustic cassette|cassette and vinyl adaptations. Even although it was developed like entirely a advertising implement, it extended the Top Ten of the Christian broadcast graphs, and gained the 1984 Grammy Award for Best Gospel Performance, Female. It was afterward highlighted onto the cartridge and CD adaptations of Grant's 1986 compiling collection The Collection (Amy Grant album)|The Collection.

The name is a mention to Grant's 1982 collection Age to Age, that is in turn a mention to a line in the words of the tune El Shaddai (song)|El Shaddai.

Compassionart - The recording

Following the withdraw, CompassionArt songwriters started transcriptioning the tunes in February at the well known Abbey Road Studios in London. Joining the songwriters remained performers Dan Needham, Tommy Sims and Akil Thompson, and designing and building remained Josiah Bell, Danny Duncan and Sam Gibson. The songwriters sustained to record tunes in March at Pentavarit Studio in Nashville, Tennessee|Nashville, joined by visitor singers Amy Grant, tobyMac and Leeland Mooring, and with Matt Bronleewe and Paul Moak making and Andy Hunt designing and building. With 14 tunes at the moment recorded, time to come transcriptioning meetings with the songwriters are designed.

The kids on tunes like 'Come to the water', 'Highly Favored' and 'There Is Always A Song', are piece of Watoto Childrens Choir and remained recorded in Kampala, Uganda at Watoto kirk studios. Engineered and recorded by Kiracho Njoroge Jude.

In extension to the songwriters, the producers, administrators, charter Institutes and representatives included altogether waived their claims and contributed their attempts on this program to CompassionArt. The tunes are to be specified via CompassionArt to aid to rise cash for the respite of hurting about the globe. One fifty per cent of the funds experienced over the songs' Lifetimes must proceed to the songwriters' aids of option, and the other 50% must proceed to a philanthropic program decided on by altogether the songwriters included.

News about CompassionArt was moved by the Associated Press, Chicago Tribune, Washington Post, Houston Chronicle, MTV, MSN, Canadian Press, ChristianMusicToday.com, Worship Musician, the fore page of Amazon.com, and additional documents worldwide.

The collection CompassionArt (album)|CompassionArt was disseminated worldwide in November 2008.

1990 in music - October–December

*October 9 - Leonard Bernstein declares his retreat as of the managing podium; he passes away 5 days afterward.
*October 20 - A Florida jury acquits 2 Live Crew of the indecency demands stemming as of a June 10 execution of their play familiar for its sensually clear and obvious words.
*October 22 – Pearl Jam, additionally designated Mookie Blaylock, play their foremost show like a group at the Off Ramp association in Seattle, Washington (U.S. State)|Washington.
***Fall – For the foremost time, Amy Grant and Gary Chapman (musician)|Gary Chapman contain a nighttime of tunes at their Franklin, Tennessee Riverstone Farm, for native adolescents. Performers contained Rich Mullins, Rick Elias, Charlie Peacock, Wes King and Michael W. Smith. The happening goes familiar like The Loft.**
*October 27 – Janet Jackson's Black Cat (song)|Black Cat extends numeral one, creating her the foremost unaccompanied creator to have 2 numeral one strikes in the 90's. It was as well the foremost tune to concurrently top on top the Billboard Hot 100 and Mainstream Rock (chart)|Mainstream Rock graph.
*November 6 - Madonna (entertainer)|Madonna deliverances her spic-and-span sole, Justify My Love. The subsequent Justify My Love (video)|music audiovisual is prohibited by MTV amid global disagreement over its sensually clear and obvious subject matter.
*November 21 - The Rolling Stones frontman Mick Jagger eventually weds long-established sweetheart Jerry Hall in a customary Hindu pomp on the isle of Bali, though the wedding's lawful bindingness is controversial.
*November 27 – Vocal cluster Milli Vanilli confesses to lip-synching strikes such like Girl You Know It's True. They afterward have their Grammy prize revoked.

*December 1 - American Broadcasting Company|ABC expresses a TV out of the ordinary subsequent the Red Hot + Blue help collection in that modern pop artists reinterpret the tunes of Cole Porter. The out of the ordinary contains audiovisual clips depicting the cultural results of AIDS.
*December 3 - Following the prohibiting of her Justify My Love (video)|Justify My Love tunes audiovisual by MTV, vocalist Madonna shows onto Nightline (US information program)|Nightline to protect the audiovisual.
*December 15 - Rod Stewart weds model Rachel Hunter.
*December 31 – The nineteenth yearly Dick Clark's New Year's Rockin' Eve with Ryan Seacrest|New Year's Rockin' Eve out of the ordinary expresses on ABC, with emergences by The Beach Boys, Bell Biv DeVoe, The Kentucky Headhunters, Nelson (band)|Nelson, The O'Jays and Sweet Sensation (band)|Sweet Sensation.

Home For Christmas (Amy Grant album)

'Home for Christmas' is the 13th collection by Contemporary Christian music|Christian tunes and pop tunes vocalist Amy Grant, disseminated within 1992 in music|1992.

Home for Christmas is Amy Grant's second break collection, the foremost being 1983's A Christmas Album (Amy Grant album)|A Christmas Album. coming off of the heels of Grant's hugely prosperous 1991 collection Heart in Motion, Home for Christmas accomplished even stronger compared to Heart in Motion on the Billboard magazine|Billboard graphs, arriving at No.2 on the Billboard 200|Billboard 200 and No.1 on the Christian collection graph. It was afterward reissued in 2003 as '20th Century Masters - The Christmas Collection: The Best of Amy Grant'. It has traded 2,542,000 duplicates as of December 2012.

Amy Grant - Special awards and recognitions

* 1992: Junior Chamber International|Junior Chamber of Commerce Young Tennessean of the Year
* 1994: St. John's University (Minnesota)|St. John University Pax Christi Award
* 1994: Nashville Symphony Harmony Award
* 1996: Sarah Cannon Humanitarian Award – The Nashville Network|TNN Awards
* 1996: Minnie Pearl Humanitarian Award – Columbia Regional Hospital|Columbia Hospital
* 1996: Voice of America Award – ASCAP
* 1996: Academy of Achievement Golden Plate Award

* 1999: an Evening with the Arts" Honor – The Nashville Chamber of Commerce, Nashville Symphony and Tennessee Performing Arts Center
*** 1999: The Amy Grant Room for Music and Entertainment – The Target House at St. Jude Children's Research Hospital|St. Jude's Children's Hospital**
* 2001: Easter Seals Nashvillian of the Year Award
* 2003: Summit Award – Seminar in the Rockies
* 2005: Hollywood stroll of celebrity induction
*** 2006: Amy Grant Performance Platform – Nashville Schermerhorn Symphony Center**
* 2007: Charter associate of Tiffany Circle – American Red Cross|Red Cross
* 2007: Inducted in to the Christian Music Hall of Fame
* 2012: Honorary Doctorate Degree of Music and Performance – Grand Canyon University

Marshall Altman - Record Producer

During his final annums like an AR head at Columbia, he as well started busily functioning as a record maker. Some of his first work contains making Marc Broussard|Marc Broussard's foremost 2 collections, Momentary Setback and Carencro (album)|Carencro, as well like an collection for the group Jupiter Sunrise. He finally left Columbia to follow being a complete time record maker in 2005, beginning the Galt Line Music label and a workshop in Burbank, California. During the manufacture of Todd Carey|Todd Carey's collection Watching Waiting he was instituted to architect Eric Robinson by Carey, and Altman and Robinson ought to resume a functioning cooperation at the Galt Line for annums afterward. At the Galt Line he ought to proceed on to make for a diversity of creators, attaining profit-oriented triumph with collections such like Kate Voegele|Kate Voegele's Don't Look Away (album)|Don't Look Away and Matt Nathanson|Matt Nathanson's Some Mad Hope. His different maker acclaims contain collections for: Bethany Dillon, Natasha Bedingfield, Gabe Dixon, Walker Hayes, Rosi Golan, Adema, Matt Wertz, Trevor Hall (singer)|Trevor Hall, Caitlin Crosby, Kimberly Caldwell, and Tom Morello and other ones.

Marshall set up the label Galt Line Music in 2007, and its foremost discharge, the eponymous collection by Curtis Peoples, appeared out in August 2008.

In 2010, Altman had a highest 10 hit in the UK of his co-write Parachute (song)|Parachute with Ingrid Michaelson for British pop vocalist Cheryl Cole's first public appearance unaccompanied collection 3 Words that proceeded #1 in the UK, Ireland, Australia and New Zealand. Marshall as well co-wrote Jessie James' 2011 sole When You Say My Name.

Altman created and co-wrote choose traces as of Amy Grant's 2013 collection How Mercy Looks as of Here, co-produced and was a co-writer on Frankie Ballard's forthcoming collection Sunshine Whiskey expected out mid-February, and co-produced Eric Paslay's collection Eric Paslay, that was disseminated on February 4.

Mosaic: Pieces of My Life So Far - Conclusion

The publication stops with Grant's own gradational stroll via her existence, devoting a section to the chief landmarks of her existence and vocation. The sequential part, allowed The Times of My Life, extends as of the author's birthing to the 2006 discharge of Time Again...Amy Grant Live on CD and DVD and her authoring of Mosaic in 2007.

Additionally, there is a discography and videography, alongside with new selling diplomas numerals, blanketing fifty Amy Grant deliverances. The discography is pursued by a limited directory of chief prizes and attainments as of Grant's vocation, containing her 6 Grammy prizes, 11 Grammy recommendations, 22 GMA Dove Award|Dove prizes, and her star on the Hollywood Walk of Fame.

Dark as a Dungeon - Recorded versions

* Merle Travis on Folk Songs of the Hills, 1946
* Cisco Houston, Early 1950s
* Tennessee Ernie Ford, (1955)
* Harry Belafonte on The Many Moods of Belafonte (1962)
* Grandpa Jones, 1963
* The Twiliters on In Concert (The Twiliters)|In Concert (1966)
* Johnny Cash on At Folsom Prison (1968)
* Merle Travis with The Nitty Gritty Dirt Band on Will the Circle Be Unbroken (1972)
* Dolly Parton on 9 to 5 and Odd Jobs (1980)
* Patrick Sky, 1985
* Wall of Voodoo on Seven Days in Sammystown (1985)
* The Seldom Scene with Charlie Waller (American musician)|Charlie Waller on 15th Anniversary Celebration (1988)
* Souled American on Sonny (1992)
* The Chieftains with Vince Gill on Down the Old Plank Road: The Nashville Sessions (2002)
* Marley's Ghost on Ghost Country (1996)
* Queens of the Stone Age, 2005
* Mark Linkous (recording as Sparklehorse) MOJO Magazine Tribute CD to Johnny

Cash (2006)
* Charlie Louvin on Sings Murder Ballads and Disaster Songs (2008)
* Kathy Mattea on Coal (2008)
* Willie Nelson on Country Music (2010)
*** Amy Grant on the Lee C. Camp Friends forte collection, Tokens 9: Back to Green (2010)**
* Maddox Brothers and Rose 1950
* John Darnielle of The Mountain Goats on The Front Porch Sessions (The Front Porch Festival, 2012)
* Slobberbone recorded a variant of Dark as a prison in 1998 on the Your apology EP

Mosaic: Pieces of My Life So Far - Lead Me On

Named following Grant's hit hit sole, Lead Me On (Amy Grant song)|Lead Me On, as of the 1988 Lead Me On (Amy Grant album)|album of the similar designation, the 3rd themed part in Mosaic is possibly the most deliberately religious in the publication, about heartfelt religious experiences with God and Grant's style to orison, Communion (Christian)|fellowship, and reverence. Included is the tale of her re-baptism ensuing her annulment, remarriage, and the birthing of her 4th kid. This part as well attributes a sixteen page, full-color outspread of pictures as of Grant's youth and 30 annum vocation.

The tune words held inside the Lead Me On (Amy Grant song)|Lead Me On part are: Lead Me On (Amy Grant song)|Lead Me On, Angels (Amy Grant song)|Angels, House of Love (Amy Grant album)|Helping Hand, 1974 (Amy Grant song)|1974, The Water (Amy Grant song)|The Water, and Breath of Heaven (Mary's Song). This produces this the second of Grant's publications to hold the perfect words to Breath of Heaven (Mary's Song)|Breath of Heaven.

1960 in music - Births

*January 3 - Mikuláš Škuta, Pianist and composer
*January 4 – Michael Stipe, head vocalist for the rock group R.E.M.
*January 8 – Dave Weckl, jazz combination drummer
*January 20 – Scott Thunes, deep-toned player
*January 22 – Michael Hutchence, singer for INXS (d. 1997)
*January 26 – Charlie Gillingham (Counting Crows)
*January 31 – George Benjamin (composer)|George Benjamin, composer
*February 3 – Tim Chandler (Daniel Amos, The Swirling Eddies)
*February 4 – Tim Booth, British rock vocalist (James (band)|James)

*February 18 – Paul Mazzolini|Gazebo, singer
*February 19 – William Holly Johnson, vocalist (Frankie Goes to Hollywood)
*February 20 – Kee Marcello, Swedish rock guitar player (Easy Action (band)|Easy Action, Europe (band)|Europe)
*February 27 – Paul Humphreys (Orchestral Manoeuvres in the Dark)
*March 4 – Thierry Pastor, French singer
*March 12 – Maki Nomiya, Japanese vocalist (Pizzicato Five)
*March 13 – Adam Clayton, bassist of rock group U2
*April 4 – Jane Eaglen, Wagnerian soprano
*April 21 – John Maher (Buzzcocks drummer)|John Maher, drum player for Buzzcocks, Flag of Convenience (band)|Flag of Convenience, The Invisible Girls
*April 23 – Steve Clark, guitar player (Def Leppard) (d. 1991)
*April 26 – Roger Andrew Taylor|Roger Taylor, English rock performer (Duran Duran)
*May 6 – John Flansburgh, American rock performer (They Might Be Giants)
*May 10 – Bono, head vocalist of U2
*June 1 – Simon Gallup, bassist of The Cure
*June 2 – Tony Hadley, singer of Spandau Ballet
*June 6 – Steve Vai, American guitarist
*June 8 – Mick Hucknall, singer of Simply Red
*June 10 – Mark-Anthony Turnage, composer
*June 12 – Meredith Brooks, American singer
*June 14 – Gary Husband, drum player, Pianist and composer
*June 20 – John Taylor (bass guitarist)|John Taylor, bassist of Duran Duran
*June 22 – Alexander Shchetynsky, composer
*July 3 – Vince Clarke, English rock composer (Depeche Mode, Yazoo (band)|Yazoo, Erasure)
*July 22
**John Prior (musician)|John Prior, Australian composer-producer-drummer (Matt Finish)
**Jon Oliva, American singer and Pianist (Savatage)
*July 23 - Billy Rutherford, Scottish singer-songwriter, performer and record maker (#Riders of the Dark|Riders of the Dark)
*July 28 – Chris Reece, drum player (Social Distortion)
*August 1 – Chuck D, Public Enemy (band)|Public Enemy
*August 7 – Jacquie O'Sullivan, Bananarama
*August 26 – Branford Marsalis, jazz musician
*August 31 – Chris Whitley, singer-songwriter (d. 2005)
*September 1 – Joseph Williams (musician)|Joseph Williams, vocalist and feature composer
*September 4 – Kim Thayil, Soundgarden
*September 8 – David Steele (musician)|David Steele, Fine Young Cannibals
*September 22 – Joan Jett, The Runaways

*October 7 – Kyosuke Himuro, Japanese vocalist (Boøwy)
*October 19 – Daniel Woodgate, Madness (band)|Madness
*October 22 – Cris Kirkwood, Meat Puppets
*October 30
**Joey Belladonna (Anthrax (American band)|Anthrax)
**Alfred Hill (composer)|Alfred Hill, composer
*November 14 - Tom Judson, American melodic playhouse actor
*November 15 - Keith Washington, American singer
*November 18 – Kim Wilde, vocalist and gardender (daughter of Marty Wilde)
*November 19 – Matt Sorum, American Drums|drummer of Guns N' Roses, Velvet Revolver and The Cult
***November 25 – Amy Grant, singer-songwriter and actress**
*December 2 – Rick Savage (Def Leppard)
*December 5 – Osvaldo Golijov, composer
*date unknown
**Greg Flesch (Daniel Amos, The Swirling Eddies)
**Priti Paintal, East Indian melodist, performing artist, tunes maker and agent

Jimmy Webb - From songwriting to larger projects

Throughout the 1970s and in to the 1980s, Webb's tunes sustained to be recorded by a few of the industry's nearly all prosperous creators. In 1977, the opening discharge of Art Garfunkel's Watermark (Art Garfunkel album)|Watermark collection comprised solely of tunes by Webb. In 1978, Donna Summer's discotheque variant of MacArthur Park grew to be a multi-million vending vinyl sole that was numeral one on the American pop tunes graphs for 3 7-day periods. In 1980, Thelma Houston recorded Before There Could Be Me, Breakwater Cat, Gone, Long Lasting Love, and What Was that Song on her collection Breakwater Cat. Leah Kunkel recorded Never Gonna Lose My Dream of Love Again and Let's Begin for her collection I Run with Trouble. The last one was accomplished live in 1980 by the born-again Bob Dylan. Tanya Tucker recorded Tennessee Woman on her collection Dreamlovers (album)|Dreamlovers.

In 1981, Art Garfunkel recorded Scissors Cut, In Cars, and That's All I've Got to Say for his collection Scissors Cut, and Arlo Guthrie recorded Oklahoma Nights on his collection Power of Love. In 1982, Linda Ronstadt recorded The Moon Is a Harsh Mistress and Easy for You to Say on her collection Get Closer (Linda Ronstadt album)|Get Closer. That similar annum, Joe Cocker recorded Just Like Always on his collection Sheffield Steel, and The Everly Brothers recorded She Never Smiles Anymore on their collection Living Legends.

From 1982 to 1992, Webb turned his center as of unaccompanied carrying out to larger-scale programs, such like feature gains, Broadway musicals, and traditional tunes. In 1982, he created the sound recording for the feature The Last Unicorn (film)|The Last Unicorn, an cartoon children's narrative, with the melodic cluster America (band)|America carrying out the tunes. That similar annum, he devised the sound recording to altogether chapters of the TV serials Seven Brides for Seven Brothers (TV series)|Seven Brides for Seven Brothers.

The subject tunes for the 1984-85 TV situation comedy E/R was authored by Webb. Then in 1985, Glen Campbell recorded Webb's Cowboy Hall of Fame and Shattered for the collection It's Just a Matter of Time. And heavyweights Johnny Cash, Waylon Jennings, Willie Nelson, and Kris Kristofferson recorded Highwayman (song)|Highwayman on the collection Highwayman. In 1988, Toto (band)|Toto recorded Home of the Brave on the collection The Seventh One. Kenny Rankin recorded She Moves, Eyes Follow for the collection Hiding in Myself. And in 1989, Linda Ronstadt recorded the collection Cry Like a Rainstorm, Howl Like the Wind, that highlighted 4 Jimmy Webb songs: Still Within the Sound of My Voice (with Webb performing piano), Adios (with symphonical plan by Webb), I Keep It Hid (with Webb performing piano), and Shattered. In 1990, John Denver recorded Postcard as of Paris on the collection The Flower That Shattered the Stone (album)|The Flower That Shattered the Stone. In 1991, Kenny Rogers recorded They Just Don't Make Em Like You Anymore on the collection Back Home Again (Kenny Rogers album)|Back Home Again.

In 1986, Webb created a oratorio, The Animals' Christmas, with Art Garfunkel, Amy Grant, and the London Symphony Orchestra. The oratorio informs the Nativity of Jesus|Christmas tale as of the outlook of creatures.

In 1987, Webb created the sound recording for the feature The Hanoi Hilton (film)|The Hanoi Hilton. That similar annum, he reunified with Campbell for the collection Still Within the Sound of My Voice, for that he authored the name tune. They pursued this up in 1988 with an collection devised nearly completely of Jimmy Webb tunes, Light Years. The collection contained the name tune, as well like Lightning in a Bottle, If These Walls Could Speak (which was recorded by Amy Grant that year) and Our Movie. Two tunes as of 1982's Seven Brides for Seven Brothers as well emerge on the collection. The record as well contained the tunes Other People's Lives, Wasn't There A Moment, I Don't Know How To Love You Anymore, and Is There Love After You. Several of those tunes afterward finished ended up on Webb unaccompanied collections.

In 1992, Webb finished a melodic named Instant Intimacy, that he elaborated with the Tennessee Repertory Theatre. The melodic held spic-and-span tunes that he and other ones ought to afterward record, containing What Does a Woman See in a Man, I Don't Know How to Love You Anymore, and Is There Love After You. That similar annum, Webb accomplished live at the association Cinegrill, carrying out What Does a Woman See in a Man and presenting some extra spic-and-span tunes, containing Sandy Cove and an aged people anthem, I Will Arise.

In 1994, Webb linked with Nanci Griffith to give the tune If These Old Walls Could Speak to the AIDS help collection Red Hot + Country created by the Red Hot Organization.

In 1997, Webb co-produced Carly Simon's Film Noir collection and donated his voices, arrangement and keyboard instrument expertises to the program that was shot for an AMC docudrama (which debuted in September 1997). He as well co-wrote the tune Film Noir with Simon. Webb repeated his part as organizer and co-producer on Simon's 2008 collection, This Kind of Love.

Brown Bannister - Credits

Bannister has created either designed and built functions for the ensuing artists:

*The Afters
*Carolyn Arends
*Susan Ashton
*Avalon (band)|Avalon
*Debby Boone
*Building 429
*Jeremy Camp
*Carman (singer)|Carman
*Bruce Carroll
*Steven Curtis Chapman
*Bryan Duncan
*Chris Eaton (British musician)|Chris Eaton
*Michael English (singer)|Michael English
Amy Grant
*Sara Groves
*Kim Hill (singer)|Kim Hill
*The Imperials
*The Katinas
*Kutless

*Rachael Lampa

*Mandisa
*David Meece
*MercyMe
*Bart Millard
*Rich Mullins
*Bebo Norman
*Out of the Grey
*Paul Overstreet
*Twila Paris
*Sandi Patty
*Charlie Peacock
*Petra (band)|Petra
*PFR
*Phillips, Craig Dean
*Point of Grace
*Kerrie Roberts
*Kenny Rogers

*Mark Schultz (musician)|Mark Schultz
*Chris Sligh
*Michael W. Smith
*Michael Tait
*John Tesh
*Third Day
*B.J. Thomas
*Kathy Troccoli
*Ronan Tynan
*Jaci Velasquez
*Steve Wariner
*Wayne Watson
*Matthew West
*Phil Wickham
*CeCe Winans
*Joy Williams (musician)|Joy Williams
*White Heart
*Darlene Zschech

GMA Dove Awards - Definition of gospel music

In 1998, expected to disagreement triggered by 2 well-liked selects by Amy Grant and Sixpence None the Richer, the GMA issued a spic-and-span meaning of canon tunes. According to the meaning, to be contemplated entitled for

the Dove Awards, canon tunes should have words that are:

* Substantially founded on with reference to past events traditional Christian veracity held in either obtained as of the Holy Bible
* An articulation of reverence of God either commend for His works; and /or
* Testimony of connection with God via Christ; and/or
* Obviously caused and enlightened by a Christian society view.

Prior to the meaning, the solely officially recognized tunes was that traded in Christian Booksellers Association associated stores. The spic-and-span norms followed in protests by a few fans and creators following thirteen items remained banned as being also nonreligious in the 1999 Dove Awards. The commands remained rescinded later, and numerous groupings banned by the rulings in 1999 remained victors in 2000.

Bartender's Blues (song) - Covers

George Jones veiled Bartender's Blues as the name trail of his 1978 collection Bartender's Blues. James Taylor chanted context voices on this variant. Allmusic commentator Stephen Thomas Erlewine calls Bartender's Blues the sturdiest tune on the collection. Janovotz rates Jones' execution further positively compared to Taylor's, asserting that Jones exhibits in what way it ought to be completed. Janovitz commendations Billy Sherrill's manufacture of Jones' interpretation, as well like Jones' vocal execution, particularly in the heart-wrenching ultimate poetry. Author Kurt Wolff calls the tune a vocal journey de influence.

Amy Grant veiled Bartender's Blues on the 2007 accolade collection George Jones Friends: 50th Anniversary Tribute Concert. Tammy Wynette chanted the tune with George Jones on the 1981 collection Encore: George Jones Tammy Wynette. Harlem Hamfats veiled the tune on Harlem Hamfats, Vol. 4.

List of Vanderbilt University people - Entertainment and fashion

* Dierks Bentley, region musician
* Joe Bob Briggs, B-movie critic
* Grandma Got Run Over by a Reindeer|Randy Brooks, composer (Grandma Got Run Over by a Reindeer)
* Paula Cale, female actor, moved to DePaul University
* Rosanne Cash, vocalist and songwriter
* George Ducas (singer)|George Ducas, region tunes artist

*** Amy Grant, modern Christian tunes creator (dropped out to follow tunes career)**
* Jill King, region tunes artist
* Lance Kinsey, actor
* Richard Kyanka, maker of comedy internet site Something Awful
* Bettie Page*, model
* Amy Ray, singer/songwriter/member of the Indigo Girls (eventually moved to Emory University)
* Dinah Shore, vocalist, female actor, and TV host
* Scott Siman, creator administrator, erstwhile presiding officer of the Academy of Country Music
* Molly Sims, model, female actor (dropped out to follow modeling)
* Brooklyn Sudano, model, female actor, and singer
* Chris Mann (singer)|Chris Mann, singer; 4th place in season 2 of The Voice (U.S. TV series)|The Voice
* Mikey Wax, singer/songwriter
* William Gray Espy, performer, The Young and The Restless

Say Once More

:For the alternating Amy Grant tune of the similar name, perceive the collection Never Alone

'Say Once More' is a 1988 sole by Contemporary Christian music|Christian tunes vocalist Amy Grant. It was disseminated like the 5th sole as of Grant's Lead Me On (Amy Grant album)|Lead Me On collection. Unlike a few of Grant's foregoing selects, this tune produced an influence on Christian broadcast however not on Pop music|pop either normal broadcast.

Say Once More is a down-tempo fancy ballad. Unlike the other 5 selects as of Lead Me On (Amy Grant album)|Lead Me On, Say Once More does not characteristic whatever clear and obvious Christian words, although it accomplished well on Christian broadcast and may possibly be interpret whichever like a nonreligious fancy tune either like a fancy message to God.

The tune ought to not be puzzled with one other Amy Grant tune of the similar designation. Grant recorded a real different-sounding tune with dissimilar words, as well named Say Once More, for her 1980 collection, Never Alone.

Christian music industry - Ghetto assertion

Christian tunes is occasionally quoted as a Ghetto, signifying that the major part of creators in the business are pigeonholed to handle only in it. These creators are separated as of the normal common, to Christian media, containing broadcast, periodicals, and publication stores. For numerous this is a aware option, nevertheless other ones, not subject matter to remain in an separated business section, aim to cross over and obtain receipt in the common trade. For numerous creators, being named Christian goes a wiktionary:stigma|stigma.

A 1997 research disclosed that a self-identified public of Christian tunes ones listening had what was contemplated a missing acknowledgment of Christian creators. The study was ordered by the Christian Music Trade Association and Z Music Television. The research ogled at some creators containing Amy Grant, BeBe Winans|BeBe and CeCe Winans, Carman (singer)|Carman, Steven Curtis Chapman, DC Talk, Sandi Patty, and Michael W. Smith. At the time of the study, every one of those creators was energetic in Christian tunes and had been thus for at minimum 9 annums, was a numerous Dove Award either-or Grammy Award victor, and had collections RIAA certification|certified Gold either developed.

Even thus, the study noticed that the Christian tunes public was no further well known with creators in the area compared to they remained with Hootie The Blowfish, a well-liked play at that time. The research decided that the expression Christian was the difficulty, bringing about a shame. It's the label, not the tunes, that dissuades, one Christian tunes head was stated like indicating, concurring with the study.

Another facet of the Ghetto is that a few creators have difficulty obtaining public with Christians expected to their non-conservative picture. Stryper is a popular illustration. Stryper experienced great sums of critique as of groupings on the Christian right, whoever reason (among additional things) that their picture as rock stars negate their espoused persuasion. One commentator authored that the wedding of nonreligious and devout components within Christian tunes contravenes altogether that God has commanded in the Bible about Doctrine of separation|separation.

The Ghetto has some results, reviewers point out that the public of such creators are frequently previously Christians, consequently restricting the influence of whatever assumed Evangelism. Another is that creators occasionally have difficulty attractive to and keeping either nonreligious and devout viewers. For example:

*One Jesus tunes creator, Randy Matthews, ran in to difficulty at an early Christian tunes fete following proclaiming an forthcoming journey with Lynyrd Skynyrd and ZZ Top. The throng, as well responding to his galvanic melodic manner, pursued him off the stage, pronouncing him to be Demonic possession|demon either Drug abuse|drug controlled. Matthews was afterward let go as of the journey.

*After Bob Dylan proclaimed his change to Christianity in 1979, he disseminated 3 collections extensively quoted as being founded on his newfound persuasion. Dylan consumed some annums touring and preaching as of stage, although he not ever grew to be a piece of the Christian tunes subculture. The effect, as one commentator bluntly places it, was that It did not work. Christian tunes fans remained distinctively dubious of Dylan's letdown to leave the planet beyond and come to be a piece of their itty-bitty Ghetto, and the planet at great exhausted swiftly of rewarding cash to perceive him chant about faith. By 1981, Dylan had let go the clear and obvious devout references; either reviewers and viewers restored his tunes to praise.

*While normally quoted as the dad of Christian rock, Larry Norman fought to obtain receipt as of the Christian tunes business, and was mostly alienated as of it for his vocation. His Upon This Rock (Larry Norman album)|1969 unaccompanied first public appearance has been depicted by nonreligious spectators as maybe the foremost sincerely established and applicable Christian rock evidence at any time recorded, and 1972's Only Visiting This Planet grew to be one of the most admired collections of altogether time in Christian tunes. Even thus, Norman grew to be, depending to CCM thus long external the normal that nearly all of today's Christian tunes fans have no thought whoever Larry Norman is.

The difficulty, as summed by one commentator, was that the tunes was also devout for nonreligious public, when concurrently also hostile for devout viewers. One commentator explains the state of affairs, expressing that for a group to be taken gravely external the Christian set, a group should remain long, long off as of that set.

Mutemath, for example charged their record label with the objective of eliminating their article as of the Christian trade. Reset (Mute Math EP)|Their foremost discharge traded nearly 30,000 duplicates, with mass of selling pending as of the Christian trade, depending to Billboard. The group had been put in the Christian trade by their record label mostly since their head vocalist, Paul Meany, was formerly with the group Earthsuit, whose Kaleidoscope Superior|only chief label discharge was disseminated on Sparrow Records|a Christian label.

This triggered the group to not get taken gravely by tunes reviewers, and by the discharge of Mutemath (album)|their complete extent collection the group started airing dissatisfaction with their state of affairs. Meany informed Tucson Weekly ...we started to perceive ourselves getting pigeonholed in to this specific society that we were not inevitably pleased to be related with... We're not attempting to sermonize via our music; we do not have a few sort of evangelistic schedule with what we are undertaking... You comprehend, you do not desire to be embarrassed of your persuasion and your faiths, however you do not desire to be advertised by that, whichever.

On the other side, a few creators handle only inside the Ghetto of Christian tunes, and notice significant triumph in undertaking thus.

Bruce Gaitsch - Other appearances

* 1977 - Jim Peterik - Don't Fight the Feeling
* 1984 - Barbra Streisand - Emotion
* 1984 - Evelyn Champagne King - So Romantic
* 1985 - Evelyn Champagne King - A Long Time Coming
* 1986 - Pauli Carman - Dial My Number
* 1986 - Madonna (entertainer)|Madonna - True Blue (Madonna album)|True Blue
* 1987 - Timothy B. Schmidt - Timothy B.
* 1987 - Richie Havens - Simple Things
* 1987 - Richard Marx - Richard Marx
* 1987 - Martha Davis (singer)|Martha Davis - Policy
* 1987 - Jody Watley - Jody Watley
* 1988 - Gary Wright - Who I Am
* 1988 - Nick Kamen - Us
* 1988 - Glenn Frey - Soul Searchin'
* 1988 - Peter Cetera - One More Story
* 1988 - Julio Iglesias - Non Stop
* 1988 - Agnetha Fältskog - I Stand Alone
* 1988 - Chicago (band)|Chicago - Chicago 19
* 1989 - Richard Marx - Repeat Offender (Richard Marx album)|Repeat Offender
* 1989 - Julian Lennon - Mr. Jordan
* 1989 - Madonna (entertainer)|Madonna - Like a Prayer (album)|Like A Prayer
* 1989 - Poco - Legacy
* 1990 - Timothy B. Schmidt - Tell Me The Truth
* 1990 - Glenn Medeiros - Glenn Medeiros
* 1990 - Marc Jordan - C.O.W.
* 1991 - Richard Marx - Rush Street
* 1991 - Tommy Page - From The Heart
* 1992 - Peter Cetera - World Falling Down
* 1992 - Freddie Jackson - Time For Love
* 1992 - Celine Dion - Celine Dion
* 1992 - Bill Champlin - Burning The House Down
* 1992 - Restless Heart (band)|Restless Heart - Big Iron Horses

* 1992 - Roger Waters - Amused To Death
* 1993 - Jay Graydon - Airplay For The Planet
* 1994 - Ednita Nazario - Pasiones
* 1994 - Richard Marx - Paid Vacation
* 1995 - Dionne Farris - Wild Seed - Wild Flower
* 1995 - Mark Winkler - Tales From Hollywood
* 1995 - Peter Cetera - One Clear Voice
* 1995 - Chicago (band)|Chicago - Night Day: Big Band
* 1995 - Sheena Easton - My Cherie
* 1995 - Michael W. Smith - I'll Lead You Home
* 1995 - Bill Champlin - He Started To Sing
* 1996 - Tamara Champlin - You Won't Get To Heaven Alive
* 1996 - Bill Champlin - Through It All
* 1996 - 4Him - The Message
* 1996 - Fee Waybill - Don't Be Scared by These Hands
* 1996 - Amy Sky - 'Cool Rain
* 1997 - Amy Morriss - Within The Sound of Your Voice
* 1997 - Lara Fabian - Pure
* 1997 - Richard Marx - Flesh Bone
* 1998 - Deborah Franco - Deborah Franco
* 1999 - Yolanda Adams - Mountain High...Valley Low
* 2000 - Wayne Watson - Wayne Watson
* 2000 - Kenny Rogers - There You Go Again
* 2000 - Elton John - The Road To El Dorado
* 2000 - Tammy Trent - Set You Free
* 2000 - Richard Marx - Days in Avalon
* 2000 - Gladys Knight - At Last
* 2001 - Kelly Keagy - Time Passes
* 2001 - Elton John - Songs as of the West Coast
* 2001 - Jim Brickman - Simple Things
* 2001 - Hanne Boel - My Kindred Sprit
* 2001 - Peter Cetera - Another Perfect World
* 2001 - Charlotte Church - Enchantment
* 2002 - Jim Brickman - Valentine
* **2003 - Amy Grant Simple Things**
* 2003 - Rodney Atkins - Honesty
* 2004 - Joshua Payne - Your Love, My Home
* 2004 - Peter Cetera - You Just Gotta Love Christmas
* 2004 - Bebo Norman - Try
* 2004 - Richard Marx - My Own Best Enemy
* 2004 - Joe Cocker - Heart Soul
* 2004 - Michael W. Smith - Healing Rain
* 2005 - Peter Cetera - Faithfully

* 2005 - Cy Curnin - Mayfly
* 2006 - Michael W. Smith - Stand
* 2006 - Kelly Keagy - I'm Alive
* 2007 - Michael Paige - Michael Paige
* 2008 - Bill Champlin - No Place Left To Fall
* 2009 - Adele Morgan - This One Life
* 2011 - George Canyon - Better Be Home Soon
* 2012 - Harry Shearer - Can't Take A Hint
* 2013 - Fergie Frederiksen - Any Given Moment
* 2013 - Lara Fabian - Le Secret
* 2014 - Waylon (Dutch singer)|Waylon - Heaven After Midnight

Rock music - Christian rock

Rock has been condemned by a few Christian devout directors, whoever have sentenced it like unethical, anti-Christian and even devilish.J. J. Thompson, Raised by Wolves: the Story of Christian Rock Roll (Toronto: ECW Press, 2000), ISBN 1-55022-421-2, pp. 30–1. However, Christian rock started to create in the belated 1960s, especially out of the Jesus motion starting in Southern California, and appeared as a sub-genre in the 1970s with creators like Larry Norman, normally noticed like the foremost chief star of Christian rock.J. R. Howard and J. M. Streck, Apostles of Rock: The Splintered World of Contemporary Christian Music (Lexington, KY: University Press of Kentucky, 2004), ISBN 0-8131-9086-X, p. 30. The category has been especially well-liked in the United States.J. R. Howard and J. M. Streck, Apostles of Rock: The Splintered World of Contemporary Christian Music (Lexington, KY: University Press of Kentucky, 2004), ISBN 0-8131-9086-X, pp. 43–4. Many Christian rock artists have links to the modern Christian tunes set, when additional groups and creators are carefully connected to autonomous tunes. Since the 1980s Christian rock artists have obtained normal triumph, containing numbers such like the American gospel-to-pop crossing creator Amy Grant and the British vocalist Cliff Richard.J. Bowden, Christianity: the Complete Guide (London: Continuum, 2005), ISBN 0-8264-5937-4, p. 811. While those creators remained mostly satisfactory in Christian groups the acceptance of weighty rock and glam alloy methods by groups like Petra (band)|Petra and Stryper, whoever attained substantial normal triumph in the 1980s, was further contentious.J. J. Thompson, Raised by Wolves: the Story of Christian Rock Roll (Toronto: ECW Press, 2000), ISBN 1-55022-421-2, pp. 66-7 and 159-161.M. B. Wagner, God's Schools: Choice and Compromise in American Society (Rutgers University Press, 1990), ISBN 0-8135-1607-2, p. 134. From the 1990s there remained expanding numerals of acts whoever endeavored to circumvent the Christian group label, favoring to be noticed like groupings whoever remained as well

Christians, containing P.O.D and Collective Soul.J. J. Thompson, Raised by Wolves: the Story of Christian Rock Roll (Toronto: ECW Press, 2000), ISBN 1-55022-421-2, pp. 206–7.

Mosaic: Pieces of My Life So Far

'Mosaic: Pieces of My Life So Far' (ISBN 0-3809-7594-7) is an memoirs authored by American performer Amy Grant, issued by Flying Dolphin Press and WaterBrook Press (subsidiaries of Random House) and disseminated within October 2007. The publication attributes tune words, biographies, first verse, images, and a limited directory of Grant's vocation attainments. The publication is devised mostly of small narratives, nearly all bridging solely a limited leafs, that supply a brief look in to a few part of Grant's existence either her private viewpoints, frequently holding a shock disclosure either turn at the conclusion.

Dann Huff - Career

Huff started his vocation as piece of the first Christian rock group White Heart in that he played with his male sibling David Huff (musician)|David Huff, and afterward in the melodious Hard Rock group Giant (band)|Giant. He has subsequently then been energetic as a meeting guitar player and maker in either rock tunes and region tunes. In the 1980s Huff has played stringed instrument on collections for Michael Jackson, Scritti Politti, Whitesnake, Roger Hodgson, Steven Curtis Chapman, Doro Pesch, George Benson,[http://www.artistdirect.com/nad/store/artist/album/0,,51091,00.html Geroge Benson 20/20, collection as of 1984] Whitney Houston's first public appearance collection Whitney Houston (album)|Whitney Houston, Barbra Streisand,[http://www.artistdirect.com/nad/store/artist/album/0,,170124,00.html Barbra Streisand, collection Emotion as of 1984] Kenny Rogers[http://www.artistdirect.com/nad/store/artist/album/0,,155866,00.html Kenny Rogers, Single 'what about me'] and further.[Songs and Albums on that Dann Huff played on][Biography of Giant/Dan Huff on Allmusic.com] Since the 1990s Huff has been functioning as a maker for different groups and creators a few of that contain Faith Hill, Megadeth, Rebecca St. James and Rascal Flatts.

Some tunes Huff has played on include:
*Begin Again (Taylor Swift song)|Begin Again, Starlight (Taylor Swift song)|Starlight Red (Taylor Swift song)|Red - Taylor Swift
*Man in the Mirror I Just Can't Stop Loving You - Michael Jackson

*My Heart Will Go On - Celine Dion
*I Could Fall In Love - Selena
* Toulouse to gain - Claude Nougaro
*Here I Go Again (US broadcast variant 1987) - Whitesnake
*Rhythm of the Night (song)|Rhythm of the Night - DeBarge
*Glory of Love|The Glory of Love - Peter Cetera
***Next Time I Fall - Peter Cetera with Amy Grant**
*I Keep Prayin - Whitecross
*One Sweet Day All I Want for Christmas Is You (Mariah Carey song)|All I Want For Christmas Is You - Mariah Carey
*Straight Up (Paula Abdul song)|Straight Up Cold Hearted - Paula Abdul
*I Found Someone - Michael Bolton
*The Heart Is A Lonely Hunter - Reba McEntire
*On My Own (Patti LaBelle and Michael McDonald song)|On My Own - Michael McDonald (singer)|Michael McDonald Patti LaBelle
*Go West Young Man (Michael W. Smith album)|Go West Young Man - Michael W. Smith

53rd Annual Grammy Awards - Gospel

;Best Gospel Performance

*'Grace – BeBe Winans|BeBe CeCe Winans'
*He Wants It All – Forever Jones
*You Hold My World – Israel Houghton
*Nobody Greater – VaShawn Mitchell
*He's Been Just That Good – Kirk Whalum Lalah Hathaway

;Best Gospel Song

*'It's What I Do'
*'Jerry Peters Kirk Whalum, songwriters (Kirk Whalum Lalah Hathaway)'
*Beautiful Things
**Lisa Gungor Michael Gungor, songwriters (Michael Gungor|Gungor)
*Better Than a Hallelujah
****Sarah Hart Chapin Hartford, songwriters (Amy Grant)**
*Our God
**Jonas Myrin, Matt Redman, Jesse Reeves Chris Tomlin, songwriters (Chris Tomlin)
*Return to Sender
**Gordon Kennedy, composer (Ricky Skaggs)

;Best Rock either Rap Gospel Album

*'Hello Hurricane – Switchfoot'
*Church Music (album)|Church Music – David Crowder Band
*For Those Who Wait – Fireflight
*Beautiful Things (EP)|Beautiful Things – Michael Gungor|Gungor
*Rehab (Lecrae album)|Rehab – Lecrae

;Best Pop/Contemporary Gospel Album

*'Love God, Love People (Israel Houghton album)|Love God. Love People. – Israel Houghton'
*Beauty Will Rise – Steven Curtis Chapman
*Pieces of a Real Heart – Sanctus Real
*Mosaic – Ricky Skaggs
*Tonight (TobyMac album)|Tonight – TobyMac

;Best Southern, Country, either Bluegrass Gospel Album

*'The Reason (Diamond Rio album)|The Reason – Diamond Rio'
*Times Like These (Austins Bridge album)|Times Like These – Austins Bridge
*Expecting Good Things – Jeff Sheri Easter
*Journey On – Ty Herndon
*Live at Oak Tree: Karen Peck New River – Karen Peck New River

;Best Traditional Gospel Album

*'Downtown Church – Patty Griffin'
*The Experience – Vanessa Bell Armstrong
*A City Called Heaven – Shirley Caesar
*Here I Am – Marvin Sapp
*All in One (Karen Clark Sheard album)|All in One – Karen Clark Sheard

;Best Contemporary RB Gospel Album

*'Still (BeBe CeCe Winans album)|Still – BeBe CeCe Winans'
*Get Ready – Forever Jones
*Love Unstoppable – Fred Hammond
*Triumphant – VaShawn Mitchell
*Aaron Sledge – Aaron Sledge

Tommy Sims - Music career

From 1987 to 1989 he was the bassist of the well-liked Christian rock group White Heart that he left to come to be a Session musician|studio performer and maker. During 1992-1993, he played deep-toned on the Bruce Springsteen and the Other Band Tour. He is as well a composer, whoever co-wrote Eric Clapton's Change the World that gained the Grammy Award for Song of the Year in 1997. Other tunes of his have been recorded by Bonnie Raitt, Susan Tedeschi, Garth Brooks, Cher, Blackstreet|BlackStreet, Toni Braxton and Babyface (musician)|BabyFace amid other ones. Tommy has as well operated with Michael Bolton, Amy Grant, Kelly Clarkson, Carman, CeCe Winans, Israel Houghton|Israel, The Neville Brothers, Michelle Williams (singer)|Michelle Williams of Destiny's Child, and other ones.

Lucky One (song) - Music Video versions

* Original collection variant, accessible on the 2004 DVD Greatest Videos 1986-2004

*** Live execution, accessible on the 2006 DVD Time Again: Amy Grant Live (DVD)|Time Again...Amy Grant Live**

Gospel Music Hall of Fame - Groups

* The Blackwood Brothers (1998)
* The Blind Boys of Alabama (2002)
* Cathedral Quartet (1999)
* DeGarmo Key (2010)
* The Fairfield Four (1999)
* Fisk Jubilee Singers (2000)
* The Hoppers (2012)
* Bill Gaither Trio (1999)
* The Imperials (1998)
* The Jordanaires (1998)
* The Kingsmen Quartet|The Kingsmen (2000)
* Mighty Clouds of Joy (1999)
* TRUTH (2000)
* The Oak Ridge Boys (2000)
* Petra (band)|Petra (2000)
* The Rambos (2001)
* Second Chapter of Acts (1999)
* The Singing LeFevres (1998)
* The Statler Brothers (2007)
* The Winans (2007)

Billy Graham (evangelist)|Billy Graham was inaugurated to the Gospel Music Hall of Fame in 1999 for delivering a program to numerous Christian creators whoever have had the merit of carrying out at the Billy Graham happenings. Graham has sermonized the canon to over 210 million folks in further compared to 185 nations and areas. These creators include: Michael W. Smith, Amy Grant, Sandi Patty, Larnelle Harris, Steven Curtis Chapman, DC Talk, Jars of Clay. Others related with Graham's ministries are as well inductees: George Beverly Shea (soloist of the Billy Graham Evangelistic Team); Cliff Barrows (inducted 1988 - tunes director and chorus principal for altogether Billy Graham Evangelistic Campaigns); Ralph Carmichael (producer for the tunes in Billy Graham features such like Mr. Texas, For Pete's Sake, The Restless Ones, and His Lane); and singers Ethel Waters and Stuart Hamblen.

Amy Grant - In the mainstream

When Heart in Motion was disseminated within 1991, numerous fans remained startled that the collection was thus plainly one of modern pop tunes. Grant's wish to broaden her public was frowned on by the restrains of the well-liked descriptions of office at the time. The trail Baby Baby (Amy Grant song)|Baby Baby (written for Grant's just born girl Millie, whose six-week-old face was my stimulation,) grew to be a pop hit (hitting No. 1 on the Billboard Hot 100), and Grant was recognized as a designation in the normal tunes world. Baby Baby experienced Grammy recommendations for Best Female Pop Vocal Performance, and Record and Song of the Year (although it disappointed to gain in whatever of these categories). Four additional strikes as of the collection produced the Pop highest 20: Every Heartbeat (No. 2), That's What Love Is For (No. 7), Good for Me (song)|Good for Me (No. 8), and I Will Remember You (Amy Grant song)|I Will Remember You (No. 20). On the Adult Contemporary graph, altogether 5 tunes remained top 10 strikes, with 2 of the 5 (Baby Baby and That's What Love Is For) arriving at No. 1. Many Christian fans stayed faithful, placing the collection on top Billboard Contemporary Christian Chart for 32 7-day periods. Heart in Motion is Grant's best-selling collection, experiencing traded over 5 million duplicates depending to the RIAA. Grant pursued the collection with her second Christmas collection, Home For Christmas (Amy Grant album)|Home For Christmas in 1992, that contained the tune Breath of Heaven (Mary's Song), authored by Chris Eaton (UK musician)|Chris Eaton and Grant, and ought to afterward be veiled by numerous creators, containing Donna Summer, Jessica Simpson (who recognized Grant as one of her best-loved artists), Vince Gill, Sara Groves, Point of Grace, and Broadway star Barbara Cook.

House of Love (Amy Grant album)|House of Love in 1994 sustained in the similar vein, claiming arresting pop tunes mingled with religious words. The collection was a Multi-platinum triumph and created the pop hit Lucky One (song)|Lucky One (No. 18 pop and No. 2 AC; No. 1 on Radio Records) as well like the name trail (a duo with region tunes star and time to come spouse Vince Gill) (No. 37 pop) and a cover of Joni Mitchell's often veiled Big Yellow Taxi (No. 67 pop) (in that she altered the line And they charged the folks a buck and a fifty per cent simply to see'em to And then they charged the folks 25 bucks simply to see'em).

After she veiled the 10cc tune The Things We Do for Love (song)|The Things We Do for Love for the Mr. Wrong (film)|Mr. Wrong sound recording, Behind the Eyes (Amy Grant album)|Behind the Eyes was disseminated within September 1997. The collection hit a a lot dimmer record, leaning further in the direction of down-tempo, auditory soft-rock tunes, with further developed (yet nevertheless optimistic) words. She named it her razor blades and Prozac collection. Although Takes A Little Time was a modest hit sole, the collection disappointed to vend like the foregoing 2 collections, that had either moved Multi-platinum. Behind The Eyes was finally endorsed Gold by the RIAA. The audiovisual for Takes A Little Time was a spic-and-span management for Grant; with a azure light sieve, auditory stringed instrument, the roads and types of New York City, and a scenario, Grant was re-cast as an grown-up light rocker. She pursued up Behind The Eyes with A Christmas To Remember, her 3rd Christmas collection, in 1999. The collection was endorsed Gold in 2000.

In 2001, Grant chanted God Bless America in fore of a Sellout throng at the Owen County Fair Grounds in Spencer, Indiana. She committed her execution to the sufferers of 9/11, and formally commenced the Demolition Derby. Following the 9/11 charges, Grant's I Will Remember You (Amy Grant song)|I Will Remember You saw a renewal in reputation as numerous broadcast DJs varied a out of the ordinary accolade variant of the tune. That similar annum, Grant gained $125,000 for almsgiving on the Rock Star Edition of Who Wants to Be a Millionaire?

James William Guercio - Other accomplishments

Guercio grew to be engrossed in motion depiction manufacture, and he was specified the occasion to make and straight the 1973 feature Electra Glide in Blue; he as well authored and created the film's melodic sound recording. The feature featured Robert Blake (actor)|Robert Blake and highlighted Peter Cetera and different participants of Chicago in bit bits. Although the feature was well experienced by reviewers and has afterward come to be a movement timeless, it saw solely moderate profit-oriented triumph. Guercio created one additional Robert Blake feature, Second-Hand Hearts, that was disseminated within 1981. Guercio is an graduate of DePaul University.

Guercio was the originator of Caribou Ranch, a well-liked transcriptioning workshop in Colorado's Rocky Mountains. The foremost genuine broadcast hit recorded at Caribou was Joe Walsh's Rocky Mountain Way. In extension to Chicago (starting with Chicago VI), the workshop has been applied by countless additional artists: Elton John (for his Caribou (album)|Caribou collection like well like Captain Fantastic and the Brown Dirt Cowboy and Rock of the Westies), Billy Joel, Rod Stewart, Carole King, Stephen Stills, Waylon Jennings, Amy Grant, Supertramp, and The Beach Boys. Unfortunately, the workshop compound was close down and not ever applied once more following a March 1985 fire demolished the command area and triggered about $3 million in harm.

After the split-up with Chicago and the Caribou Ranch fire, Guercio grew to be disenchanted with the transcriptioning business and moved gears, following a prosperous vocation in extensive livestock farming, assets creation, and oil and gas investigation, drilling and manufacture, especially coalbed methane wells. In the belated 1980s, Guercio bought the Country Music Television (CMT) delivery method. In one of his further well-publicized undertakings, in the first 1990s he traded CMT to media magnate Ed Gaylord and Westinghouse Electric Corporation|Westinghouse Broadcasting.

Vanderbilt University - Notable faculty and alumni

Vanderbilt has about 114,000 exisiting graduates, with 31 graduates societies recognized international. Many Vanderbilt graduates have moved on to create important donations within political affairs. Lamar Alexander (Bachelor's degree|B.A. 1962) is a present U.S. Senator, erstwhile List of Governors of Tennessee|Governor of Tennessee, erstwhile U.S. Secretary of Education, and erstwhile U.S. Head of state candidate; he packed the Senate chair left empty by the retreat of Fred Dalton Thompson|Fred Thompson (J.D. 1971). Two Vice President of the United States|U.S. Vice premiers, John Nance Garner and Al Gore, tended to the Uni, however did not alumna. However, Gore's former wife, Tipper Gore|Tipper, is herself an alumna, getting a master's level as of Peabody in 1975. Other graduates whoever are either have been included in political affairs contain erstwhile United States Supreme Court Associate Justice and erstwhile U.S. Attorney General James Clark McReynolds (B.S. 1882), Executive Vice President of the Cato Institute David Boaz (B.A. 1975), and erstwhile White House Chief of Staff John R. Steelman (M.A.

1924). Bill Frist, a cardiothoracic doctor and erstwhile U.S. Senate Majority Leader, is a power associate at Vanderbilt University Medical Center. The President of Puntland and erstwhile Prime Minister of Somalia, Abdiweli Mohamed Ali (M.A. 1988), is as well an graduate of Peabody College.

Within the trade world, Vanderbilt graduates have moved on to service in a numeral of key management roles; graduates contain Ann S. Moore (B.A. 1971), erstwhile Chairman and CEO of Time, Inc.; Doug Parker (M.B.A. 1986), President and CEO of US Airways; and Matthew J. Hart (B.A. 1974), erstwhile President/COO of Hilton Hotels. Vanderbilt as well has an intimate link to the modern administration advising business. In specific, the creators of 2 of the 3 nearly all important administration advising businesses graduated with freshman grades as of the Uni. Bruce Henderson, originator of The Boston Consulting Group, graduated with a level in automatic designing and building in 1937, when Bill Bain (consultant)|Bill Bain, originator of Bain and Company, graduated in 1959 with Phi Beta Kappa merits in past, and nowadays helps on the Vanderbilt University Board of Trust.[http://www.vanderbilt.edu/boardoftrust/cmembers/bain.html]

Three graduates, biochemist Stanford Moore (B.A. 1935), economic expert and microcredit trailblazer Muhammad Yunus (Ph.D. 1971), and erstwhile Vice President Al Gore have gained the Nobel Prize. Four present either erstwhile participants of the power as well share that distinction: biochemist Stanley Cohen (neurologist)|Stanley Cohen, physiologist Earl Sutherland, and trailblazer molecular Biologist Max Delbrück; Nobel Laureate and neuroscientist Paul Greengard was a stopping by academic. Alain Connes and Vaughan Jones, either Fields Medalists, are Distinguished Professors of Mathematics at the Uni. In extension, the Uni has a affluent erudite and journalistic bequest. Most especially, the Southern Agrarians remained a cluster of important American authors and writers of poetry in the 1920s and 1930s founded at Vanderbilt. Three Poet Laureate Consultant in Poetry to the Library of Congress|U.S. Poets Laureate are Vanderbilt alums: Allen Tate (B.A. 1922), Robert Penn Warren (B.A. 1925), and Randall Jarrell (M.A. 1938). Warren afterward proceeded on to the gain the Pulitzer Prize. Novelists James Dickey (B.A. 1949) and James Patterson (M.A. 1970) as well graduated as of Vanderbilt. Two popular sportswriters, Grantland Rice (B.A. 1901) and Fred Russell (B.A. 1927), have a grant designated following them at the Uni, and Buster Olney (B.A. 1988) records for ESPN.com and The New York Times. Journalist David Brinkley tended to momentarily. Skip Bayless (B.A. 1974) of ESPN First Take tended to Vanderbilt as a beneficiary of the Russell-Rice grant. Willie Geist (B.A. 1997) is a service of MSNBC's Morning Joe. Vanderbilt alumna Hildy Kuryk is the director of information exchanges at Vogue (magazine)|Vogue and erstwhile elder New York funding adviser for Barack Obama's 2008 head of state drive.

Current Chicago Bears field general Jay Cutler (American football)|Jay Cutler (B.S. 2005) is as well a Vanderbilt alum and was prepared a preliminary version of in the foremost round of the 2006 NFL Draft by the Denver Broncos. Cutler's colleague and invasive address Chris Williams (offensive lineman)|Chris Williams (B.S. 2008) was a foremost round choose by the Bears in 2008.

Vanderbilt as well created the foremost altogether draft choose of Major League Baseball in 2007 with David Price (baseball)|David Price and the second altogether draft choose of Major League Baseball in 2008 with Pedro Alvarez (baseball)|Pedro Alvarez. Price and Alvarez remained prepared a preliminary version of by the then-named Tampa Bay Rays|Tampa Bay Devil Rays and the Pittsburgh Pirates, correspondingly. Pitcher Josh Zeid produced his chief alliance first public appearance with the Houston Astros in 2013. ESPN basket ball expert Carolyn Peck was a exceptionally good associate of the Commodores' basket ball programme as of 1985–1988, finally getting to be a head tutor and directing the Purdue Boilermakers women's basket ball group to a national title in 1999.

Given the university's place in Nashville, numerous of its graduates come to be included in the tunes business. Dinah Shore (B.A. 1938), Rosanne Cash (B.A. 1979), Amy Grant (B.A. 1982), and Dierks Bentley (B.A. 1997) are altogether graduates. Shore afterward proceeded on to star in a diversity of films; additional Vanderbilt graduates with Hollywood links contain Academy Award-winners Delbert Mann (B.A. 1941) and Tom Schulman (B.A. 1972) and performers Molly Sims (B.S. 1995) and Joe Bob Briggs (B.A. 1974).

Heart in Motion

'Heart in Motion' is the Twelfth collection by Contemporary Christian music|Christian pop vocalist Amy Grant, disseminated on March 5, 1991.

In juxtaposition to its forerunner, the further auditory Lead Me On (Amy Grant album)|Lead Me On, Heart in Motion comprised of tunes that remained further deeply treated, as was the manner of normal tunes at the time. In extension, dissimilar Lead Me On, Heart in Motion held limited deliberately devout tunes, with nearly all of the words for the tunes on the collection transacting with fancy either different existence subjects that ought to not be the unique concern of pious Christians. A pair of tunes on the collection, nevertheless, remained publicly Christian in their subject matter, such like Ask Me, that

explains in what way a woman's persuasion assists her to cure as of kid intimate misuse, and Hope Set High, either of that remained strikes on Christian broadcast. Another tune with an deliberately Christian subject was You're Not Alone that mentioned a considerable power notwithstanding tense attributes like whipcracks and a shrieking stringed instrument unaccompanied.

Otherwise, Heart In Motion was a pop tunes megahit on its discharge going to the Top Ten of the Billboard 200|Billboard 200 (as well like No.1 of the Christian collections graph for 32 weeks), and vending 5 million duplicates by the conclusion of 1997. The foremost sole as of the collection, Baby Baby – further either fewer Baby Baby (Amy Grant song)|the name cut, as the album's name is drawn as of this trail – hit the No. 1 placing on the Billboard Hot 100 and the Hot Adult Contemporary Tracks|Adult Contemporary graph. The ensuing 4 selects as well accomplished well on the pop and AC charts: Every Heartbeat (No.2 Hot 100, No.2 AC), That's What Love Is For (No.7 Hot 100, No.1 AC), Good for Me (song)|Good for Me (No.8 Hot 100, No.4 AC), and I Will Remember You (Amy Grant song)|I Will Remember You (No.20 Hot 100, No.2 AC). It was recorded at No.30 in the 2001 publication, CCM Presents: The 100 Greatest Albums in Christian Music and was endorsed 5x platinum by the RIAA for selling of over 5 million duplicates, creating it the best-selling Contemporary Christian music|Christian tunes collection at any time disseminated.

The collection as well experienced a recommendation at the Grammy Awards of 1992 for Grammy Award for Album of the Year|Album of the Year, that was granted to Unforgettable... With Love by Natalie Cole.

I Will Remember You (Amy Grant song) - Official Versions

*Rhythm Remix
*Album Remix
*Album Version
***Time Again Live Version (live musical performance transcriptioning as of the 2006 Time Again...Amy Grant Live album)**

How Mercy Looks from Here

'How Mercy Looks as of Here' is the Seventeenth workshop collection as of

Contemporary Christian tunes singer-songwriter and transcriptioning creator Amy Grant. The collection was disseminated by Capitol Christian Music Group|EMI CMG and Sparrow Records on May 14, 2013. The collection is created by marked maker Marshall Altman, grading his foremost cooperation with Grant. The foremost sole disseminated within aid of the collection is Don't Try So Hard, a faith-based ballad presenting James Taylor crooning harmonized context addition.

Adult Contemporary (chart) - Other formats

Relatively limited urban modern and Hip jump music|hip-hop creators run to with success cross over to AC, though there have been a limited new exclusions, such like Beyoncé Knowles|Beyoncé's Irreplaceable, Fergie (singer)|Fergie's ballad Big Girls Don't Cry (Fergie song)|Big Girls Don't Cry, Gnarls Barkley's Crazy (Gnarls Barkley song)|Crazy, Rihanna's Take a Bow (Rihanna song)|Take a Bow and Timbaland's rehash of OneRepublic's Apologize (song)|Apologize. RB creators whoever have attained chief triumph on the AC graph in the bygones contain Dionne Warwick, Aaron Neville, Diana Ross (with her unaccompanied career), James Ingram, Lionel Richie and Whitney Houston.

Crossover as of the region music|country graphs has as well been commonplace on the AC graph eversince the graph started. Among the region stars whoever had a numeral of selects cross over to the AC graph (and the pop graph as well) as of the 1960s via the 1980s contained Brenda Lee, Ray Price (musician)|Ray Price, Patsy Cline, Ronnie Milsap, Barbara Mandrell, Dolly Parton, Kenny Rogers, Eddie Rabbitt, Crystal Gayle, Willie Nelson, and Juice Newton. The enormous development of region tunes as a broadcast setup within the 1990s accompanied a numeral of spic-and-span region crossovers on to the AC airwaves, containing Martina McBride, Wynonna Judd, LeAnn Rimes, Shania Twain, Faith Hill, Lonestar, Mary Chapin Carpenter, and Garth Brooks. More not long ago, a spic-and-span wave of region artists has been crossing over to AC, containing Tim McGraw, the Dixie Chicks (who exceeded the AC graph with their cover of Fleetwood Mac's Landslide (song)|Landslide), Rascal Flatts, Carrie Underwood, Taylor Swift, Sugarland, Lady Antebellum, Jason Aldean (whose AC triumph appeared by means of his duo with Kelly Clarkson, Don't You Wanna Stay), and The Band Perry.

The Contemporary Christian tunes trade has as well been comparatively prosperous in crossing over to normal broadcast. In the mid-1980s, the most prosperous CCM creator at the time, Amy Grant, traversed over in to nonreligious tunes with the 1985 sole Find a Way (Amy Grant song)|Find a Way, that grew to be a Top Ten AC hit and a No.1 Christian sole concurrently. In the 1990s and in to the 2000s period of 10 years, additional creators such like Lifehouse

(band)|Lifehouse, MercyMe, Natalie Grant, Kathy Troccoli, Sixpence None the Richer, Steven Curtis Chapman, and Michael W. Smith have traversed in amid the Christian and nonreligious worlds with itty-bitty disapprobation as of their fan bases.

Traditional black gospel - Representative songwriters and artists

* Charles A. Tindley (1851–1933) is normally contemplated the Father of Gospel Music.Petrie, Phil. The History of Gospel Music He devised numerous Christian hymns, containing I Shall Overcome, that was the base for the now-famous song for the Civil Rights Movement of the 1960s, We Shall Overcome. Other well known tunes contained We'll Understand It Better By And By|We'll Understand It Better By and By and Leave It There amid numerous other ones. His soulful words, entrenched in the deepness of understanding that arises as of an Oppressed folks, fancy, forbearance and acceptance, somewhat compared to dislike, vengeance either revenge. His hymns nevertheless emerge in hymnals and songbooks applied by altogether Christian denominations.
* Thomas A. Dorsey (1899–1993) had such a pronounced result on the Golden Age of canon that leaf tunes for tunes authored in his rhythmical, bluesy manner remained named dorseys at the time.Waterman, Richard Alan. (1951) Gospel Hymns of a Negro Church in Chicago Journal of the International Folk Music Council. Dorsey was an American Pianist, organizer and melodist of such norms like Peace in the Valley|Peace In The Valley, that was one of the foremost canon recordings to vend one million duplicates. Originally concentrated on nonreligious tunes, Dorsey started to record tunes with a devout subject following gathering Tindley at a National Baptist Convention. Initially, his mixturing of holy subjects with the nonreligious melodic methods of Blues and jazz was sentenced as the devil's tunes and avoided by traditionalist Christians. After some years' perseverance, nevertheless, his manner obtained in reputation. Perhaps the most well known is Take My Hand, Precious Lord, authored following dropping his spouse to labor and his just born boy the following day.Ely, Don [http://www.starrgennett.org/stories/profiles/georgia_tom_dorsey.htm Georgia Thomas A. Dorsey]. Starr Gennett Foundation. Dorsey authored over 1000 tunes in his life span and set up The National Convention of Gospel Choirs and Choruses in 1932.
* Sallie Martin (1895–1988), whoever was announced The Mother of Gospel by the National Convention of Gospel Choirs and Choruses, operated with Dorsey first in her vocation. Her executions remained distinguished by her uneven Alto vocal and the yelling and overjoyed motions related with the Pentecostal Holiness custom. After connecting Dorsey's chorus in 1932, Martin as well took over Dorsey's fighting tunes store, to its help. During the 1930s, Martin journeyed to arrange choruses all over the South and Midwest. In 1940 Martin left Dorsey's cluster and started tour-

ing. Martin and canon melodist Kenneth Morris created Martin and Morris, Inc., a issuing corporation that grew to be the largest of its sort within the United States. She additionally created her own group, the foremost feminine cluster in canon past, named the Sallie Martin Singers. Martin was busily included in the secular claims motion, and a Nigerian political authority constructing was designated within merit of her aid aimed at the Nigerian Health Program.
* Mother Willie Mae Ford Smith (1906–1994)
* Mahalia Jackson (1911–1972)
* Clara Ward (1924–1973)
* James Cleveland (1931–1991)
* **Andrae Crouch (born 1942) aided demonstrate the post-Dorsey manner of urban modern Christian tunes. Andraé Crouch was a key figure in the Jesus Music motion of the 1960s and 1970s, and burly affected time to come American creators such like Michael W. Smith and Amy Grant. Though his modern tunes is nevertheless topic to the aged critique of diluting the holy dispatch with modern tunes methods, his tunes, such like Soon and Very Soon, The Blood Will Never Lose Its Power, Bless His Holy Name, and My Tribute have come to be pins in churches altogether about the planet and recorded by normal creators such like Elvis Presley and Paul Simon. He was one of the foremost African-American Gospel creators to crossing to normal modern Christian tunes. Crouch has gained countless prizes and merits over the annums containing 8 Grammy Awards, 4 GMA Dove Awards, and ASCAP, Billboard Music Award|Billboard and NAACP Awards. In 2004, he grew to be the third-ever canon creator to have a star enshrined on the Hollywood Walk of Fame. http://www.npr.org/templates/story/story.php?storyId=1943907 Andrae Crouch granted star on Walk of Fame**

House of Love (Amy Grant song) - Tracklisting

;U.S. Advertising CD single
#House of Love (LP Version)
#House of Love (The Classic Philly Soul mix)
#House of Love (The South Street Remix)

;U.S. Trade CD single
#House of Love (The Classic Philly Soul mix)
#House of Love (The South Street Remix)
#House of Love (LP Version)
#Lucky One (Kupper 12 mix)

;U.K. CD single
#House of Love (Radio mix) [by Al Clay]

#Baby Baby (Amy Grant song)|Baby Baby (No Getting Over You mix)
#Good for Me (song)|Good For Me
#House of Love

;U.K. CD sole II
#House of Love (Radio mix)
#Big Yellow Taxi (Paradise mix)
#That's What Love Is For
#Lead Me On

Janis Ian - Music career

At the age of 13, Ian authored and chanted her foremost hit sole, Society's Child|Society's Child (Baby I've Been Thinking), about an interracial amorousness prohibited by a girl's mom and frowned on by her peers and educators. Produced by Shadow Morton|George Shadow Morton and disseminated 3 periods as of 1965 to 1967, Society's Child eventually grew to be a national hit on its 3rd discharge following Leonard Bernstein highlighted it in a CBS TV out of the ordinary named Inside Pop: The Rock Revolution. The song's poetic subject matter was forbidden for a few broadcast stations, and they removed either prohibited it as of their playlists accordingly; in her 2008 memoirs Society's Child, Ian recollects getting dislike post and demise menaces as a reply to the tune, and references that a broadcast facility in Atlanta that played it was scorched down. In the summertime of 1967, Society's Child extended #14 on the Billboard Hot 100, the sole experiencing traded 600,000 duplicates, and the collection 350,000.Life Magazine, October 27, 1967 p. 53

Ian relays on her internet site that, though the tune was initially designed for Atlantic Records and the label compensated for her transcriptioning meeting, the label afterward restored the Master recording|master to her and silently declined to discharge it. Years afterward, Ian speaks, Atlantic's leader at the time, Jerry Wexler, openly said sorry to her for this. The sole and Ian's 1967 eponymous first public appearance collection remained eventually disseminated on Verve Forecast; her collection was as well a hit, arriving at #29. In 2001, Society's Child was inaugurated in to the List of Grammy Hall of Fame Award receivers Q-Z|Grammy Hall of Fame, that merits recordings contemplated lasting and essential to tunes past. Her first tunes was assembled on a duple Compact Disc|CD allowed Society's Child: The Verve Recordings in 1995.

Society's Child stigmatized Ian as a One-hit marvel till her nearly all prosperous sole in the United States, At Seventeen, a bittersweet explanation on teenager brutality, the delusion of reputation, and adolescent angst, as mirrored on as of the outlook of a 24-year-old, was disseminated within 1975. At Seventeen was a chief hit, getting huge praise as of reviewers and record purchasers alike—it charted at #3 on the Billboard Hot 100 and hit #1 on the Adult Contemporary graph. It gained the 1975 Grammy Award for Best Pop Vocal Performance - Female whipping out Linda Ronstadt, whoever was proposed for her Heart Like a Wheel album; Olivia Newton-John; and Helen Reddy. Ian accomplished At Seventeen as a melodic visitor on the first public appearance of Saturday Night Live on October 11, 1975. The song's collection, Between the Lines (Janis Ian album)|Between the Lines, was as well a hit and hit #1 on Billboard's Album graph. It was swiftly endorsed Gold and afterward received a 'Platinum' credential for selling of over one million duplicates traded in the US. Another amount of her triumph is anecdotal: on Valentine's Day 1977, Ian experienced 461 Valentine cards, experiencing specified in the words to At Seventeen that she not ever experienced whatever as a adolescent.

Fly Too High (1979), created by discotheque maker Giorgio Moroder, was her donation to the sound recording of the Jodie Foster feature Foxes (film)|Foxes, as well highlighted onto Ian's 1979 collection Night Rains. It received her a Grammy recommendation and grew to be a hit sole in numerous nations, containing South Africa, Belgium. Australia, Israel, and the Netherlands.

Another region wherever Ian has attained a elevated layer of reputation is Japan. She had 2 highest 10 selects on the Japanese Oricon graphs, Love Is Blind in 1976, and You Are Love in 1980; and her collection Aftertones exceeded Oricon's collection graph in October 1976. You Are Love (Toujours Gai Mon Cher) is the subject tune of Kinji Fukasaku's 1980 film Virus (1980 film)|Virus. Ian has cut some different selects especially for the Japanese trade, containing 1998's The Last Great Place.

Ian extended the pop graphs solely at one point further following At Seventeen (Under the Covers (song)|Under the Covers, #71 in 1981), although she had some further tunes get to the Adult Contemporary selects graph via 1980 (all flunking to create the Top 20, however). She walked off as of her CBS agreement in 1982 when it nevertheless had 3 collections to proceed. Ian intentionally consumed a lot of the 1980s and first 1990s short of a record transact. During the 1982–1992 time she sustained to record tunes, frequently in cooperation with songwriting collaborator Kye Fleming, that remained veiled by the likes of Amy Grant, Bette Midler and Marti Jones. She as well learned under performing tutor Stella Adler and hit up a close amity with her, that sustained till the latter's demise in 1992.

Ian eventually grew to be one of the foremost indie creators, resurfacing in 1993, with the discharge of Breaking Silence and its name tune regarding incest. She as well Coming out|came out like a homosexual at the time of the discharge of that collection. On 6/25/1993, Ian emerged on The Howard Stern Show, wherever she accomplished a spic-and-span variant of At Seventeen about Jerry Seinfeld.

Ian's collection, Folk Is The New Black, was disseminated together by the Rude Girl and Cooking Vinyl tags in 2006. It is the foremost in over 20 annums wherever she did altogether the songwriting herself.

Other creators have recorded Ian's compositions, nearly all especially Roberta Flack, whoever had a hit in 1973 with Ian's tune Jesse, as well recorded by Joan Baez and Dottie West; Ian's own variant is highlighted onto her 1974 collection Stars (the name tune of that has as well been oft-covered, containing adaptations by Cher, Nina Simone and Barbara Cook). Other creators whoever have recorded either accomplished tunes authored either co-written by Janis Ian contain Amy Grant, Jeanette (singer)|Jeanette Dimech, Sheena Easton, Michele Pillar, Mel Torme, Michelle Wright, Bette Midler (Some People's Lives, a tune authored by Ian and her then-partner Kye Fleming, grew to be the name tune of her Some People's Lives|1990 album), Jann Arden, and Japanese vocalist Shiina Ringo (covered Ian's success Japanese hit, Love Is Blind).

Ian resumes to journey, with a round of musical performances planned for the United Kingdom in the Spring of 2014, and a serials of emergences in the US following that.

Galileo (disambiguation) - Music

*Galileo (song)|Galileo (song), a tune by the Indigo Girls
***Galileo, a tune by Amy Grant as of Heart in Motion**
*Galileo (Someone Like You), a tune by Declan O'Rourke as of Since Kyabram

Grammy Awards of 1989 - Gospel

*Grammy Award for Best Gospel Vocal Performance, Female|Best Gospel Performance, Female
****Amy Grant for Lead Me On**
*Grammy Award for Best Gospel Vocal Performance, Male|Best Gospel Performance, Male
**Larnelle Harris for Christmas
*Grammy Award for Best Gospel Vocal Performance by a Duo either Group, Choir either Chorus|Best Gospel Performance by a Duo either Group, Choir either Chorus
**The Winans for The Winans Live at Carnegie Hall
*Grammy Award for Best Soul Gospel Performance, Female|Best Soul Gospel Performance, Female
**Aretha Franklin for One Lord, One Faith, One Baptism
*Grammy Award for Best Soul Gospel Performance, Male|Best Soul Gospel Perfor-

mance, Male
**BeBe Winans for Abundant Life
*Grammy Award for Best Soul Gospel Performance by a Duo either Group, Choir either Chorus|Best Soul Gospel Performance by a Duo either Group, Choir either Chorus
**Take 6 for Take 6

Charlie Peacock - 1978 to 1999

In 1978, composer Stephen Holsapple recorded Peacock's vocal compositions and they started authoring tunes alltogether. Peacock commenced carrying out at Maurice's American Bar and his tune So Attractive was put with a tunes producer. Vocalist and composer Sal Valentino questioned Peacock to unite his group and gave Peacock's tunes to his business acquaintances. Finally in 1980 AM Records signed Peacock for a demonstration transcriptioning with maker David Kahne.

Peacock created a group named The Charlie Peacock Group with Erik Kleven (bass), Jim Caselli (drums), Darius Babazadeh (tenor saxophone) and guitar player, Mark Herzig. Peacock as well recorded with David Kahne at the Automatt and at Moon Studios with Stephen Holsapple throughout this time and these recordings grew to be the collection Last Vestiges of Honor that was disseminated within 1998. Peacock contractiled with a manufacture imprint corporation named Exit Records in first 1983 and disseminated his personal first public appearance unaccompanied collection Lie Down In The Grass in 1984. Later that annum Peacock started touring as an beginning play for The Fixx, Let's Active, General Public, Missing Persons (band)|Missing Persons, and the Red Hot Chili Peppers.

Peacock repositioned to Island Records and recorded a self-titled collection that was disseminated within 1986. During this time Peacock as well started performing jazz in an galvanic ad hoc group named, Emperor Norton. The group comprised of Peacock, Brent Bourgeois, Larry Tagg, Bongo Bob Smith, Henry Robinett, and Aaron Smith. After being disseminated as of Island records in 1988 Peacock joined Jimmy Abegg and Vince Ebo to shape an auditory triad that visited the USA and Europe.

In 1987, Peacock's tune (Down In The Lowlands) was recorded by modern Christian creator Russ Taff with Peacock crooning context voices. That similar annum Peacock created the Christian group, The Choir (alternative rock band)|The Choir. He additionally co-wrote tunes with Margaret Becker in the fall of 1988 and the following collection, Immigrant's Daughter was proposed for a Grammy prize. Peacock repositioned to Nashville in the Summer of 1989 and experienced a transcriptioning agreement with Sparrow Records. His

transcriptioning, The Secret of Time was proposed for a Grammy Award in 1990 (Best Rock Gospel) as Peacock sustained to accomplish manufacture and meeting performer work with Al Green, Twila Paris, and Amy Grant. He co-wrote Grant's No.2 sole Every Heartbeat.

From 1990 to 1999 Peacock created over fifty collections in the Christian and canon tunes category and set up the record corporation, re:think (EMI/Sparrow) and signed the creators Sarah Masen and Switchfoot.Trinkner, Alex (2010, April 1). Switchfoot: New Way to Be Human. Sputnik Music. Retrieved 2011-05-23, as of [http://www.sputnikmusic.com/review/35898/Switchfoot-New-Way-to-Be-Human/ SputnikMusic.com] Peacock's publication, At the Crossroads, a explanation on the category of modern Christian tunes, was issued by Broadman Holman in 1999.

El Shaddai (song) - Lyrics

Michael Card's first words contained a line Though the Jews simply could not see/ What Messiah require to be; Amy Grant altered this to Though the folks could not see/ What Messiah require to be. Most covers integrate Grant's change.

Amy Grant - Personal life

Born in Augusta, Georgia, Grant is the least old of 4 female siblings. Her kin worked out in Nashville, Tennessee, in 1967.

Grant tended to Furman University in 1979 and 1980. There she accomplished one of her early compensated, non-amateur musical performances, beginning for Gene Cotton at McCalister Auditorium on the Furman grounds. She left Furman and restored to Nashville to be closer to the transcriptioning studios and her then-boyfriend, Gary Chapman (musician)|Gary Chapman.

Grant wedded companion Christian performer Gary Chapman on June 19, 1982. Their wedding created 3 kids. Article written material as of The Tennessean contained within Lam's Amy Grant internet site. Citing irreconcilable dissimilarities, Grant recorded for annulment as of Chapman in March 1999, and the annulment was ultimate in June 1999.

On March 10, 2000, Grant wedded Vince Gill, whoever had been formerly wedded to region vocalist Janis Oliver of Sweethearts of the Rodeo. Grant and Gill have a girl alltogether, Corinna Grant Gill, born March 12, 2001.

In the December 1999 Baptist Standard, Grant clarified wherefore she left Chapman and wedded Gill:

I did not get a annulment since I had a significant wedding and then alongside appeared Vince Gill. Gary and I had a Rocky way as of day one. I consider what was thus hard—and this is (what) one of our counselors said—sometimes an guiltless party may come in to a state of affairs, and they are like a great limelight. What they undertake is disclose, by juxtaposition, the irritating kinetics that are previously in being.

Contemporary Christian - History

The category grew to be familiar like Contemporary Christian tunes as a effect of the Jesus motion resurgence in the last one 1960s and first 1970s, and was initially named Jesus tunes. About that time, numerous youthful folks as of the sixties' counter culture avowed to trust in Jesus. Convinced of the emptiness of a way of life founded on narcotics, gratis intercourse, and revolutionary political affairs, 'hippies' grew to be 'Jesus people'.Frame, John M. Contemporary Worship Music. Phillipsburg, NJ: PR Publishing, 1997. However there remained folks whoever sensed that Jesus was one other journey.John M. Contemporary Worship Music. Phillipsburg, NJ: PR Publishing, 1997. It was throughout the 1970s Jesus motion that Christian tunes commenced to come to be an business inside its normal self. Jesus Music commenced by performing tools and crooning tunes regarding fancy and tranquility, that additionally interpreted in to fancy of God. Paul Wohlegemuth, whoever authored the publication Rethinking Church Music, indicated [the] 1970s must perceive a pronounced receipt of rock-influenced tunes in altogether degrees of kirk tunes. The rock manner tend to come to be further well known to altogether folks, its rhythmical superfluity must come to be sophisticated, and its earliest non-religious relationships must be fewer recalled.Baker, Paul. Page 140. Contemporary Christian Music: Where it appeared as of What it is Where It's Going. Westchester, Illinois: Crossway Books, 1985. Print.

Though there remained Christian collections in the 1960s that held contemporary-sounding tunes, there remained 2 collections recorded in 1969 that are contemplated to be the foremost perfect collections of Jesus rock: Upon This Rock (Larry Norman album)|Upon This Rock (1969) by Larry Norman originally disseminated on Capitol Records,John J. Thompson, Raised by Wolves: The Story of Christian Rock Roll (2000):49. And Mylon – We Believe by Mylon LeFevre, disseminated by Cotillion, that was LeFevre's aim at mixturing canon tunes with southern rock. Unlike customary either southern canon tunes, this spic-and-span Jesus tunes was birthed out of rock music|rock and people tunes.

Pioneers of this motion as well contained Keith Green, 2nd Chapter of Acts,

Benny Hester, Barry McGuire, Andrae Crouch|Andraé Crouch and the Disciples Evie (singer)|Evie, The Imperials and Love Song (band)|Love Song, amid other ones. The not so large Jesus tunes intellectual/artistic awareness had extended in to a multi-million-dollar Christian tunes industry|industry by the 1980s.By the '80s, the special-interest net-work that Jesus tunes had seeded had elaborated in to a multimullion-dollar business. Contemporary Christian tunes had its personal periodicals, broadcast stations, and prize exhibits. The Jesus motion resurgence was over: p. 10 Many CCM creators such like Benny Hester, Amy Grant, DC Talk, Michael W. Smith, Stryper, and Jars of Clay noticed Crossover (music)|crossover triumph with Top 40 normal broadcast play.

Beginning in July 1978, CCM Magazine started blanketing Contemporary Christian Music creators and a ample span of religious subjects till it started on the web documents in 2009.

Amy Grant - Looking ahead

Grant joined the actuality TV occurrence by servicing Three Wishes (TV series)|Three Wishes, a show in that she and a group of helpers create desires come genuine for small-town inhabitants. The show launched on NBC in the fall of 2005 however was abandoned at the conclusion of its foremost season since of elevated manufacture outlays. After Three Wishes was abandoned, Grant gained her 6th Grammy Award for Rock of Ages... Hymns Faith. In a February 2006 webchat, Grant declared she understands her finest tunes is nevertheless in front.

In April 2006, a live CD/DVD named Time Again...Amy Grant Live was recorded in Fort Worth, Texas, at Bass Performance Hall. (Grant's foremost compensated common execution was at the Will Rogers Auditorium in Fort Worth.) The musical performance was disseminated on September 26, 2006. In extension to getting a star on the Hollywood Walk of Fame, media emergences contained write-ups in CCM Magazine, and a execution on The View (U.S. TV series)|The View.

In a February 2007 net talk on her net site, Grant deliberated a publication she was functioning on named Mosaic: Pieces of My Life So Far, indicating, It's not an memoirs, however further a gathering of recollections, tune words, verse and a limited images. The publication was disseminated on October 16, 2007. In November, it launched at No. 35 on the New York Times Best Seller catalog. In the similar net talk, Grant marked that she is worried to get back in the workshop following the publication is completed, and recreate myself as an almost-50 carrying out female.

2007 was Grant's 30th annum in tunes. She left Word/Warner, and contractiled with EMI CMG whoever re-released her frequent workshop collections as re-mastered adaptations on August 14, 2007. Marking the commence of Grant's spic-and-span agreement is a career-spanning Greatest Hits (Amy Grant album)|greatest strikes collection, with altogether the tunes digitally remastered. The collection was disseminated like either a single-disc CD issue, and a 2-Disc CD/DVD Special Edition, the DVD presenting tunes recordings and talks.

Grant emerged with Gill on The Oprah Winfrey Show for a break out of the ordinary in December 2007. Grant has designs to emerge on Country Music Television|CMT, a Food Network out of the ordinary, the Gospel Music Channel, and The Hour of Power.

In February 2008, Grant joined the authoring group as of Compassion-art as a visitor singer at the Abbey Road studios, London, to record a tune named Highly Favoured, that was contained on the collection CompassionArt (album)|CompassionArt.

On June 24, 2008, Grant re-released her 1988 collection, Lead Me On, in merit of its 20th day of remembrance. The two-disc discharge contains the first collection and a second disc with spic-and-span auditory recordings, live executions as of 1989, and talks with Amy. Grant reproduced the Lead Me On journey in the fall of 2008.

On June 27, 2008, Grant startled everybody at the Creation Festival|Creation Northeast Festival by being the out of the ordinary visitor. She accomplished Lead Me On and a limited additional tunes sponsored with the Hawk Nelson group. At the conclusion of the musical performance, Grant restored to the stage and chanted Thy Word. She emerged on the 2008 collection Anne Murray Duets: Friends Legends crooning Could I Have This Dance.

In May 2009 for Mother's Day, Grant disseminated an EP on iTunes holding 2 spic-and-span tunes, She Colors My Day, and Unafraid, as well like the aged tunes Baby Baby and Oh How The Years Go By.

In 2010, Grant disseminated Somewhere Down the Road (Amy Grant album)|Somewhere Down the Road, presenting the hit sole Better Than a Hallelujah, that reached its highest point at No. 8 on Billboard Top Christian Songs graph. When questioned about the spic-and-span collection throughout an conference with CBN.com, Grant speaks, ... My desire is simply for these tunes to supply friendship, prompt myself and whoever other is paying attention what is essential. I sense like tunes have the capacity to link up

us to ourselves and to every one other, and to our persuasion, to the fancy of Jesus, in a means that chat does not do. Songs sort of slide in and turn you beforehand you understand it.[http://www.cbn.com/cbnmusic/interviews/amy-grant-somewhere-down-the-road-goodwyn.aspx Amy Grant: Somewhere Down the Road]. CBN.

In September 2012, Grant took part in a drive named 30 Songs / 30 Days to aid Half the Sky: Turning Oppression in to Opportunity for Women Worldwide, a multi-platform media program motivated by Nicholas Kristof and Sheryl WuDunn's publication.

Grant's following collection, named How Mercy Looks as of Here, was disseminated on May 14, 2013. The collection was created by Marshall Altman.[http://www.emicmgdistribution.com/products/detail.aspx?iid=1985134 How Mercy Looks as of Here]. EMI. Retrieved March 8, 2013. The collection extended No.12 on the Billboard 200|Billboard 200 graph, creating it her biggest graphing collection eversince 1997's Behind the Eyes. Two selects remained disseminated as of the collection, Don't Try So Hard and If I Could See with graphing inside the top 40 of US Billboard Christian Singles graph.

Grammy Awards of 2006 - Gospel music

;Grammy Award for Best Gospel Performance|Best Gospel Performance
*'Pray-CeCe Winans'
;Grammy Award for Best Gospel Song|Best Gospel Song
*'Be Blessed-Yolanda Adams'
**'Yolanda Adams, James Harris III, Terry Lewis James 'big Jim' Wright, songwriters'
;Grammy Award for Best Pop/Contemporary Gospel Album|Best Pop/Contemporary Gospel Album
*'Lifesong-Casting Crowns'
;Grammy Award for Best Rock Gospel Album|Best Rock Gospel Album
:Audio Adrenaline for Until My Heart Caves In
;Grammy Award for Best Southern, Country either Bluegrass Gospel Album|Best Southern, Country either Bluegrass Gospel Album
:Amy Grant for Rock of Ages...Hymns Faith
;Grammy Award for Best Traditional Soul Gospel Album|Best Traditional Soul Gospel Album
:Donnie McClurkin for Psalms, Hymns Spiritual Songs
;Grammy Award for Best Contemporary Soul Gospel Album|Best Contemporary Soul Gospel Album
:CeCe Winans for Purified
;Grammy Award for Best Gospel Choir either Chorus Album|Best Gospel Choir

either Chorus Album
:Gladys Knight, chorus director Saints Unified Voices for One Voice

List of awards and nominations received by Amy Grant

'Amy Grant' is an United States|American singer-songwriter, performer, writer, media character and female actor, finest familiar for her Christian tunes. She has been referenced to like The Queen of Christian Pop. As of 2009, Grant stays the best-selling modern Christian tunes vocalist at any time, experiencing traded over 30 million components international.

Grant produced her first public appearance as a adolescent, and obtained celebrity in Christian tunes throughout the 1980s with such strikes as Father's Eyes, El Shaddai (song)|El Shaddai, and Angels (Amy Grant song)|Angels. In 1986, she netted her foremost numeral one graphing Billboard Hot 100 hit tune in a duo with Peter Cetera The Next Time I Fall. During the 1980s and 1990s, she grew to be one of the foremost canon creators to Crossover (music)|cross over in to normal pop on the heels of her prosperous collections Unguarded and Heart in Motion, the last one of that contained the number-one sole Baby Baby (Amy Grant song)|Baby Baby.

Grant has gained 6 Grammy Awards, 25 Gospel Music Association Dove Awards, and had the foremost Christian collection at any time to proceed Platinum album|Platinum. Heart in Motion is her biggest vending collection, with over 5 million duplicates traded in the United States only. She was respected with a star on Hollywood Walk of Fame in 2005 for her donations to the amusement business.

2000 in country music - Events

* March 4 — Amazed by Lonestar goes the foremost region tune to have exceeded either the Hot Country Songs|Billboard Hot Country Singles Tracks and the Hot 100|Billboard Hot 100 graph eversince the Kenny Rogers-Dolly Parton duo, Islands within the Stream (song)|Islands In The Stream within October 1983. The country-leaning Amazed — that had a brief run in the Hot 100 throughout the summertime of 1999 — had been remixed for Top 40 broadcast, starting it to its run of pop-radio triumph.
* **March 10 — Vince Gill and Christian vocalist Amy Grant are wedded.**
* December – RFD-TV, a wire net-work dedicated to bucolic American intellectual/

artistic awareness, is started. In extension to agriculture- and farming-centric exhibits, a great program design chunck is dedicated to timeless country|classic region tunes TV exhibits.

Amy Grant - Return to gospel

Grant restored to her canon tunes origins with the 2002 discharge of Legacy... Hymns and Faith. The collection highlighted a Vince Gill-influenced mixture of Bluegrass music|bluegrass and canon and pronounced Grant's 25th day of remembrance within the tunes business. Grant pursued this up with the pop discharge Simple Things (Amy Grant album)|Simple Things in 2003. The collection did not have the triumph of her foregoing pop either canon attempts. However, shortly following Simple Things, Grant and Interscope/AM separated methods. The similar annum, Grant was inaugurated in to the Gospel Music Hall of Fame by the Gospel Music Association, an business commerce business of that she is a well-established associate, in her foremost annum of qualification. Grant disseminated a follow-up to her hymns gathering in 2005 named Rock of Ages...Hymns and Faith|Rock of Ages... Hymns Faith.

I Love the '80s (U.S. TV series) - 1986

* Ferris Bueller's Day Off
* Wheel of Fortune (U.S. Game show)|Wheel of Fortune
* Hands Across America
* Teddy Ruxpin
* ALF (TV series)|ALF
* Pretty in Pink
* Madonna (entertainer)|Madonna's Papa Don't Preach
* Swatch
* 1986 World Series and the Bill Buckner Fielding error
* The Cosby Show
* Baby On Board
* Crocodile Dundee
* Hollywood marriage|Celebrity marriages
* Whitney Houston
* Comic Relief (charity)|Comic Relief
* Janet Jackson
* Stand by Me (film)|Stand by Me
* Run-D.M.C.|Run-D.M.C.'s Walk This Way
* Top Gun

Makeout tunes of 1986: Berlin (band)|Berlin- Take My Breath Away, Peter Cet-

era Amy Grant - The Next Time I Fall, Atlantic Starr - Secret Lovers

End Credit Video is Mr. Mister's Kyrie (song)|Kyrie

Chris Rodriguez - Biography

Rodriguez was born on March 7, 1960, in Bronx New York, and repositioned to Nashville, getting to be a old hand of the set in the first 1990s. His first public appearance collection, Beggar's Paradise, was disseminated by Sony in 1999, by that time he had co-operated on programs with region and CCM acts such like Amy Grant, Michael W. Smith, Wynonna Judd, and Shania Twain. He resumes to work as a meeting performer with different creators on the Nashville set, such like Kenny Rogers, Kenny Loggins, and Lee Ann Womack. Chris is as well the idea beyond the Nashville founded group The Alternators that attributes a few of Nashville's finest meeting participants that exchange as their plans permit.

Chris is wedded and they have 2 kids, Nicole and Andre.

Chris was piece of Shania Twain's the Woman in Me TV journey group 1995-96 carrying out picked global sites and TV exhibits with different esteemed performers Randy Thomas (musician)|Randy Thomas (co-writer of the tune Butterfly Kisses (song)|Butterfly Kisses), Daniel Joseph Schafer|Dan Schafer, Russ Taff, Dave Malachowski, Allison Cornell Will Owsley.

As of 2007, he is touring with Kenny Loggins. From 2005 to 2010, he visited with Keith Urban.

As of 2010, he is touring with Kenny Loggins as well like formally for LeAnn Rimes.

As of 2011, Chris was functioning with Don Moen (singer)|Don Moen and spic-and-span creator Jessica Ridley.

As of 2012, Chris is performing Rhythm Guitar for Faith Hill.

From July to November 2012, Chris played Rhythm Guitar for Kelly Clarkson.

Wise Up (Amy Grant song)

'Wise Up' is a 1985 sole by Contemporary Christian music|Christian tunes vocalist Amy Grant. It was disseminated like the 3rd sole as of her Unguarded collection. The tune extended The Billboard 100, as well like the Adult Contemporary and Contemporary Christian Music|Christian tunes graphs in the United States.

Wise Up is an increased tempo, motivational tune with a Rock music|rock sound, presenting weighty Percussion instrument|percussion and guitars. The tune delivers the Unguarded collection with its name within the words stronger employ your head to watch your heart. That words basically abridges the song's principal subject.

1988 in music - Top hits

* 1-2-3 (Gloria Estefan and Miami Sound Machine song)|1-2-3 – Gloria Estefan the Miami Sound Machine
* Acid Man – Jolly Roger
* Age Of Reason – John Farnham
* All Fired Up (Pat Benatar song)|All Fired Up – Pat Benatar
* Angel of Harlem – U2
* Angel (Aerosmith song)|Angel – Aerosmith
* Another Lover – Giant Steps (band)|Giant Steps
* Another Weekend – Five Star
* Any Love (Luther Vandross song)|Any Love – Luther Vandross
* Anything for You (Gloria Estefan song)|Anything For You – Gloria Estefan
* Atmosphere (Joy Division song)|Atmosphere – Joy Division (re-release)
* Bad Medicine (song)|Bad Medicine – Bon Jovi
* Bass (How Low Can You Go) – Simon Harris
* Bad Young Brother – Derek B
* Beat Dis – Bomb The Bass
* Behind the Wheel – Depeche Mode (released in 1987)
* Better Be Home Soon – Crowded House
* Big Fun (song)|Big Fun – Inner City (band)|Inner City
* The Blood That Moves The Body – a-ha
* Blue Monday (New Order song)|Blue Monday 1988 – New Order (remix)
* Born to Be My Baby – Bon Jovi
* Boys (Summertime Love) – Sabrina Salerno (released in 1987)
* Breakfast in Bed – UB40 presenting Chrissie Hynde
* Bring the Noise – Public Enemy (band)|Public Enemy
* Buffalo Stance – Neneh Cherry
* Burn It Up – Beatmasters presenting PP Arnold
* Candle In The Wind#1986 live version|Candle In The Wind – Elton John (live)
* Car Wash (song)|Car Wash/Is It Love You're After – Rose Royce (re-release)

* Cars and Girls|Cars And Girls – Prefab Sprout
* Can You Party – Todd Terry|Royal House
* Catch My Fall – Billy Idol
* Chains of Love (Erasure song)|Chains of Love – Erasure
* Check This Out – LA Mix
* Circle in the Sand – Belinda Carlisle
* Come Into My Life – Joyce Sims (released in 1987)
* Copperhead Road – Steve Earle
* Crash (The Primitives song)|Crash – The Primitives
* Cross My Heart – Eighth Wonder
* Cult of Personality (song)|Cult of Personality – Living Colour
* Desire (U2 song)|Desire – U2
* Devil Inside (INXS song)|Devil Inside – INXS
* Dignity (Deacon Blue song)|Dignity – Deacon Blue
* Dirty Diana – Michael Jackson
* Divine Emotions – Narada Michael Walden
* Doctorin the House – Coldcut presenting Yazz|Yazz and the Plastic Population
* Doctorin' the Tardis – The KLF|The Timelords
* Domino Dancing – Pet Shop Boys
* Don't Believe the Hype – Public Enemy (band)|Public Enemy
* Don't Blame It on that Girl / Wap-Bam-Boogie – Matt Bianco
* Bomb the Bass|Don't Make Me Wait/Megablast – Bomb The Bass
* Don't Worry, Be Happy – Bobby McFerrin
* Dreaming (OMD song)|Dreaming – Orchestral Manoeuvres in the Dark|OMD
* Drop the Boy – Bros
* Edge of a Broken Heart – Vixen (band)|Vixen
* Endless Summer Nights – Richard Marx
* Everlasting (Natalie Cole album)|Everlasting – Natalie Cole
* Everyday Is Like Sunday – Morrissey
* Every Rose Has Its Thorn – Poison (American band)|Poison
* Everything Your Heart Desires – Hall Oates
* Express Yourself (N.W.A song)|Express Yourself – N.W.A. (released in 1990 in the UK)
* Fake 88 – Alexander O'Neal (remix)
* Fast Car – Tracy Chapman
* Fiesta (The Pogues song)|Fiesta – The Pogues
* The Flame (Cheap Trick song)|The Flame – Cheap Trick
* Fine Time – New Order
* First Time (Robin Beck song)|First Time – Robin Beck
* Follow the Leader – Eric B. Rakim
* Foolish Beat – Debbie Gibson
* Four Letter Word – Kim Wilde
* Forever Young (Rod Stewart song)|Forever Young – Rod Stewart

* Get Outta My Dreams, Get in to My Car – Billy Ocean
* Girlfriend (Pebbles song)|Girlfriend – Perri Pebbles Reid|Pebbles (released in 1987)
* Giving You the Best That I Got (song)|Giving You the Best That I Got – Anita Baker
* Got My Mind Set on You – George Harrison
* Goodgroove – Derek B
* Good Life (Inner City song)|Good Life – Inner City (band)|Inner City
* Good Tradition – Tanita Tikaram
* The Great Commandment – Camouflage (band)|Camouflage
* Hands to Heaven – Breathe (band)|Breathe
* Happy Ever After – Julia Fordham
* Heart (Pet Shop Boys song)|Heart – Pet Shop Boys
* Heat It Up – Wee Papa Girl Rappers presenting Two Men A Drum Machine
* Heatseeker (song)|Heatseeker – AC/DC
* Heaven is a Place on Earth – Belinda Carlisle (released in 1987)
* Hey Manhattan! – Prefab Sprout
* Hey Mister Heartache – Kim Wilde
* Hold On to the Nights – Richard Marx
* Hole in My Heart (All the Way to China) – Cyndi Lauper
* Hot in the City – Billy Idol
* House Arrest (song)|House Arrest (The Beat Is Law) – Krush (released in 1987)
* Hungry Eyes – Eric Carmen
* Hustle! (To the Music...) – The Funky Worm
* I Don't Wanna Go on with You Like That – Elton John
* I Don't Want to Live Without You – Foreigner (band)|Foreigner
* I Don't Want to Talk About It – Everything however the Girl
* I Gave It Up (When I Fell In Love) – Luther Vandross
* I Get Weak – Belinda Carlisle
* I Know You Got Soul (Eric B. Rakim song)|I Know You Got Soul – Eric B. Rakim
* I Hate Myself for Loving You – Joan Jett and the Blackhearts
* I Owe You Nothing – Bros
* I Need You – BVSMP
* I Saw Him Standing There – Tiffany (American singer)|Tiffany
* I Should Be So Lucky – Kylie Minogue
* I Want You Back – Bananarama
* I Want Your Love – Transvision Vamp
* I'll Always Love You (Taylor Dayne song)|I'll Always Love You – Taylor Dayne
* I'll Be There for You (Bon Jovi song)|I'll Be There for You – Bon Jovi
* I'll Be With You – T'Pau (band)|T'Pau
* I'll House You – Richie Rich encounters The Jungle Brothers
* I'm Not Scared – Eighth Wonder
* I'm Real – James Brown (musician)|James Brown presenting Full Force
* I'm Too Scared – Steven Dante

* Im Nin'Alu – Ofra Haza
* In My Dreams – Will Downing
* In The Air Tonight – Phil Collins (remix)
* Is This Love (Whitesnake song)|Is This Love – Whitesnake
* It Must Have Been Love – Magnum (band)|Magnum
* It Takes Two (Rob Base DJ E-Z Rock song)|It Takes Two – Rob Base DJ E-Z Rock
* The Jack That House Built – Jack 'N' Chill (released in 1987)
* Jack To The Sound Of The Underground – Peter Slaghuis|Hithouse
* Joe le Taxi – Vanessa Paradis (released in 1987)
* John Skero Goes West – John Skero
* Johnny B. Goode – Judas Priest
* Jour de neige – Elsa Lunghini
* Just Got Paid (Johnny Kemp song)|Just Got Paid – Johnny Kemp
* Just Like Paradise – David Lee Roth
* The King of Rock 'N' Roll – Prefab Sprout
* Kokomo – The Beach Boys
* **Lead Me On – Amy Grant**
* Left to My Own Devices – Pet Shop Boys
* A Little Respect – Erasure
* Look Away – Chicago (band)|Chicago
* Love Bites (song)|Love Bites – Def Leppard (released in 1987)
* Love Changes (Everything) – Climie Fisher (remix/released in 1987)
* The Lover in Me (Sheena Easton song)|The Lover In Me – Sheena Easton
* The Lovers (Alexander O'Neal song)|The Lovers – Alexander O'Neal
* Lucretia My Reflection – The Sisters of Mercy
* Make It Real – The Jets (band)|The Jets
* Make Me Lose Control (song)|Make Me Lose Control – Eric Carmen
* Mary's Prayer – Danny Wilson (band)|Danny Wilson (released in 1987)
* Man in the Mirror – Michael Jackson
* Maybe (We Should Call It a Day) – Hazel Dean
* Mercedes Boy – Perri Pebbles Reid|Pebbles
* Mistletoe and Wine – Cliff Richard
* Monkey (song)|Monkey – George Michael
* Moonchild – Fields of the Nephilim
* Mountain Song – Jane's Addiction
* My Prerogative – Bobby Brown
* Mystify (song)|Mystify – INXS (released 1989 in the UK)
* Need You Tonight – INXS (released in 1987)
* Never Gonna Give You Up – Rick Astley (released in 1987)
* Never Knew Love Like This – Alexander O'Neal
* Never Tear Us Apart – INXS
* Never Trust a Stranger – Kim Wilde
* New Sensation – INXS

* Nothin' however a Good Time – Poison (American band)|Poison
* Nothing Can Divide Us – Jason Donovan
* Nothing's Gonna Change My Love for You – Glenn Medeiros (United Kingdom peak)
* Nuit de Folie – Début de Soirée
* One More Try (George Michael song)|One More Try – George Michael
* One (Metallica song)|One – Metallica
* The Only Way Is Up – Yazz|Yazz and the Plastic Population
* Orange Crush (song)|Orange Crush – R.E.M. (released 1989 in the UK)
* Orinoco Flow – Enya
* Pamela (song)|Pamela – Toto (band)|Toto
* Paradise (Sade song)|Paradise – Sade (band)|Sade
* Paradise City – Guns N' Roses
* Parents Just Don't Understand – DJ Jazzy Jeff and the Fresh Prince
* The Payback Mix – James Brown (musician)|James Brown
* People Are Strange – Echo the Bunnymen
* People Have the Power – Patti Smith
* Perfect Strangers (Anne Murray song)|Perfect Strangers – Anne Murray
* Piano in the Dark – Brenda Russell
* Pink Cadillac (song)|Pink Cadillac – Natalie Cole
* Pour Some Sugar on Me – Def Leppard (released in 1987)
* Pourvu qu'elles soient douces – Mylène Farmer
* The Promise – When in Rome
* Push It (Salt-n-Pepa song)|Push It/Tramp – Salt-N-Pepa
* Put a Little Love in Your Heart – Annie Lennox Al Green
* Quelque selected dans Mon cœur – Elsa Lunghini
* Quelque piece Au Soleil – Dalida
* The Race – Yello
* Rag Doll – Aerosmith
* Real Gone Kid – Deacon Blue
* Revolution Baby – Transvision Vamp
* Rise To The Occasion (Hip Hop Mix) – Climie Fisher (remix/released in 1987)
* Rockin' Around the Christmas Tree – Mel Smith|Mel Kim Wilde|Kim (released December 1987)
* Rok Da House – The Beatmasters presenting The Cookie Crew (remix/released in 1987)
* Roll with It (Steve Winwood song)|Roll With It – Steve Winwood
* Roses Are Red – Mac Band presenting McCampbell Brothers
* Run's House (song)|Run's House – Run-D.M.C.
* **Saved By Love – Amy Grant**
* I Say a Little Prayer – Bomb The Bass
* Shaday – Ofra Haza
* Shake for the Sheik – The Escape Club

* Shake Your Thang (It's Your Thing) – Salt-N-Pepa presenting Experience Unlimited|E.U.
* Shattered Dreams – Johnny Hates Jazz (USA release)
* Ship of Fools (Erasure song)|Ship of Fools – Erasure
* Sidewalking – The Jesus and Mary Chain
* Sign Your Name – Terence Trent D'Arby (released in 1987)
* Simply Irresistible (song)|Simply Irresistible – Robert Palmer (singer)|Robert Palmer
* Smooth Criminal – Michael Jackson (released in 1987)
* Stakker Humanoid – Brian Dougans|Humanoid
* Stand (R.E.M. Song)|Stand – R.E.M.
* Stand Up for Your Love Rights – Yazz
* Stay on These Roads – a-ha
* Stop! (Erasure song)|Stop! – Erasure
* Stop This Crazy Thing – Coldcut presenting Junior Reid The Ahead Of Our Time Orchestra
* Straight Outta Compton – N.W.A.
* Stutter Rap (No Sleep 'Til Bedtime) – Morris Minor and the Majors
* Superfly Guy – S-Express
* Suedehead – Morrissey
* Superstitious (song)|Superstitious – Europe (band)|Europe
* Sweet Child o' Mine – Guns N' Roses (released in 1987)
* Teen Age Riot – Sonic Youth
* Tell Me True – Juice Newton
* That's the Way I Wanna Rock 'n' Roll – AC/DC
* There's More To Love – The Communards
* Theme as of S-Express – S-Express
* This Is Your Life – The Blow Monkeys
* Tougher Than the Rest – Bruce Springsteen
* Together Forever (song)|Together Forever – Rick Astley
* Touched by the Hand of God – New Order
* The Twist (Yo Twist) – Fat Boys Chubby Checker
* Twist in My Sobriety – Tanita Tikaram
* Twist and Shout – Salt-N-Pepa
* Two Hearts – Cliff Richard
* Two Strong Hearts – John Farnham
* Un Roman d'amitié|Un Roman d'amitié (Friend You Give Me a Reason) – Elsa Lunghini and Glenn Medeiros
* Waiting For A Star To Fall – Boy Meets Girl (band)|Boy Meets Girl (released on December 10, 1988)
* Walking Away (Information Society song)|Walking Away – Information Society
* We Call it Acieeed! – D Mob presenting Gary Haisman
* Wee Rule – Wee Papa Girl Rappers

* Welcome to the Jungle – Guns N' Roses (released in 1987)
* (What Can I Say) To Make You Love Me – Alexander O'Neal
* Whats' On Your Mind (Pure Energy) – Information Society (band)|Information Society
* What I Am – Edie Brickell New Bohemians (released 1989 in the UK)
* When We Was Fab – George Harrison
* When Will I Be Famous – Bros
* When You Come – Crowded House
* When You Put Your Heart In It – Kenny Rogers
* Wild World – Maxi Priest
* Wishing Well – Terence Trent D'Arby (released in 1987)
* Yé Ke Ye Ke – Mory Kanté
* You Are the One (A-ha song)|You Are the One – a-ha
* You Came – Kim Wilde
* You Have Placed a Chill in My Heart – Eurythmics

1986 Grammy Awards - Gospel

*Grammy Award for Best Gospel Vocal Performance, Female|Best Gospel Performance, Female
Amy Grant for Unguarded
*Grammy Award for Best Gospel Vocal Performance, Male|Best Gospel Performance, Male
**Larnelle Harris for How Excellent Is Thy Name
*Grammy Award for Best Gospel Vocal Performance by a Duo either Group, Choir either Chorus|Best Gospel Performance by a Duo either Group, Choir either Chorus
**Larnelle Harris Sandi Patty|Sandi Patti for I've Just Seen Jesus
*Grammy Award for Best Soul Gospel Performance, Female|Best Soul Gospel Performance, Female
**Shirley Caesar for Martin
*Grammy Award for Best Soul Gospel Performance, Male|Best Soul Gospel Performance, Male
**Marvin Winans for Bring Back the Days of Yea and Nay
*Grammy Award for Best Soul Gospel Performance by a Duo either Group, Choir either Chorus|Best Soul Gospel Performance by a Duo either Group, Choir either Chorus
**The Winans for Tomorrow
*Grammy Award for Best Inspirational Performance|Best Inspirational Performance
**Jennifer Holliday for Come Sunday

I'll Be Home For Christmas - Other recordings

I'll Be Home for Christmas was recorded by Perry Como (1946), Frank Sinatra (1957), Sara Evans (Hear Something Country - Christmas 2007, 2007), Kelly Clarkson (ITunes Session (Kelly Clarkson EP)|iTunes Session Wrapped in Red) and numerous different creators.[http://www.secondhandsongs.com/work/7893 I'll Be Home For Christmas: Second Hand Songs.] These creators include:

*98 Degrees
*Aimee Mann (One More Drifter in the Snow, 2006)
*Al Green
*78violet|Aly AJ (Acoustic Hearts of Winter, 2006)
***Amy Grant**
*Andy Williams
*Anna Gilbert (musician)|Anna Gilbert
*Anne Murray
*Aqua Teen Hunger Force (Have Yourself A Meaty Little Christmas, 2009)
*Art Paul Schlosser Parody: (I'll Be a Gnome for Christmas (Words of Cheese and Other Parrot Trees, 2003)
*B.B. King
*Barbra Streisand
*BarlowGirl (Home for Christmas (BarlowGirl album)|Home for Christmas, 2008)
*The Beach Boys (The Beach Boys' Christmas Album, 1964)
*Bette Midler (Cool Yule)
*Blake Shelton (Cheers, It's Christmas)
*Bob Dylan (Christmas in the Heart, 2009)
*Brad Johner
*Brad Paisley
*Brian Littrell
*Brian McKnight
*The Brothers Four Note: 1966 Billboard graph single
*Carl Brutananadilewski
*The Carpenters
*Carrie Underwood with Elvis Presley (Christmas Duets (Elvis Presley album), 2008)
*Cascada (It's Christmas Time (album)|It's Christmas Time)
*Celtic Woman singer Lisa Lambe
*Chicago (band)|Chicago (Chicago XXXIII: O Christmas Three, 2011)
*Connie Francis
*Crystal Lewis Holiday!: A Collection of Christmas Classics, 2002
*Crystal Shawanda
*Damien Leith (Where We Land (Limited Special Christmas Edition))
*Dannii Minogue
*David Archuleta (Christmas as of the Heart (David Archuleta album)|Christmas as

of the Heart, 2009)
*Dean Martin (The Dean Martin Christmas Album, 1966)
*Diana Krall
*Diamond Rio
*Diane Schuur
*Dolly Parton
*Donna Summer (Christmas Spirit Album, 1984)
*Doris Day (The Doris Day Christmas Album, 14 September 1964)
*Drew Seeley (Disney Channel Holiday, 2007)
*Dwight Yoakam
*Eddie Rabbitt
*Elvis Presley (Elvis' Christmas Album, 1957)
*Fats Domino
*The Forester Sisters
*Gary Hoey
*Girl in a Coma (A Blackheart Christmas - *Blackheart Records, 2008) *Joan Jett's Record Label
*Glen Campbell
*Glenn Miller Orchestra
*Gloria Estefan
*Hampton String Quartet
*Harry Connick, Jr. (Harry for the Holidays, 2003)
*Jaci Velasquez
*Jackie Evancho (Heavenly Christmas, 2011)
*Jackie Gleason
*Jackie Wilson (Merry Christmas From Jackie Wilson, 1963)
*Jeffrey Osborne
*Jennifer Warnes (The Tradition of Christmas, 1991)
*Jessica Simpson (Happy Christmas (Jessica Simpson album)|Happy Christmas , 2010)
*Jillian Hall (A Jingle with Jillian, 2007)
*Jimmy Buffett
*Joe Williams (jazz singer)|Joe Williams
*John Berry (singer)|John Berry
*John Gary (1964)
*Johnny Cash
*Johnny Mathis
*Jonathan Butler (2013)
*Jordin Sparks (This Christmas (film)|This Christmas Soundtrack, 2007)
*Josh Groban (Noël (Josh Groban album)|Noël, 2007)
*Justin Guarini
*Katharine McPhee (Single, 17 November 2009)
*Kelly Clarkson (iTunes Session (Kelly Clarkson EP)|iTunes Session, 2011 and

Wrapped in Red, 2013)
*Kenneth Copeland
*Kenny Chesney
*Kokia (singer)|Kokia (Christmas Gift (album)|Christmas Gift, 2008)
*Kristin Chenoweth (A Lovely Way to Spend Christmas, 2008)
*Lady Antebellum (On This Winter's Night, 2012)
*Lana Cantrell (Vinyl LP VA Christmastime in Carol and Song, 1968; Christmas in California 1968,)
*Lea Michele (Glee: The Music, The Christmas Album Volume 3)
*Leon Redbone
*Linda Ronstadt (A Merry Little Christmas (Linda Ronstadt album)|A Merry Little Christmas, 2000)
*Lisa Leuschner
*Lonestar
*Martina McBride
*Matchbook Romance (A Santa Cause: It's a Punk Rock Christmas)
*Mauro Calderón
*Michael Bublé
*Mindy Smith
*Neil Diamond
*Nora Aunor Christmas Songs (Nora Aunor Album)|Christmas Songs collection 1972
*The Nylons
*The Oak Ridge Boys
*The Osmonds
*Overboard (a cappella)|Overboard (Tidings, 2008)
*Pam Tillis
*Pat Boone
*Peabo Bryson and Roberta Flack
*Percy Faith
*Perry Como
*Phil Driscoll
*Plácido Domingo, containing a duo with Tony Bennett (Concert: Our Favourite Things: Christmas in Vienna Vienna, 2000)
*The Platters
*Plus One (band)|Plus One (Medley in Christmas (Plus One album)|Christmas album)
*Rascal Flatts (Greatest Hits Volume 1 (Rascal Flatts album)|Greatest Hits Volume 1 (Bonus Track), 2008)
*Reba McEntire
*Ricky Van Shelton (Ricky Van Shelton Sings Christmas, 1989)
*Ronan Tynan
*Ronnie Milsap

* Royce Campbell
*Sara Evans
*Sarah McLachlan
*Scott Weiland (The Most Wonderful Time of the Year (Scott Weiland album)|The Most Wonderful Time of the Year (album), 2011)
*She Him
*Slim Whitman
*Smokey Robinson The Miracles (Christmas with The Miracles, 1963)
*Spyro Gyra
*The Statler Brothers
*Sufjan Stevens
*Suzy Bogguss
*Take 6 (The Most Wonderful Time of the Year (Take 6 album)|The Most Wonderful Time of the Year, 2010)
*The Three Tenors
*Tierney Sutton with Erich Kunzel and the Cincinnati Pops Orchestra
*Tift Merritt
*Toby Keith
*Tony Bennett (A Swingin' Christmas (Featuring The Count Basie Big Band)|A Swingin' Christmas, 2008)
*Twisted Sister with Lita Ford (A Twisted Christmas, 2006)
*Vanessa L. Williams
*Vince Gill
*Whitney Houston
*Wynonna Judd

House of Love (Amy Grant song) - Official versions

***Original collection variant (4:38), accessible on the House of Love (Amy Grant album)|House Of Love album**
*The Classic Philly Soul mixture (4:37)
*The South Street Remix (4:38)
*United Kingdom|UK broadcast mix
*Alternate variant, accessible like a extra audiovisual on Greatest Videos 1986-2004

Linda Thompson (actress) - Songwriting

She started her melodic vocation as a songwriter with the Kenny Rogers sole Our Perfect Song as of his 1985 collection The Heart of the Matter (album)|The Heart of the Matter. Thompson proceeded on to co-operate with writers such like Richard Marx to pen Josh Groban's foremost hit record To Where You Are, Composer Steve Dorff for the Celine Dion hit Miracle (Ce-

line Dion song)|Miracle, Andreas Carlsson for Drowning (Backstreet Boys song)|Drowning by the Backstreet Boys, and other ones containing her numerous collaborations as songwriter to melodist David Foster's melodic compositions. (The 2 remained wedded in 1991). Their cooperative triumphs contain No Explanation for the 1990 feature Pretty Woman, and I Have Nothing sung by Whitney Houston in the 1992 motion depiction, The Bodyguard (1992 film)|The Bodyguard, for that they remained proposed either for the Academy Award for Best Song in 1993 and the Grammy Award for Best Song Written Specifically for a Motion Picture either for Television in 1994. They as well authored what has come to be a Christmas timeless, Grown Up Christmas List, recorded by Natalie Cole, Barbra Streisand, Kelly Clarkson, Amy Grant, Michael Buble', and numerous other ones. In 2011, Thompson, Foster and Jackie Evancho co-operated on the name trail for Evancho's collection Dream With Me.

Thompson and Foster parted the 2003 Emmy for Outstanding Music and Lyrics for Aren't They All Our Children for the The Concert for World Children's Day (2002 television).

Tapestry Revisited: A Tribute to Carole King - Track listing

I Feel the Earth Move – 4:59 (performed by Eternal (band)|Eternal)
So Far Away (Carole King song)|So Far Away – 4:25 (performed by Rod Stewart)
 # It's Too Late (Carole King song)|It's Too Late – 3:59 (performed by Amy Grant)
Home Again – 3:41 (performed by Curtis Stigers)
Beautiful (Carole King song)|Beautiful – 3:46 (performed by Richard Marx)
Way Over Yonder – 3:54 (performed by Blessid Union of Souls)
You've Got a Friend – 6:03 (performed by BeBe CeCe Winans presenting Aretha Franklin)
Where You Lead – 3:32 (performed by Faith Hill)
Will You Love Me Tomorrow – 5:02 (performed by Bee Gees)
Smackwater Jack (song)|Smackwater Jack – 4:37 (performed by The Manhattan Transfer)
Tapestry – 3:12 (performed by All-4-One)
(You Make Me Feel Like) A Natural Woman – 3:43 (performed by Celine Dion)

Michael Omartian - Producer

*1974: White Horse (album)|White Horse Michael Omartian

*1975: Young Frankenstein (original soundtrack)
*1976: I've Got a Reason The Richie Furay Band
*1976: Streetheart Dion DiMucci|Dion
*1977: Crackin' Crackin'
*1977: Love at First Sight Dionne Warwick
*1978: Special Touch Crackin'
*1978: Sweet Salvation Jim Krueger
*1978: Roger Voudouris Roger Voudouris
*1979: Christopher Cross Christopher Cross
*1979: One More Song for You The Imperials
*1979: Radio Dream Roger Voudouris
*1981: Maxus Maxus
*1981: Nobody Knows Me Like You Benny Hester
*1981: Priority The Imperials
*1981: Still Feels Good Tom Johnston (musician)|Tom Johnston
*1983: Another Page Christopher Cross
*1983: She Works Hard for the Money Donna Summer
*1984: Camouflage (Rod Stewart album)|Camouflage Rod Stewart
*1984: Cats Without Claws Donna Summer
*1985: Choose Life (Debby Boone album)|Choose Life Debby Boone
*1985: Every Turn of the World Christopher Cross
*1985: Vox Humana (Kenny Loggins album)|Vox Humana Kenny Loggins
*1986: About Last Night... (original soundtrack)
*1986: Conversations Michael Omartian
*1986: The Karate Kid, Part II|The Karate Kid, Pt. 2 (original soundtrack)
*1986: Passion Jennifer Rush
*1986: Precious Moments Jermaine Jackson
*1986: Solitude/Solitaire Peter Cetera
*1987: Friends for Life (Debby Boone album)|Friends for Life Debby Boone
*1988: Back of My Mind Christopher Cross
*1988: Rock Solid The Commodores
*1989: Bowling in Paris Stephen Bishop (musician)|Stephen Bishop
*1989: Sing (1989 film)|Sing (original soundtrack)
*1990: Downtown Train Rod Stewart
*1991: For Our Children Disney
***1991: Heart in Motion Amy Grant**
*1991: Power of Jennifer Rush Jennifer Rush
*1991: The Race Michael Omartian
*1991: T.E.V.I.N. Tevin Campbell
*1992: Countess Countess Vaughn
*1992: Sarafina! The Sound of Freedom (original soundtrack)
*1993: The Standard Carman (singer)|Carman
*1993: Taking Heaven by Storm Steve Camp

*1994: Christmas Spirit Donna Summer
***1994: House of Love (Amy Grant album)|House of Love Amy Grant**
*1994: Kathy Troccoli Kathy Troccoli
*1994: The Light Inside Gary Chapman (musician)|Gary Chapman
*1994: Maverick (film)|Maverick (original soundtrack)
*1994: Mercy in the Wilderness Steve Camp
*1994: Razon de Cantar First Call
*1994: The Ride (4Him album)|The Ride 4Him
*1994: Sizzlin' Sounds Collection different artists
*1994: Slow Revival Bryan Duncan
*1995: Come Together: America Salutes the Beatles different artists
*1995: Field of Souls Wayne Watson
*1995: Helen Darling Helen Darling (singer)|Helen Darling
*1995: One Love Jonathan Pierce
*1996: The Birdcage (original soundtrack)
*1996: Come on Back Billy and Sarah Gaines
*1996: Distant Call Susan Ashton
*1996: Life Love Other Mysteries Point of Grace
*1996: The Message 4Him
*1996: Mission Accomplished: Themes for Spies different artists
*1996: Shelter Gary Chapman
*1996: Summer of '78 Barry Manilow
*1996: Tribute: The Songs of Andrae Crouch different artists
*1997: Amazing Grace, Vol. 2: A Country Salute to Gospel different artists
*1997: Anastasia (1997 film)|Anastasia (original soundtrack)
*1997: Let Us Pray: National Day of Prayer different artists
*1997: The Way in a Manger: Country Christmas different artists
*1998: Almighty God different artists
*1998: Civil War: The Nashville Sessions different artists
*1998: Movies Greatest Love Songs different artists
*1998: Obvious (4Him album)|Obvious 4Him
*1998: The Prince of Egypt (soundtrack)|Prince of Egypt (original soundtrack)
*1998: Visions of Love Jim Brickman
*1998: The Way Home Wayne Watson
***1999: Christmas to Remember Amy Grant**
*1999: Fade Into Light Boz Scaggs
*1999: In the Moon of Wintertime: Christmas with Michael Crawford
*1999: Learning to Breathe (Larry Stewart album)|Learning to Breathe Larry Stewart (singer)|Larry Stewart
*1999: Love Takes Time Bryan Duncan
*1999: Touched by an Angel: The Christmas Album [original TV soundtrack]
*2000: Brand New Dream Danny Gans
*2000: Heart of a Champion Carman

*2000: Hymns: A Place of Worship 4Him
*2000: Nicol Smith Nicol Smith (Sponberg)
*2000: Organ-Ized: All-Star Tribute to the Hammond B3 Organ different artists
*2000: Wayne Watson Wayne Watson
*2001: Angel Eyes (film)|Angel Eyes (original soundtrack)
*2001: Another Perfect World Peter Cetera
*2001: Love Songs Michael Bolton
*2003: Pass the Love Larnelle Harris
*2003: Cliff at Christmas Cliff Richard
*2003: 24 Point of Grace
*2003: Visible 4Him
*2004: '70s: From Acoustic to the Wall of Sound Dion DiMucci|Dion
*2004: Prayer That Changes Everything Stormie Omartian
*2005: Christmas Reunion Tony Orlando Dawn
*2005: Duets Sandi Patty
*2005: Something's Goin' On Cliff Richard
*2006: Collections Kenny Loggins
*2009: Where's Our Revolution Matt Brouwer
*2009: Beloved Lara Landon
*2010: Bold as Brass (album)|Bold As Brass Cliff Richard
*2012: Till The Sunrise Matt Brouwer

Something to Talk About (Bonnie Raitt song)

'Something to Talk About' is a tune authored by Canadian singer-songwriter Shirley Eikhard and recorded by Bonnie Raitt in 1990, for her 1991 in music|1991 collection Luck of the Draw (album)|Luck of the Draw. It was disseminated to U.S. Broadcast on June 3, 1991. Three sole adaptations remained released: the promotional b/w the similar tune, the 7 sole b/w One Part Be My Lover a tune authored by Raitt with her additionally spouse performer Michael O'Keefe, that was as well off Luck of the Draw, and a 12 sole with those 2 tunes and I Ain't Gonna Let You Break My Heart Again off her foregoing collection Nick of Time (album)|Nick of Time. In turn, this tune was contained on the EP variant of Raitt's 2000 sole of The Fundamental Things taken as of her 1998 collection Fundamental (Bonnie Raitt album)|Fundamental. It was as well contained within 2003's largest strikes compiling The Best of Bonnie Raitt. Live adaptations as well emerged on 1995's Road Tested and 2006's Bonnie Raitt and Friends.

The tune was well-liked onto numerous setups of radio: it reached its highest point at numeral 5 on Billboard magazine|Billboard's Adult Contemporary graph, numeral

12 on Billboard's Mainstream Rock graph, and numeral 5 on the Billboard Hot 100. It is amid one of Bonnie Raitt's nearly all well-liked tunes, alongside with I Can't Make You Love Me.

Raitt gained the Grammy Award for Best Female Pop Vocal Performance|Best Female Pop Vocal Performance at the Grammy Awards of 1992 for her transcriptioning of this tune (Oleta Adams, Mariah Carey, Amy Grant and Whitney Houston remained the other finalists). The trail as well experienced a recommendation for Grammy Award for Record of the Year|Record of the Year, dropping to Unforgettable (song)|Unforgettable by Nat King Cole and Natalie Cole.

Anne Murray desired to record this tune in 1986, however her creators did not consider it ought to be a hit. She nevertheless named the collection that she disseminated that annum Something to Talk About (album)|Something to Talk About even although it did not contain this tune.

Inspirational music - Style and artists

Contemporary Christian tunes has effects as of people, canon, pop and rock tunes. Genres of tunes such like malleable rock, people rock, alternate, hip-hop, etcetera. Have played a great impact on CCM. Mumford, Lawrence R. A diversity of devout composition: the tunes we chant, in and out of kirk, is further diverse and absorbing compared to we have been guided to trust. Christianity Today June 2011: 42+. Fine Arts and Music Collection. Web. 8 Feb. 2014.

Charismatic churches have had a great impact on modern Christian tunes and are one of the greatest creators of CCM. Hillsong Church is one of the numerous important CCM creators.Evans, Mark. Studies in Popular Music : Open up the Doors : Music in the Modern Church. London: Equinox Publishing Ltd , 2006. Ebook. Contemporary Christian tunes has as well developed within that there are sub-genres of CCM such like Christian punk, Christian diehard, Christian alloy and Christian hip jump, though not usually contemplated CCM, may as well come under the genre's parasol. Contemporary reverence tunes is as well integrated in contemporary CCM. Contemporary reverence is either recorded and accomplished throughout kirk facilities.

Artists whoever helped CCM to come to be well-liked remained Amy Grant, Michael W. Smith, Phil Keaggy and John Elefante. Several normal creators, such like The Byrds, Bob Dylan, Van Morrison, Elvis Presley, Creed (band)|Creed, Lifehouse (band)|Lifehouse and U2, have dealt with Christian subjects in their tunes, up till now are not piece of the CCM business. Other creators depicting the category include

MercyMe, Casting Crowns, Jeremy Camp, Third Day, Matthew West, tobyMac, Chris Tomlin, Brandon Heath and Aaron Shust. Historically, Jars of Clay, DC Talk, Steven Curtis Chapman and Newsboys have as well belonged to this category.

Merry Christmas Darling - Other versions

The tune was sung by female actor Lea Michele for the second season Christmas chapter of the hit TV serials, Glee (TV series)|Glee, allowed A Very Glee Christmas, in 2010.http://www.imdb.com/title/tt1628280/ This variant was disseminated like piece of the series' foremost Glee: The Music, The Christmas Album|Christmas collection.

The tune has as well been veiled by Natalie Cole, Amy Grant, Glenn Medeiros, Kimberley Locke, Vanessa L. Williams, Phil Vassar, Boyz II Men, Kyle Vincent, Kealii Reichel|Keali'i Reichel, Briana Cash, Christina Perri, Deanna Carter, Jane Monheit, and Chicago (band)|Chicago, as well like Filipino people|Filipino rock vocalist Kitchie Nadal, Filipino people|Filipino pop balladeer Rico J. Puno, and Filipino people|Filipino pop balladeer Richard Poon.

Crossover music - Christian crossover artists

The expression crossing creator might allude to melodic artists and groupings that are Christian tunes creators, whoever numerous periods initially are advertised via List of Christian record labels|Christian record labels, broadcast stations, churches and different Christian media however whoever commence vending in normal nonreligious markets as well. Other periods, crossing creators might commence out in the normal trade however have Christian undertones either subjects if not deliberately Christian. The expression crossing over is applied to report once an creator whoever had commenced mainly in Christian markets begins getting normal triumph. Some folks might sense that the creator is exposing the kirk for celebrity either splendor, when other ones might perceive this like a significant occasion for the creator outspread the communication of their Christian faiths.

The foremost chief creator crossing was by Amy Grant, with her 1985 collection Unguarded and 1991 hit tune Baby Baby (Amy Grant song)|Baby Baby as of the highest-selling Christian collection Heart in Motion. The collections and sole remained dispersed by a Christian label however experienced weighty play on pop broadcast stations and remained chart-toppers on the Billboard graphs. Since then, numerous creators have been tagged as crossing creator notwithstanding of if they initially designed to trade to the Christian trade, nonreligious trade, either either. The most noteworthy new Christian cross-

ing creators are Kirk Franklin, Switchfoot, The Afters, Relient K, and numerous of the creators on Tooth Nail Records such like MxPx, Underoath, Emery (band)|Emery, Lifehouse (band)|Lifehouse, Zao (American band)|Zao, and Dead Poetic.

A further uncommon illustration of a cross-over creator is Katy Perry. She disseminated a itty-bitty familiar, monetarily stillborn Christian collection in 2001 under her birthing designation, Katy Hudson. She additionally proceeded on to discharge monetarily prosperous nonreligious collections in 2008, 2010, and 2013. There are nevertheless a few obvious Christian components within her nonreligious tunes, especially her afterward work, such like Who Am I Living For (2010) and By The Grace of God (2013).

Amy Grant - Grammy Awards

;Wins
* 1982: Best Gospel Performance, Contemporary either Inspirational – Age to Age
* 1983: Best Gospel Performance, Female – Ageless Medley
* 1984: Best Gospel Performance, Female – Angels
* 1985: Best Gospel Performance, Female – Unguarded
* 1988: Best Gospel Performance, Female – Lead Me On
* 2006: Best Southern, Country, either Bluegrass Gospel Album – Rock of Ages... Hymns Faith

;Nominations
* 1979: Best Gospel Performance, Contemporary either Inspirational – My Father's Eyes
* 1980: Best Gospel Performance, Contemporary either Inspirational – Never Alone
* **1981: Best Gospel Performance, Contemporary either Inspirational – Amy Grant In Concert**
* 1990: Best Gospel Vocal Performance, Female – 'Tis So Sweet to Trust in Jesus
* 1992: Album of the Year – Heart in Motion
* 1992: Song of the Year – Baby Baby
* 1992: Record of the Year – Baby Baby
* 1992: Pop Performance Female – Baby Baby
* 1994: Children Spoken Word – Lion the Lamb
* 2008: Album of the Year (as highlighted artist) – These Days
* 2011: Best Gospel Song – Better Than a Hallelujah
* 2012: Best Country Song – Threaten Me with Heaven[http://www.cmt.com/news/country-music/1675195/grammy-award-nominations-revealed.jhtml Grammy Award Nominations Revealed]. Country Music Television

Christian rock - Controversy

In his publication Controversies of the Music Industry (2001), Richard D. Barnet states, numerous fundamentalist devout groupings and denominations bad-mouth rock tunes in common. Such groupings might review recognized modern Christian creators such like Amy Grant, Petra (band)|Petra, Steve Green (singer)|Steve Green and Twila Paris as blamable as nonreligious groups like White Zombie (band)|White Zombie and Marilyn Manson (band)|Marilyn Manson. And that, Christian rock groups also have come under critique for evidently advancing Satanism.

Barnet asserts that Christian rock acts are contentious since they undertake not encounter the Fundamental Evangelistic Association's (FEA) standards for a sincerely Christian tune. That is, it ought to be doctrinally right depending to the FEA's explanation of the Bible; it ought to not hold syncopation (Does it hustle the flesh to 'boogie,' either the will to commend the Lord?), and it ought to be dogmatically right (The type of a lot what is named Christian tunes might finest be distinguished as charming... Universalist, social democrat, idealistic, romantic.).organizations such like Dial-the-Truth Ministries trust Christian rock groups disappoint to cohere to the prohibitions of II Corinthians 6:14, that directs Christians opposed to uniting the good with the unrighteous.

Despite such critique, Barnet concludes: It ought to be marked that Christian rock as well has many million of advocates, even amid the office. Frank Breeden, leader of the Gospel Music Association, the business beyond the Dove Awards, states that There actually is no such object as a Christian B□ (musical note)|B-flat. Music in its normal self is an morality|amoral means of transport.

Julie Miller - Biography

Miller's foremost in a professional manner disseminated transcriptioning was with the cluster Streetlight, that comprised of Julie, Buddy and Ron Krueger. The self-titled collection was disseminated within 1983 and Julie and Buddy presented a few songwriting to the LP, that contained the first variant of Jesus in Your Eyes (later re-recorded for Orphans and Angels). How Could You Say No (written by Mickey Cates) was as well initially accomplished on this collection, and afterward contained within Julie's unaccompanied first public appearance Meet Julie Miller.

An eight-track 1985 demonstration as of Miller recorded 8 tunes, however grasped 11. Of the tunes on the tape, 2 tunes remained afterward contained on Meet Julie Miller, however the still existing 9 tunes remained not re-recorded. The tunes on this tape are: I Don't Need Anything Else, Mystery Love (Synth Pop Version), Love Is, I

Look to You, I Don't Need, What Does it Take, I Wanna Be Ready, King of my Heart (not the similar like that that emerged afterward on her foremost Myrrh release), My New Psychiatrist (Synth Pop Version with dissimilar lyrics), Debby Came Back, Dangerous Place (Synth Pop Version). Only one duplicate of this tape has noticed flow, it's unidentified if Julie applied them to shop for a record label either traded them at musical performances.

In 1987 Julie donated context voices to the tune Remember Me on Benny Hester's collection Through the Window.

Miller's melodic vocation originally took off following vocalist Sam Phillips (singer)|Sam Phillips ascertained a demonstration tape by the creator and turned it over to acquaintances at Myrrh Records. Miller was signed to a agreement and recorded her foremost unaccompanied collection, Meet Julie Miller for the label, disseminated within 1990. This collection contained supporting voices as of Shawn Colvin, Victoria Williams, Amy Grant, Kelly Willard and Russ Taff.

Miller's second unaccompanied collection, He Walks Through Walls (1991) as well contained supporting voices as of Colvin, Williams, Grant and Willard as with her first public appearance. Mark Heard and Reverend Dan Smith as well donated voices. This collection contained the first variant of the tune Broken Things, that was afterward re-recorded.

In 1992, Miller engaged in the collection, Cry of the Heart: Emily's Eyes, an collection disseminated to carry desire to sufferers of kid misuse, by delivering the name trail. Julie alluded to following a 2002 musical performance in Kentucky that the tune Emily's Eyes had one line checked out of it, as there was concern concerning the consequences. No additional particulars remained specified clarifying.

Miller's 1993 collection Orphans and Angels contained a duo with Emmylou Harris on the tune All My Tears, that has come to be one of Miller's nearly all well-liked tunes. Jazz singer Jimmy Scott as well donated voices. The tune was authored following the demise of Mark Heard. Miller as well veiled Heard's tune Treasure of the Broken Land. Shawn Colvin at one point more donated context voices. The tune S.O.S. As of this collection was disseminated like a audiovisual to Christian TV.

In 1994, Julie and her spouse Buddy Miller recorded Mark Heard's Orphans of God that was the name trail for the sole CD Mark Heard Tribute collection Strong Hand of Love. As well, they aided out Victoria Williams on her variant of What Kind of Friend for this program. Later that similar annum, either tunes remained contained on the two-CD Mark Heard Tribute Orphans of God, with the tune What sort of Friend extended by almost a complete minute.

Miller's 4th unaccompanied collection, Invisible Girl, was disseminated by Street Level Records, a retreat as of Word Records that disseminated her foremost 3 unaccompanied collections. Julie veiled The Williams Brothers tune Can't Cry Hard Enough on this collection. Victoria Williams, Mark Olson (musician)|Mark Olson and the Electrics presented context voices.

In 1997, Julie Miller shifted to Hightone Records and disseminated Blue Pony, an wide-ranging gathering that contains donations as of Emmylou Harris, Buddy Miller, Valerie Carter. This was pursued by her nearly all new unaccompanied collection Broken Things in 1999 that contains spic-and-span adaptations of Broken Things and All My Tears as well like noteworthy spic-and-span tunes I Know Why The River Runs, Orphan Train, Out In The Rain and I Still Cry. The tune By means of Sorrow was a duo with Innocence Mission's Karen Peris.

The foremost Duo collection of Buddy and Julie Miller, allowed Buddy Julie Miller was disseminated within 2001, this was pursued by Love Snuck Up a compiling of the Millers' Hightone Recordings in 2002.

After the 1998 Omagh bombarding in Northern Ireland, native vocalist Juliet Turner accomplished a variant of Miller's tune Broken Things at a commemorative facility for the sufferers of the bombarding.

Julie and Buddy Miller linked up with Victoria Williams, Mark Olson, and Jim Lauderdale for a European journey billed as The Rolling Creek Dippers in the 90s.

The Dixie Chicks, Linda Ronstadt, Ann Savoy, Lee Ann Womack, Emmylou Harris, Jars of Clay, Julie Roberts, Selah, Brooks Dunn, Lucy Kaplansky, Miranda Lambert, Kelly Willard and Ilse DeLange have recorded the tunes of Julie Miller, as well like tunes authored by either her and Buddy.

Buddy Miller proclaimed that this fall, a Julie Miller compiling is designed, that tend to contain traces selected by Julie as of her foremost 4 collections, that have been out of print for numerous annums.

Christian music industry - Downplayed religious content

An early Christian record label, Lamb Lion Records (founded by Pat Boone) announced in 1978 that it was their objective to make crossing creators, however they remained restricted by absence of dispersion to the nonreligious market. Both difficulties influenced Christian tags in to the 1990s. Since folks do not comprehend [the term] 'Blood of Christ|the Blood of Jesus, ' declared a administrator for Lamb Lion, ...music that interfaces should style it one other means. We've received to here and now a pleasantly understated however delicate Christian dispatch. Lyrics with muted devout subject matter have come to be ordinary in the industry; One commentator details out that the nonreligious hit Spirit in the Sky has further clear and obvious devout mentions compared to do numerous new Christian broadcast strikes.

Some reviewers have supposed that CCM frequently utilizes negligible straight divinity, and promotes a Jesus is my lover picture of God. Using downplayed devout subject matter in words has permitted a few creators to cross over and create important influence in to the common trade. Some Christian groups are capable to undertake this when keeping their ID in the Christian trade. For instance, MercyMe, whose duple platinum collection Almost There (MercyMe album)|Almost There created the Christian and nonreligious graph hit I Can Only Imagine (MercyMe song)|I Can Only Imagine. However, the words of the sole, when Christian in essence, hold what one commentator calls somewhat wiktionary:vacuous|vacuous divinity.

Sometimes crossing over produces vagueness over if an creator is Christian (a Christian band), either the creator is devised of Christians and creates tunes that pleas to Christian tunes fans however does not provide to the Christian trade (Christians in a band). Such creators are:

***Chevelle, whose Point No. 1|debut collection was disseminated to Christian tunes markets, experienced 3 Dove prizes. However, the group is not normally contemplated to be a Christian group this day. On that subject the group states We initially signed with Squint Entertainment|a record corporation that was sponsored by Word Records|Word (a Christian label lodging John Tesh and Amy Grant), thus the record was in Christian book stores. It was actually an accidental object.**

*Project 86 has occasionally been tagged a Christian group, though the group its normal self eschewed the label. The group contemplates its handcraft to be the finest transport of their dispatch. Frontman Andrew Schwab has presented some declarations on the subject. We're not going to proceed in there and utter 'Hey we are the Christian group. We're going to take ourselves like a usual group. Hopefully folks must like our tunes and examine in to the group [...] and they tend to absorb our faiths. If we are performing at Ozzfest either on Family Values Tour|Family Values..., the group informed 7ball following the discharge of Drawing Black Lines|their second collection, there is a considerable layer of diplomacy required in line to reach that type of public. In a 2007 conversation, Schwab additional pronounced We on every relevant occasion inform folks that the objective has been to simply record tunes that we fancy, and record tunes optimistically that is demanding and stirring to folks and does not sound like all things other out there.

*Switchfoot is frequently referenced to like a Christian group, mainly expected to their participation with the Christian rock set in their first days. But the group has on every relevant occasion avoided this label: For us, it's a persuasion, not a category,... Speaks Jon Foreman. ...these tunes are for everybody. Calling us 'Christian rock' inclines to be a container that shuts a few folks out and precludes them. And that is not what we are attempting to undertake. Music has on every relevant occasion unlocked my mind—and that is what we desire. Duly, Foreman's words direct clear of preachiness, unique announcements of persuasion, either even whatever reference of Jesus|Jesus Christ, in lieu Social commentary|questioning the condition quo, investigating Existentialism|existential subjects via Socratic conversation in that he replies queries with further queries, investigating frustrations, either plainly being motivational. Even thus, this placing has not estranged their Christian fans. As in their Indie (music)|indie days, they are nevertheless dispersed to Christian trade outlet vents via Sparrow Records, highlighted onto Christian broadcast and graphs, and offered GMA Music Awards|Dove Awards, even following experiencing been signed to the normal Columbia Records. Spin (magazine)|Spin author Andrew Beaujon bears the view that their words frequently have 2 dissimilar definitions, one signifying for a Christian public and one signifying for the respite of us. They attempt to connect to 2 dissimilar groupings of folks at at one point.

My Best Christmas

'My Best Christmas' (2005) is an Amy Grant compiling collection of her 3 foregoing Christmas collections. It was disseminated by YMC Records (Your Music Channel Records). It attributes 2 hard-to-find Christmas songs: Merry Christmas Darling, a cover of the Carpenters tune, that was solely accessible on the Target store variant of A Christmas to Remember, and Child of God, that shows onto the various-artists compiling collection One Silent Night (2000). A dissimilar variant of Child of God emerged on a limited-edition Christmas maxi-single in 1999 disseminated to advance A Christmas to Remember.

Oh How the Years Go By - Amy Grant cover

The tune was then veiled by singer-songwriter Amy Grant and disseminated on her 1994 collection House of Love (Amy Grant album)|House of Love. It was the 6th discharge as of that collection.

*** Original collection variant (5:15), accessible on the House of Love (Amy Grant album)|House of Love album**
* Radio correct, accessible on the sole with an acoustic introduction
* Original collection variant with acoustic start, accessible on the single
*** Live variant (4:35), accessible on the Time Again...Amy Grant Live collection**

Say Once More - Background

The foremost 2 selects as of Lead Me On (Amy Grant album)|Lead Me On broken the normal pop graphs in extension to topping the U.S. Christian graphs. The album's 4 still existing selects, nevertheless, charted solely on Christian broadcast. The discharge of Say Once More appeared at a time once Grant was at what appeared to be the stature of her vocation, experiencing not long ago come to be the foremost Contemporary Christian tunes creator to attain triumph on pop broadcast (though she ought to afterward attain long considerable triumph in the 1990s). The Lead Me On (Amy Grant album)|Lead Me On collection is extensively contemplated one of the largest and nearly all prosperous Christian collections at any time recorded and was designated the largest of altogether time by CCM Magazine.

Half the Sky movement - 30 Songs / 30 Days

Legendary and upcoming feminine performers as of about the planet come alltogether to aid [http://www.halftheskymovement.org/30-songs-30-days Half the Sky]: Turning Oppression in to Opportunity for Women Worldwide, a multi-platform media program motivated by Nicholas Kristof and Sheryl WuDunn's best-selling publication.

For 30 successive days (Sept. 3rd to Oct. 2nd), a spic-and-span tune as of a highlighted feminine creator must be presented for gratis down-load for twenty-four hours onto www.halftheskymovement.org. Visitors to the Half the Sky Movement site whoever involve with the drive tend to be renumerated with a tune that that talks to the subjects of Half the Sky: Turning Oppression in to Opportunity for Women Worldwide, motivated by the best-selling publication.

Confirmed partaking creators include: A Fine Frenzy, India.Arie, Brandi Carlile, Sheryl Crow, Kimya Dawson, Fatoumata Diawara, Karen Elson, Frally, Amy Grant, Patty Griffin, Gemma Hayes, Emmylou Harris, Katie Herzig, Norah Jones, Alicia Keys, Angelique Kidjo, Ingrid Michaelson, The McCrary Sisters, Mountain Man, Joan Osborne, Corinne Bailey Rae, Bonnie Raitt, Oumou Sangare, Ana Tijoux, Rokia Traore, St. Vincent, Julia Stone, Brooke Waggoner, Abigail Washburn, and Lucinda Williams.

Mosaic: Pieces of My Life So Far - Release and reception

The publication was disseminated on October 16, 2007 in hardcover press by Flying Dolphin Press and WaterBrook Press. Mosaic experienced rave appraisals as of a diversity of outlet vents, containing Entertainment Weekly and Christianity Today. In November, the publication launched on the New York Times Bestseller catalog at #35, growing to #27 in December. The publication as well consumed some 7-day periods in the Amazon.com Top 100 best-selling publications catalog.

Grant downplayed the media's portrayal of the publication as a tell-all, indicating, It's not an memoirs, however further a gathering of recollections, tune words, verse, and a limited images. Still, she has recognized in talks that the publication attributes a numeral of frank narratives. On her internet site, Grant informed her fan association that she is worried to get back in the workshop following the publication is completed, and recreate myself as an almost-50 carrying out female and specified that she designs to record once more in the time to come.

To advance the publication, Grant started a national publication journey and WaterBrook Press backed a chief on the web weblog journey. Grant's publication journey concurred with her own musical performance journey and Symphony journey at the time, that as well advanced Mosaic alongside with her spic-and-span Greatest Hits (Amy Grant album)|Greatest Hits collection.

In December, Amy Grant emerged on The Oprah Winfrey Show in an chapter allowed Heading Home for the Holidays. The Christmas-themed chapter highlighted an encompassing conversation with either Grant and spouse Vince Gill as well like altogether 5 of the couple's kids. Grant gave a journey of her home and of her authoring cottage on the show. During the chapter, Grant deliberated Mosaic at extent and service Oprah Winfrey interpret extracts as of her best-loved segments. The 2 launched the tune True Love (Amy Grant song)|True Love, that has not ever been recorded however was contained within poetic shape in Mosaic, as a live duo. Additionally, Amy chanted an extract of What the Angels See, one other uncataloged tune with perfect words inner Mosaic. The workshop public experienced present duplicates of Mosaic, Grant's Greatest Hits (Amy Grant album)|Greatest Hits collection, and Gill's These Days (Vince Gill album)|These Days collection. Following the show, the book's placing on the Amazon.com and New York Times bestsellers catalogs spiked. The chapter pronounced Grant's 3rd emergence on The Oprah Winfrey Show and the foremost in almost 10 annums. It was Vince Gill's foremost emergence.

Other TV emergences contained The View (U.S. TV series)|The View, Paula's Party with service Paula Deen, Today (NBC program)|The Today Show, The 700 Club, CMT Insider, CMT Loaded, CNN's Showbiz Tonight, Hour of Power, and Fox Friends. Additionally, the upstart Gospel Music Channel screened a docudrama on Amy Grant as piece of their Faith and Fame serials.

At the time of Mosaic's discharge, Grant, a one-time representative for Land O'Lakes|Land O'Lakes Butter, grew to be a representative for Country Crock butter and the organization's Spread the Sharing drive. The publication, the drive, and Grant's Greatest Hits (Amy Grant album)|Greatest Hits CD remained cross-promoted. In extension, in aid of the spic-and-span publication and CD, Amy Grant started her own 10 chapter podcast on iTunes, wherever it was produced accessible aimed at gratis. The podcast veiled spotlights of the artist's existence and vocation and was a chief piece of a greater iTunes advertising drive that pronounced the start of Grant's whole index in digitally remastered, digital claims management-free setup onto the iTunes Music Store.

Mosaic: Pieces of My Life So Far - Contents

The publication is split in to an start, a vocation directory, and 4 themed segments, every one designated following one of Grant's songs: Every Road, Heirlooms, Lead Me On (Amy Grant song)|Lead Me On, and Takes a Little Time (maxi single)|Takes a Little Time. Inside every one are different narratives as of Grant's existence, first verses, not so large black and white images, and words to tunes that Grant in person authored, normally associated to either motivated by the tale right away foregoing either ensuing the words. There are no tunes as of whatever of Grant's foremost 3 collections. However, the publication holds words to 4 tunes that Grant has up till now to record.

Say Once More - 20th Anniversary Edition

In 2007, Grant had left Word Records and AM Records, the 2 tags that had supervised the first discharge of Lead Me On. That annum, her spic-and-span record label, EMI Records, reissued a spic-and-span digitally remastered issue of Lead Me On. In 2008, EMI Records|EMI once more reissued the collection, this time as a double-disc 20th Anniversary Edition. The second disc of that re-release highlighted a spic-and-span transcriptioning of Say Once More by Amy Grant with Owsley (musician)|Will Owsley on stringed instrument. Grant depicted the spic-and-span transcriptioning as a songwriter's variant, with the tunes cleared down to additional highlight the words. In advancing the re-release, Grant accomplished the spic-and-span auditory variant throughout

different media emergences.

Target Corporation - Holiday advertising

Promoting Christmas selling is a ensign of Target's marketing. Target has enlisted numerous crooning characters to advance its break selling. Amy Grant and Charlotte Church have been amid the spokespersons noticed over the annums. One specific Christmas drive highlighted LeAnn Rimes and the Looney Tunes types (Bugs Bunny, etcetera.).

Jesu, Joy of Man's Desiring - Cover versions

Chloe Agnew (solo variant on her Walking In The Air album), Méav Ní Mhaolchatha, Órla Fallon and Máiréad Nesbitt as of Celtic Woman.
*Apollo 100, at elevated pace on microelectronic keyboards (1972). This variant reached its highest point at numeral 6 on the Hot 100 and numeral 2 on the Hot Adult Contemporary|Easy Listening graph, and was highlighted in the feature Boogie Nights (1997).
*Claudio Baglioni's tune Per incanto e per amore was motivated by this work.
*The Beach Boys, as a base for the tune Lady Lynda, however short of the terms.
*Frida Boccara's tune L'enfant AUX cymbales (Dans Les rues de Rio) utilizes the tune.
*Jim Brickman, noticed on his collection Grace (though he recorded the melodist asTraditional in lieu of Bach).
*Sarah Brightman on her collection, A Winter Symphony
*Wendy Carlos, on her collection, Switched-On Bach
*Leon Fleisher, on his 2004 collection Two Hands.
*Renée Fleming, on her Sacred Songs collection as of 2005.
***Amy Grant, an involved bit noticed on her 1992 collection, Home for Christmas (Amy Grant album)|Home for Christmas.**
*Josh Groban, on the 2001 eponymous collection Josh Groban (album)|Josh Groban.
*Gary Hoey, as Desire on the Bug Alley collection.
*Jigsaw (band)|Jigsaw, on their 1970 first public appearance collection Letherslade Farm
*Leo Kottke, noticed on his 1969 collection 6- and 12-String Guitar.
*Sissel Kyrkjebø (on her Northern Lights collection as of 2007).
*Roger McGuinn, in the audiovisual Guitar Lesson speaks this motivated the introduction to, Mr Tambourine Man
*Mormon Tabernacle Choir, on their collection Jesu, Joy of Man's Desiring: 20 Great Bach Handel Choruses
*The Move on their collection, Shazam, the tune Cherry Blossom Clinic Revisited

utilizes extracts as of this bit.
* Paulinho Nogueira, on his self-titled 1967 LP and then on his 1999 collection Coração Violão.
*Popa Chubby, on the collection Back to New York City
* Baden Powell, recorded the tune numerous periods throughout his vocation, the foremost one being on his 1966's live collection next to Vinícius de Moraes.
*Rebecca St. James
*The Brian Setzer Orchestra's tune Bach's Bounce utilizes the tune.
*Isao Tomita on the collection Dawn Chorus (performed on synthesizers).
*TVXQ, on their 2004 collection Christmas Gift as of TVXQ
*Grover Washington, Jr. (on his Breath Of Heaven: A Holiday Collection collection as of 1997).
*George Winston, noticed on his collection December (George Winston album)|December.
*Shirō Sagisu, for the 1997 feature The End of Evangelion.

The tune was applied within a 2011 TV advertisement for a Japanese cell telephone, wherever a colossus gravity-driven Xylophone was created within a Kyushu woods to play the tune.http://www.youtube.com/watch?v=C_CDLBTJD4Mfeature=player_embedded

Amy Grant - Early career

In 1976, Grant authored her foremost tune (Mountain Man), accomplished in common for the foremost time at Harpeth Hall School, the all-girls educational institution she tended to, recorded a demonstration tape for her father and mother with kirk youth-leader Brown Bannister, additionally afterward once Bannister was dubbing a duplicate of the tape, Chris Christian, the possessor of the transcriptioning workshop, perceived the demonstration and named Word Records. He played it over the telephone, and she was presented a transcriptioning agreement, 5 7-day periods beforehand her 16th anniversary. In 1977, she recorded her foremost collection named Amy Grant (album)|Amy Grant, created by Brown Bannister, whoever ought to as well make her following 11 collections. It was disseminated within first 1978, one month beforehand her high-school graduation. Toward the conclusion of 1978 she accomplished her foremost ticketed musical performance following starting her foremost annum at Furman University. In May 1979, when at the album-release party for her second collection, My Father's Eyes (album)|My Father's Eyes, Grant encountered Gary Chapman (musician)|Gary Chapman, whoever had authored the name trail and ought to come to be her foremost spouse. Grant and Chapman visited alltogether in mid-1979. In belated 1980, she moved to Vanderbilt University, wherever she was a associate of the fraternity

Kappa Alpha Theta. Grant additionally produced a limited further collections beforehand relinquishing out of school to follow a vocation in music—Never Alone, pursued by a couple of live collections in 1981 (In Concert (Amy Grant album)|In Concert and In Concert Volume Two (Amy Grant album)|In Concert Volume Two), either sponsored by an increased issue of the DeGarmo and Key|DeGarmo Key group. It was throughout those first exhibits that Grant as well recognized one of her musical performance trademarks: carrying out Barefoot. To date, Grant resumes to take off her footwear Midway via executions, as she has indicated it is simply further comfy.Preston and Steve broadcast show excerpt; May 2008

1982 saw the discharge of her success collection Age to Age. The collection holds the autograph trail, El Shaddai (song)|El Shaddai (written by Michael Card) and the Grant-Chapman wrote tune, In a Little While. El Shaddai was afterward granted one of the Songs of the Century by the RIAA in 2001. Grant experienced her foremost Grammy Award for Best Contemporary Gospel Performance, as well like 2 GMA Dove Awards for Gospel Artist of the Year and Pop/Contemporary Album of the Year. Age to Age grew to be the foremost Christian collection by a unaccompanied creator to be endorsed gold (1983) and the foremost Christian collection to be endorsed platinum (1985).

In the mid-1980s, Grant started touring and transcriptioning with youthful up-and-coming composer Michael W. Smith. Grant and Smith resume to have a forceful amity and originative connection, frequently authoring tunes for either donating voices to every one other's collections. During the 1980s, Grant was as well a back-up vocalist for Bill Gaither (gospel singer)|Bill Gaither.

Grant pursued this collection with the foremost of her Christmas albums—-albums that afterward ought to be the base for her break exhibits. In 1984, she disseminated one other pop-oriented Christian hit, Straight Ahead (Amy Grant album)|Straight Ahead, receiving Grant her foremost emergence at the Grammy Awards display in 1985. The head of NBC took notice of Grant's execution and named her administrator to publication her for her own Christmas out of the ordinary.

Myrrh Records

'Myrrh Records', as well familiar like 'Myrrh Worship', is a Christian tunes record label. According to Encyclopedia of American Gospel Music, the label was involved in elaborating a well-liked ensuing for Contemporary Christian tunes as the label that foremost issued tunes by Barry McGuire, 2nd Chapter of Acts, Randy Matthews and Nancy Honeytree. The label is as well familiar

for servicing like the foremost label for well-liked Christian crossing vocalist Amy Grant, whoever joined the label in 1977.
The label has as well issued such creators as B.J. Thomas, Benny Hester, Billy Preston, The Choir (alternative rock band)|The Choir, Cliff Richard, Crystal Lewis, Dakoda Motor Company, David and the Giants, pleased (band)|GLAD, Jaci Velasquez, Malcolm and Alwyn, Mark Heard, Michael Omartian|Michael and Stormie Omartian, Mike Warnke, One Bad Pig, Petra (band)|Petra, Phil Keaggy, Randy Stonehill, Richie Furay, Salvation Air Force, Sam Phillips (musician), Steve Archer, Steve Taylor, Rev. Milton Brunson and The Thompson Community Singers, and The 77s

The label started as Myrrh Records in 1972, however took a 5 annum pause starting in 2000 beforehand being relaunched by progenitor corporation Word Entertainment under the designation Myrrh Worship in 2005.

ReJoyce: The Christmas Album

'ReJoyce: The Christmas Album' is the 4th workshop collection by American pop vocalist Jessica Simpson. Released by Columbia Records on November 23, 2004. The collection attributes cover adaptations of well-liked Christmas, it contains a duo (music)|duet with her female sibling, Ashlee Simpson, on the tune Little Drummer Boy. Additionally, it as well contains a duo with Nick Lachey, Simpson's spouse at the time, on Baby, It's Cold Outside. The cover of Amy Grant's Breath of Heaven (Mary's Song) is noteworthy, as Simpson has indicated that Amy Grant is one of her best-loved transcriptioning creators and her part model.
Its selects are Let It Snow, Let It Snow, Let It Snow and What Christmas Means To Me (although no subsequent audiovisual was produced); the tune O Holy Night has a audiovisual.

ReJoyce: The Christmas Album was disseminated following Simpson's nearly all prosperous workshop collection of vocation In This Skin (2003). The collection has traded 669,000 duplicates within the United States, as of February 23, 2009, depending to Nielsen SoundScan, and has been endorsed RIAA certification|gold by the Recording Industry Association of America in January 2005. Rejoyce has traded over 2 million duplicates international.

Scissors Cut - History

In August 1981, Garfunkel disseminated his 5th unaccompanied collection Scissors Cut (U.S. #113, U.K. #51). This collection contained the Gallagher Lyle hit A Heart in New York (U.S. #61). The U.K. Variant holds the trail The Romance somewhat compared to Bright Eyes (Art Garfunkel song)|Bright Eyes. The collection was co-produced by Roy Halee, whoever as well co-produced the Simon Garfunkel collections, containing Bridge over Troubled Water. Paul Simon produces a brief emergence on In Cars carrying out context voices. Near the conclusion of the tune, Art sings, somewhat mystically, rules as of Girl as of the North Country|Girl From The North Country (Remember myself to one whoever lives there, she at one point was a genuine fancy of mine that its normal self appears as of Scarborough Fair - an aged English ballad veiled by Simon and Garfunkel on the collection Parsley, Sage, Rosemary and Thyme - a words taken out as of this tune.) The collection is committed to Laurie Bird and contains a limited picture of Ms. Bird on the back cover.

Garfunkel was wrecked by Ms. Bird's demise in his New York flat in June 1979 when he was in Europe shooting Bad Timing|Bad Timing - A Sensual Obsession. Art was stated at the time, Laurie was the largest object I at any time realized in my existence, at the moment I've missed it. In 1988, he appended, I took her demise extremely and stayed Moody over it via a lot of the 80's. He grew to be a little of a recluse ensuing the disaster and would not discharge one other unaccompanied collection till 1988's Lefty (album)|Lefty (excluding 1986's The Animals' Christmas with Amy Grant).

Word Records - History

Word Records was set up in Waco, TX|Waco, Texas, in 1951 by Jarrell McCracken. The label's designation is founded on a 16-minute conversed expression transcriptioning authored and recounted by McCracken, the foremost transcriptioning disseminated by the label, allowed the The Game of Life. The 23-year aged KWTX sportscaster in Waco had interpreted an item by Jimmy Allen, a erstwhile sportsperson whoever grew to be a Baptist cleric, and founded his transcriptioning on the item that as well is named The Game of Life. The happening is founded on a complete extent matchup amid the drives of Good and Evil with Jesus Christ and Satan instructing the 2 groups. McCracken was well known with detailed running commentary transmitting, experiencing generated virtual baseball game diversions for broadcast transmit founded on cable outlines. McCracken initially offered his The Game of Life presentment on Sunday Nights at different churches about the principal Texas zone. Everywhere he offered The Game of Life, he received calls for duplicates. Eventually, he had a small run of records forced to proffer at churches wherever he talked. The fictitious broadcast facility in the transcriptioning has the call letters WORD, thus that was hard-copied on the label of the custom record.

After being questioned by a pal once he was going to discharge a continuation, McCracken additionally determined to follow the label on a further important layer. Based on an conference with Jarrell McCracken, May 1997, Waco, TX

Subsequent records concentrated on different conversed expression recordings, however Word shortly branched out in to southern canon tunes. Early staff members for the label contained Tom Norfleet, Kurt Kaiser and Ralph Carmichael.

The label fought originally till Marvin Norcross grew to be an assets collaborator. By 1954, Word had come to be a issuing home as well.

Several subordinate tags remained commenced over the years: Canaan Records in the 60s, Myrrh Records (1972) and DaySpring Records in 1977, and Rejoice Records in the 80's. Two of those tags no more subsist this day in their first shape. The Myrrh Label was resurrected in 2005 as a commend and reverence record label: Myrrh Worship. Canaan Records was as well re-opened in first 2007 with Dave Clark at the controls.

Larry Norman's Solid Rock Records had a dispersion transact with Word as of 1975 to 1980. Artists on Solid Rock contained Norman, Randy Stonehill, Daniel Amos, Tom Howard (musician)|Tom Howard and Mark Heard.

In 1983, Chris Christian signed a dispersion transact to turn his label Home Sweet Home Records as of Benson Records to Word Records, this day it is nevertheless energetic and stays under the autonomous possession of Chris Christian.

Light Records was dispersed in the 1970s by Word Records beforehand being traded to Ralph Carmichael in the 1980s.

Reunion Records signed a dispersion and encouragement agreement in the 80s, the accord lasted well in to the 1990s. Today, Reunion Records is dispersed via Provident Music Group.

Star Song was dispersed by Word Records but left their dispersion transact in the belated 1980s to mark with Sparrow Records that was taken over by Chordant Distribution and then by EMI.

Distribution transacts with different tags in the 1970s, 1980s, and first 1990s permitted Word Records to ascend to the top, nearly lodging a who's-who in Christian tunes. They dispersed, advanced, and publicized the largest designations in modern Christian tunes. Artists such like Amy Grant, Michael W. Smith, Rich Mullins, Russ Taff|Russ and Tori Taff, Benny Hester, Paul Smith (Christian tunes performer)|Paul Smith, The Imperials, Petra, Sandi Patti,

Kenny Marks, Wayne Watson, Carman (singer)|Carman, The Archers presenting Steve Archer, White Heart, Gaither Vocal Band, Bill Gaither Trio, Point of Grace, Love Song (band)|Love Song, Sweet Comfort Band, The Nelons, Happy Goodman Family presenting Rusty Goodman, Florida Boys, Guardian (band)|Guardian and different creators.

In the 1976, McCracken traded piece attention in his label to the American Broadcasting Company. 10 annums afterward, ABC amalgamated with Capital Cities Communications|Capital Cities, Inc. And enforced McCracken out of the corporation.

From 1984 to 1990, Word was dispersed in the common trade by AM Records and then by Epic Records till 2002.

In 1992, Capital Cities ABC traded Word to Thomas Nelson (publisher)|Thomas Nelson, Inc. For $72 Million, and Nelson produced 2 chief changes—developing the here and now whirling W emblem for publication articles that was unwrapped in 1995, and as well moving its head offices as of Waco, Texas, to its here and now head offices in Nashville. Nelson cut the record label and publication issuing arms in 1996 once the tags remained traded to Gaylord Entertainment. In an accord with Gaylord, Thomas Nelson sustained to employ the Word Publishing designation for its publication imprint till 2002, at which time it grew to be W Publishing Group and kept the whirling W emblem. A extremely contentious advertisement drive instituted at the CBA gathering in 2002 generated judicial proceeding, worked out afterward.

After Colin Reed took over Gaylord Entertainment in 2001, the Hotelier produced business amends at the corporation, containing the ousting of well-established leader Roland Lundy, and traded off the Word Entertainment cluster to then-AOL Time Warner in 2002. In 2002, erstwhile Atlantic Records Christian division administrator Barry Landis momentarily took the placing of leader of the label cluster division. Word proceeded via a time of reorganization, ending their Los Angeles tunes issuing function, consuming Myrrh Records, Squint Entertainment, and Everland Entertainment in to the Word Label Group, and decreasing In-house workforce. Curb Records as well obtained a interest in the corporation throughout this time. In 2004, the corporation was traded once more as piece of Time Warner divestiture of its tunes division, vending it to a cluster of financiers guided by Edgar Bronfman, Jr.|Edgar Bronfman to shape a recently autonomous Warner Music Group.

Love Beyond Reason - Personnel

* Randy Stonehill: Vocals, Acoustic Guitar
*Milo Carter: Guitar.

*Don Griffin: Guitar.
*Steve Wilkinson: Bass.
*David Raven: Drums.
*Barry Miller Kaye: Fairlight C.M.I.
***Amy Grant: Second head voices on I Could Never Say Goodbye.**
*Danny Jacob: Lead Guitars, Guitar Solo, Sweaty, Golden, Guitars.
*Rick Geragi: Congas, Bongos, Claves, Tambourine, Cabasa Percussion.
*Denver Smith: Additional Synthesizers And M.I.D.I. Technician.
*Andrea Saparoff: Fairlight C.M.I., Orchestral Arrangement Programming
*Barry The Bear Liss: Harmonica Solo.
*Jay Leslie: Soprano Sax Solo
*Mark Heard: Additional Guitar
*Background vocals: Randy Stonehill, Caryn Robin, Táta Vega, Bryan Duncan, Richie Furay, Tonio K..

Vince Gill - Personal life

Gill wedded region vocalist Janis Oliver of Sweethearts of the Rodeo celebrity, in 1980, and they had one girl. Gill sometimes varied sound for his wife's group at musical performances. They detached in the mid-1990s and finally separated in June 1998. Gill wedded Christian/pop vocalist Amy Grant in March 2000. They have one girl. Gill, alongside with his spouse Grant, is a fan of the Nashville Predators. They have been season tag bearers eversince the beginning season and are frequently presented on the large screen. In the 2007 playoffs, they chanted the national song for every one game. On Sunday, September 8, 2013, Gill's musical performance at the Kansas City, MO Kauffman Center was picketed by the Topeka, Kansas-based Westboro Baptist Church founded on asserts that he is an fornicator eversince he separated his foremost spouse and wedded Grant.

Though Gill not ever tended to school, he's a great fan of the University of Oklahoma football game group. He as well joins almost any men's basket ball game at Belmont University in Nashville. Gill is as well an keen golfer, with a impairment about 1 either 2.

Worship music - Popularity

As a commonplace category of Christian tunes noticed in Western churches CWM has confirmed prosperous. Its ease intents that nearly anybody with a few level of capability on a melodic tool might unite in the directing of it. It is in a manner befitting to the melodic palate of a propagation whoever have developed up paying attention to pop tunes and notice traditional tunes fewer attainable.

Some tunes at the moment emerge in further customary hymnals. Evangelical Lutheran Worship (published in 2006 by the Evangelical Lutheran Church in America) contains Lord, I Lift Your Name on High by Rick Founds and Shout to the Lord by Darlene Zschech. The United Methodist Hymnal (1989) contains Thy Word Is a Lamp by Amy Grant and Take Our Bread by Joe Wise.

Christmas album - Other popular Christmas songs

Other well-liked Christmas tunes frequently perceived include: I've Got My Love to Keep Me Warm (1937), Happy Holiday (song)|Happy Holiday (1942), Baby It's Cold Outside (1944), Merry Christmas Baby (1947), Mary's Boy Child (1956), and We Need a Little Christmas (1966)—all recorded by a numeral of acts. Bing Crosby and the Andrews Sisters had a hit with Mele Kalikimaka in 1950, and Crosby instituted Marshmallow World (backed by The Lee Gordon Singers and the Sonny Burke Orchestra) in the similar annum. In 1951 he recorded Christmas in Killarney. Frank Sinatra set The Christmas Waltz on the B-side of his variant of White Christmas (song)|White Christmas in 1954, and contained Mistletoe and Holly on his 1957 collection A Jolly Christmas From Frank Sinatra. Nat King Cole set his stamp on The Happiest Christmas Tree, Buon Natale (Means Merry Christmas to You), and The Little Boy that Santa Claus Forgot on different Christmas collection deliverances.

Other Christmas tunes include:
*My Favorite Things (song)|My Favorite Things veiled by The Supremes|Diana Ross The Supremes in 1965.
*Run Rudolph Run disseminated by Chuck Berry in 1958.
*Pretty Paper sung by Roy Orbison in 1963; composer Willie Nelson afterward had a hit with his personal tune in 1978.
*Little Saint Nick and Merry Christmas, Baby disseminated by the Beach Boys on The Beach Boys' Christmas Album|their Christmas collection in 1964.
*Please Come Home for Christmas is at the moment related with The Eagles' 1978 discharge, however it was authored and disseminated by Charles Brown (musician)|Charles Brown in 1960.
*Give Love on Christmas Day disseminated by the Jackson 5 in 1970.
*This Christmas (Donny Hathaway song)|This Christmas is finest familiar for the Chris Brown (American entertainer)|Chris Brown 2007 variant, however Donny Hathaway initially disseminated the tune in 1970.
*Christmas Is the Time to Say I Love You by Billy Squier in 1981.
*Suzy Snowflake recorded by Rosemary Clooney in 1951.
*Christmas (Baby Please Come Home) disseminated by Darlene Love in 1963.
*Jingle Bells? veiled by Barbra Streisand in 1967.
*Merry Christmas Darling by The Carpenters in 1970.

*River (Joni Mitchell song)|River by Joni Mitchell in 1971.
*This Christmas (Patti LaBelle album)|If Everyday Could Be Like Christmas by Patti Labelle in 1990.
***Grown Up Christmas List|My Grown Up Christmas List veiled by Amy Grant on her break collection Home for Christmas (Amy Grant album)|Home for Christmas in 1992.**
*"All I Want for Christmas Is You" disseminated by Mariah Carey in 1994.

Christmas Time is Here, authored by Lee Mendelson and Vince Guaraldi for the 1965 A Charlie Brown Christmas cartoon TV out of the ordinary, was made fashionable by the chorus of St. Paul's Episcopal Church in San Rafael, California. From the British Isles have come such well-liked names as: Happy Xmas (War Is Over) (1971) by John Lennon, Step Into Christmas (1973) by Elton John, I Believe In Father Christmas (1975) by Greg Lake, Wonderful Christmastime (1979) by Paul McCartney, Thank God It's Christmas (1984) by Queen (band)|Queen, Fairytale of New York (1987) by The Pogues, and Mistletoe and Wine by Cliff Richard in 1988.

Adult contemporary - History

Many broadcast stations played top-40 strikes, notwithstanding of category, till the mid-1970s (when they started to mark specific statistic groups). Specialized broadcast stations additionally played concrete melodic categories.

When rock and spin grew to be well-liked throughout the mid-1950s, traditionalist broadcast stations desired to play non-rock hits; those stations contained grown-up norms and great group names to interest to ones listening whoever had developed up with these tunes. This setup was familiar like middle-of-the-road (MOR), played on WJR in Detroit, WGN (AM)|WGN and WBBM (AM)|WBBM in Chicago, KGO (AM)|KGO in San Francisco, WBBR|WNEW in New York, and WCCO (AM)|WCCO in Minneapolis. Billboard periodical foremost issued an Hot Adult Contemporary Tracks|adult-contemporary tunes graph in 1961, though it did not employ the designation Adult Contemporary till 1979.

While nearly all well-liked MOR stations at the time remained on AM, beautiful-music and traditional music|classical stations started to turn to FM since of its senior acoustic caliber. Although nearly all easy-listening tunes was involved, grown-up modern tunes aim to produce a alike (lite) setup with harmonious traces by well-liked creators.

Early illustrations of the adult-contemporary setup contained WHAS (AM)|WHAS in Louisville, Kentucky and KDKA (AM)|KDKA in Pittsburgh, erstwhile MOR stations that started performing less norms and further modern, non-hard-rock tunes. During the mid-1970s WHAS named its setup Good and Gold, containing rock-and-roll oldies on its playlist and performing harder-rock tunes on Saturday and Sunday. Mellow rock stations (such as WMGK in Philadelphia, WBBM-FM in Chicago, KCBS-FM|KNX-FM in Los Angeles and KMNB|WCCO-FM in Minneapolis) appeared on FM, blending adult-contemporary strikes with collection traces by singer-songwriters such like James Taylor, Carly Simon, Carole King, Janis Ian, Paul Simon and Elton John.

VH1 started as an adult-contemporary variant of MTV, attractive to spectators in their 30s and 40s. During the mid-1990s, it started performing recordings by Hootie The Blowfish, the Gin Blossoms, Alanis Morissette, Melissa Etheridge, the Spin Doctors, Amy Grant and Ace of Base.

Adult modern tunes has evolved; creators such like Barbra Streisand, the Carpenters, Barry Manilow, Captain Tennille and Olivia Newton-John reached its highest point in reputation in the 1970s, getting to be fewer well-liked in the 1980s once creators whose tunes recordings experienced weighty gyration on MTV, such like Phil Collins, Madonna (entertainer)|Madonna, Janet Jackson, Culture Club, Cyndi Lauper, Tears for Fears and Whitney Houston, started materializing on the adult-contemporary graphs. Phil Collins has been depicted by AllMusic as one of the most prosperous pop and grown-up modern singers of the '80s and past. VH1 has repositioned off as of its adult-contemporary setup with Destiny's Child, Eminem, Jay-Z and Snoop Dogg. Since the middle 2000s (decade)|2000s, groups such like Wilco and Feist (singer)|Feist have thrusted indie rock in to the adult-contemporary setup.

54th Annual Grammy Awards - Country

;Best Country Solo Performance
*'Mean (song)|Mean – Taylor Swift'
* Dirt Road Anthem – Jason Aldean
* I'm Gonna Love You Through It – Martina McBride
* Honey Bee (Blake Shelton song)|Honey Bee – Blake Shelton
* Mama's Song – Carrie Underwood

;Best Country Duo/Group Performance
*'Barton Hollow (song)|Barton Hollow – The Civil Wars'
* Don't You Wanna Stay – Jason Aldean Kelly Clarkson
* You and Tequila – Kenny Chesney presenting Grace Potter and the Nocturnals|Grace Potter
* Are You Gonna Kiss Me either Not – Thompson Square

;Best Country Song

*'Mean (song)|Mean'
**'Taylor Swift, composer (Taylor Swift)'
* Are You Gonna Kiss Me either Not
** Jim Collins (singer)|Jim Collins David Lee Murphy, songwriters (Thompson Square)
* God Gave Me You
** Dave Barnes, composer (Blake Shelton)
* Just Fishin'
** Casey Beathard, Monty Criswell Ed Hill, songwriters (Trace Adkins)
* Guitar Slinger (Vince Gill album)|Threaten Me with Heaven
**** Vince Gill, Amy Grant, Owsley (musician)|Will Owsley Dillon O'Brian, songwriters (Vince Gill)**
* You and Tequila
** Matraca Berg Deana Carter, songwriters (Kenny Chesney presenting Grace Potter and the Nocturnals|Grace Potter)

;Best Country Album
*'Own the Night – Lady Antebellum'
* My Kinda Party – Jason Aldean
* Chief (album)|Chief – Eric Church
* Red River Blue – Blake Shelton
* Here for a Good Time – George Strait
* Speak Now – Taylor Swift

Hee Haw - Guest appearances

Hee Haw highlighted at minimum 2, and occasionally 3 either 4, visitor famous persons every one 7 days. While nearly all of the visitor stars remained of course region tunes creators, a ample span of different well known leading lights remained highlighted. Those creating visitor emergences contained, however remained not restricted to:
Alabama (band)|Alabama,
Atlanta (band)|Atlanta,
Buddy Alan,
The Aldridge Sisters,
Jed Allan,
Rex Allen,
Paul Anka,
Bill Anderson (singer)|Bill Anderson,
John Anderson (musician)|John Anderson,
Lynn Anderson,
Garner Ted Armstrong,

Eddy Arnold,
Chet Atkins,
Gene Autry,
Hoyt Axton,
Baillie the Boys,
Razzy Bailey,
Butch Baker,
Moe Bandy,
Ava Barber,
Billy Barty,
Molly Bee,
Johnny Bench,
Matraca Berg,
Byron Berline,
Amanda Blake,
Suzy Bogguss,
Randy Boone,
Tony Booth (musician)|Tony Booth,
actor Ernest Borgnine,
former ace football game participant and present FOX NFL Sunday co-host Terry Bradshaw,
comedian Foster Brooks,
Garth Brooks,
Brooks Dunn,
the Bellamy Brothers,
Clarence Gatemouth Brown,
Family Brown,
Jim Ed Brown,
Marty Brown (singer)|Marty Brown,
T. Graham Brown,
The Buckaroos (Buck Owens' band),
Kenneth C. Burns|Jethro Burns,
Johnny Bush,
comedianne Ruth Buzzi,
West Virginia senate member Robert Byrd,
Glen Campbell,
Eric Carmen,
Billy Carter,
June Carter,
Lionel Cartwright,
Johnny Cash,
Bill Caswell,
Ray Charles,

Don Cherry (singer/golfer)|Don Cherry,
comedian Jerry Clower,
Mark Collie,
Jessi Colter,
John Conlee,
David L Cook,
Helen Cornelius,
Beverly Cotten-Dillard,
Billy Crash Craddock,
Floyd Cramer,
Rob Crosby,
Scatman Crothers,
Vic Damone,
Charlie Daniels,
Dave Sugar,
Desert Rose Band,
Gail Davies,
Danny Davis (country musician)|Danny Davis,
Linda Davis,
singer/actor Sammy Davis, Jr.,
Skeeter Davis,
Billy Dean,
pro baseball game participant and reviewer Dizzy Dean,
Jimmy Dean,
Diamond Rio,
Dillard Clark,
The Dillards,
Al Downing (musician)|Al Downing,
Connie Eaton,
Dale Evans,
Exile (American band)|Exile,
Barbara Fairchild,
Donna Fargo,
pool participant Minnesota Fats,
Freddy Fender,
Lester Flatt,
Bela Fleck,
The Flying Burrito Brothers,
Eugene Fodor (violinist)|Eugene Fodor,
Tennessee Ernie Ford,
The Forester Sisters,
Janie Fricke,
David Frizzell,

Larry Gatlin,
Crystal Gayle,
Will Geer,
Don Gibson,
TV character Kathie Lee Gifford,
Vince Gill,
Mickey Gilley,
Johnny Gimble,
Tompall The Glaser Brothers|The Glaser Brothers,
George Gobel,
Southern canon quartette Gold City,
Bobby Goldsboro,
Billy Grammer,
Amy Grant,
Lee Greenwood,
Clinton Gregory,
Lewis Grizzard,
Oscar the Grouch,
Merle Haggard,
Gus Hardin,
Phil Harris,
Freddie Hart (musician)|Freddie Hart,
John Hartford,
Tom T. Hall,
Dick Haynes,
Roy Head,
Hugh Hefner,
John Hiatt,
Highway 101,
Becky Hobbs,
David Holt (musician)|David Holt,
David Houston (singer)|David Houston,
David Huddleston,
Tommy Hunter,
Southern canon cluster The Inspirations,
Alan Jackson,
Wanda Jackson,
Jana Jae,
Sonny James,
Waylon Jennings,
Jim and Jesse|Jim Jesse,
George Jones,
The Judds,

Kieran Kane,
Stan Kann,
The Kendalls,
Hal Ketchum,
Merle Kilgore,
Alan King (comedian)|Alan King,
Alison Krauss,
k.d. Lang,
pro baseball game administrator Tommy Lasorda,
Brenda Lee,
Dickey Lee,
Johnny Lee (singer)|Johnny Lee,
Robin Lee,
Jerry Lee Lewis,
Lloyd Lindroth,
George Lindsey,
LaWanda Lindsey,
Eddie London,
Trini Lopez,
Kenny Lovelace,
Lyle Lovett,
Loretta Lynn,
Shelby Lynne,
Larry Mahan,
Barbara Mandrell,
Louise Mandrell,
Mickey Mantle,
Kathy Mattea,
C. W. McCall,
Charly McClain,
O. B. McClinton,
Mel McDaniel,
Pake McEntire,
Reba McEntire,
The McGuire Sisters,
Catherine McKinnon,
TV character Ed McMahon,
Terry McMillan (musician)|Terry McMillan,
actress Ethel Merman,
Jody Miller,
Roger Miller,
the Million Dollar Band (country tunes group)|Million Dollar Band,
Mission Mountain Wood Band,

Ronnie Milsap,
Bill Monroe,
Lorrie Morgan,
Gary Morris,
Dude Mowrey,
comedian Gary Mule Deer,
pro baseball game participant Stan Musial,
Willie Nelson,
actor Leslie Nielsen,
The Nitty Gritty Dirt Band,
The Oak Ridge Boys (including the time once they remained nevertheless a canon cluster, beforehand Joe Bonsall grew to be a member),
Mark O'Connor,
Marie Osmond,
Tommy Overstreet,
Patti Page,
Dolly Parton,
Stella Parton,
Johnny Paycheck,
Carl Perkins,
TV character Regis Philbin,
Vernon Presley (Elvis Presley|Elvis' father),
Ray Price (musician)|Ray Price,
Charley Pride,
Ronnie Prophet,
Jeanne Pruett,
Eddie Rabbitt,
Boots Randolph,
Wayne Raney,
Eddy Raven,
Susan Raye,
Shotgun Red,
Jerry Reed,
The Remingtons,
Charlie Rich,
Riders in the Sky (band)|Riders in the Sky,
Jeannie C. Riley,
John Ritter (actor and boy of Tex Ritter),
Marty Robbins,
TV missionary Oral Roberts,
Dale Robertson,
Johnny Rodriguez,
Linda Ronstadt,

Kenny Rogers,
Roy Rogers,
John Schneider (screen actor)|John Schneider,
TV character Willard Scott,
Doc Severinson,
Victoria Shaw (singer)|Victoria Shaw,
Jean Shepard,
T. G. Sheppard,
actor Sonny Shroyer,
Ricky Skaggs,
Cal Smith,
Connie Smith,
Margo Smith,
Sons of the Pioneers,
Billie Jo Spears,
Jim Stafford,
Joe Stampley,
Kenny Starr,
The Statler Brothers,
Keith Stegall,
Skip Stephenson,
Ray Stevens,
Roni Stoneman,
George Strait,
Sweethearts of the Rodeo,
Sylvia (singer)|Sylvia,
Dub Taylor,
Les Taylor (singer)|Les Taylor,
comedian Rip Taylor,
B.J. Thomas,
Hank Thompson (musician)|Hank Thompson,
Sue Thompson,
Mel Tillis,
Pam Tillis,
Aaron Tippin,
Diana Trask,
Merle Travis,
Randy Travis,
Buck Trent,
Travis Tritt,
Ernest Tubb,
Tanya Tucker,
Mary Lou Turner,

Conway Twitty,
Donna Ulisse,
Conny Van Dyke,
Bobby Vinton,
Steve Wariner,
former NASCAR race automobile driver and present NASCAR reviewer Darrel Waltrip,
B. B. Watson,
Gene Watson,
actor Dennis Weaver,
Kitty Wells,
Dottie West,
Shelly West,
former Dallas Cowboys field general Danny White,
The Whites,
Boxcar Willie,
Don Williams,
Leona Williams,
Paul Williams (songwriter)|Paul Williams,
Hank Williams, Jr.,
Sheb Wooley,
Tom Wopat,
Tammy Wynette,
Faron Young,
Henny Youngman, and
Red Zellner, alongside with countless slighter familiar creators and youthful seeking artists. Also, some blocking groupings often accomplished on the show, and sometimes the show highlighted kid singers whoever ought to accomplish highest region tunes of the day.

In extension to holds Buck Owens and Roy Clark, whoever ought to accomplish at minimum one tune every one 7 days, additional cast members—such as Gunilla Hutton, Misty Rowe, Victoria Hallman, and Diana Goodman—would sometimes accomplish a tune on the show; and the show ought to nearly on every relevant occasion open with a tune accomplished by the whole cast.

A set of an inside of a shed was applied like the principal stage for nearly all of the melodic executions as of the show's opening till the first public appearance of the Hee Haw Honky Tonk sketch in the first 1980s. Afterwards, the Hee Haw Honky Tonk set ought to service like the principal stage for the respite of the series' run. Other surroundings for the melodic executions all over the series' run contained a hayrick (where the whole cast accomplished songs), the exisiting area of a Victorian architecture|Victorian home, the fore gallery and grass of the Samuel B. Sternwheeler home, and a Grist factory (where Roy Clark accomplished numerous of his tunes in earliest seasons).

Elvis Presley was a fan of Hee Haw and desired to emerge like a visitor on the programme in the 1970s, however his administrator, Colonel Tom Parker, ought to not permit him to undertake thus. A alike state of affairs happened once Elvis' pal Johnny Cash questioned Presley to emerge on The Johnny Cash Show (TV series)|his show. Two of the Hee Haw Honeys dated Presley: Linda Thompson in the first 1970s and Diana Goodman soon later. Shortly following Presley's demise, his dad, Vernon Presley, produced an emergence on the show and compensated accolade to his belated boy, considering in what way a lot he relished ogleing the show.

Sheb Wooley, one of the first cast participants, authored the show's subject tune. After shooting the opening 13 chapters, additional non-amateur forcefully requests triggered him to leave the show, however he restored as of time to time as a visitor.

Loretta Lynn was the foremost visitor star of Hee Haw and produced further visitor emergences compared to whatever different creator. She as well joint hosted the show further compared to whatever different visitor co-host and consequently shows onto further of the DVD deliverances for trade deal compared to whatever different visitor star.

From 1990-1992, region Superstar Garth Brooks emerged on the show 4 periods. In 1992, maker Sam Lovullo attempted without success to interaction Brooks since he desired him for the ultimate show. Brooks startled Lovullo by displaying up final minute, set to Don his overalls and accomplish for the ultimate chapter.Martin, Jeff [http://thislandpress.com/01/15/2011/return-to-kornfield-kounty-why-hee-haw-still-matters/], This Land, January 2011, entered July 6, 2011.

House of Love (Amy Grant song)

'House of Love' is a tune by Contemporary Christian music|Christian tunes vocalist Amy Grant, recorded as a duo with Country music|country vocalist Vince Gill. It was disseminated within November 1994 as the second sole (after Lucky One) as of her House of Love (Amy Grant album)|House of Love collection in the United States and the 4th and ultimate sole as of the collection in the United Kingdom.

Simple Things (Amy Grant song)

'Simple Things' is the 19th collection by Contemporary Christian music|Christian tunes and pop tunes singer-songwriter Amy Grant, disseminated within 2003 in music|2003.

Grant's foremost nonreligious collection (while holding Christian themes) eversince 1997's Behind the Eyes (Amy Grant album)|Behind the Eyes, Simple Things did not perceive the normal triumph alike to Grant's collections as of the 1990s. While the collection exceeded Billboard (magazine)|Billboard's Christian collection graph and the name trail grew to be a Top Ten Christian sole, Simple Things reached its highest point simply external the Top 20 on the Billboard 200, at #23. The name trail reached its highest point at the similar placing on the Adult Contemporary graph.

Expo 86 - Entertainment and famous visitors

'Royalty': Charles, Prince of Wales|Prince Charles Diana, Princess of Wales for the beginning ceremonies; Harald V of Norway|Crown Prince Harald Queen Sonja of Norway|Crown Princess Sonja of Norway; Saudi-Arabian Prince Sultan Bin Salman al-Saud

'Prime Minister': Brian Mulroney (Canada) Margaret Thatcher (United Kingdom) Pierre Trudeau (former Prime Minister - Canada)

'Vice-President': George H. W. Bush|George Bush (United States)

'Concerts': Einstürzende Neubauten, Harry Belafonte, Anne Murray, Billy Ocean, Bruce Cockburn, Miles Davis, Wynton Marsalis, Annie Lennox - Eurythmics, Julio Iglesias, Amy Grant, Loverboy, A-ha, Liberace, Mormon Tabernacle Choir, Lawrence Gowan|Gowan, Parachute Club (band)|Parachute Club, Joan Baez with Don McLean, Kenny Loggins, Lou Rawls The 5th Dimension, Honeymoon Suite, Kim Mitchell, Johnny Cash, Depeche Mode, Joe Jackson (musician)|Joe Jackson, George Thorogood + the Delaware Destroyers, Smokey Robinson, George Benson, John Denver, The Beach Boys, Air Supply, Peter, Paul Mary, The Manhattan Transfer, The Temptations, René Simard, K.d. Lang (opening for Rockin' Ronnie Hawkins), Peter Allen, Sheena Easton, Trooper (band)|Trooper, Bryan Adams, The Romaniacs, Tangerine Dream, Youssou N'Dour, Rolf Harris, Kool The Gang, Roy Orbison,
Fats Domino with Jerry Lee Lewis, Donovan

Leilehua High School, Layton High School Lancer Marching Band, College Park High School Marching Band as of Pleasant Hill, CA, Gustine High School Marching, Concert and Jazz Band as of Gustine, CA, World Drums musical performance (led by John Wyre), Shannon Gunn, Skywalk (band)|Skywalk, Kent-Meridian Jazz Ensemble, Images In Vogue, Peter Noone, Alvin Lee unlocked for Donovan. Many of the musical performances remained hosted by Red Robinson, Vancouver DJ. These musical performances remained grasped at the Open air Expo Theatre.

The Festival of Independent Recording Artists, a musical performance serials advancing native groups, was scrapped on the foremost nighttime following a execution by Slow (band)|Slow devolved in to a uprising.Michael Barclay, Ian A.D. Jack and Jason Schneider, Have Not Been the Same: The Can-Rock Renaissance 1985-1995. ECW Press. ISBN 978-1-55022-992-9. Other creators whoever had been planned to emerge in that serials contained Art Bergmann.

'Comedians': Bill Cosby, Bob Newhart, Bob Hope, Red Skelton, Joan Rivers, Howie Mandel, George Burns and Danny Kaye

'Dance': Mikhail Baryshnikov, The Royal Ballet, Cheremosh Ukrainian Dance Company

'Directors': Norman Jewison, George Cosmatos (Rambo: First Blood Part II)

'Oceanographer': Jacques Cousteau

1974 (We Were Young)

'1974 (We Were Young)' is a 1988 sole by Christian tunes vocalist Amy Grant. It was disseminated like the 3rd sole as of her collection, Lead Me On (Amy Grant album)|Lead Me On.

Natalie Grant - Personal life

Natalie Grant was born December 21, 1971 in Seattle, Washington. She registered at Northwest University (United States)|Northwest College (Now Northwest University) in Kirkland, Washington, learning to be a educator. She allegedly figured that her melodic presents remained only for parting with her native kirk till she absorbed in what way to notice God's genuine naming for her existence, and thus shifted guidance and joined the melodic cluster Truth.

In following her tunes vocation, Grant repositioned to Nashville, Tennessee wherever she at the moment lives with her Canadian maker spouse, Bernie Herms, and their 3 daughters; Grace Ana and Isabella Noelle (born February 16, 2007) and Sadie Rose (born December 17, 2010)

In an conference with The 700 Club, Natalie disclosed that she endured as of bulimia. She speaks God aided her get over her consuming chaos. She afterward authored a publication in 2005 named The Real Me: Being the Girl God Sees, about her fight and in what way she overcame it.

She is not associated to companion Christian performer Amy Grant, though at the 2010 Dove prizes, Natalie Grant indicated, Even although we are not associated, Amy has been an stimulation to myself.

Rock (music) - Christian rock

Rock has been condemned by a few Christian devout directors, whoever have sentenced it like unethical, anti-Christian and even devilish.J. J. Thompson, Raised by Wolves: the Story of Christian Rock Roll (Toronto: ECW Press, 2000), ISBN 1-55022-421-2, pp. 30–1. However, Christian rock started to create in the belated 1960s, especially out of the Jesus motion starting in Southern California, and appeared as a sub-genre in the 1970s with creators like Larry Norman, normally noticed like the foremost chief star of Christian rock.J. R. Howard and J. M. Streck, Apostles of Rock: The Splintered World of Contemporary Christian Music (Lexington, KY: University Press of Kentucky, 2004), ISBN 0-8131-9086-X, p. 30. The category has been especially well-liked in the United States.J. R. Howard and J. M. Streck, Apostles of Rock: The Splintered World of Contemporary Christian Music (Lexington, KY: University Press of Kentucky, 2004), ISBN 0-8131-9086-X, pp. 43–4. Many Christian rock artists have links to the modern Christian tunes set, when additional groups and creators are carefully connected to autonomous tunes. Since the 1980s Christian rock artists have obtained normal triumph, containing numbers such like the American gospel-to-pop crossing creator Amy Grant and the British vocalist Cliff Richard.J. Bowden, Christianity: the Complete Guide (London: Continuum, 2005), ISBN 0-8264-5937-4, p. 811. While those creators remained mostly satisfactory in Christian groups the acceptance of weighty rock and glam alloy methods by groups like Petra (band)|Petra and Stryper, whoever attained substantial normal triumph in the 1980s, was further contentious.J. J. Thompson, Raised by Wolves: the Story of Christian Rock Roll (Toronto: ECW Press, 2000), ISBN 1-55022-421-2, pp.66–7 and 159-161.M. B. Wagner, God's Schools: Choice and Compromise in American Society (Rutgers University Press, 1990), ISBN 0-8135-1607-2, p. 134. From the 1990s there remained

expanding numerals of acts whoever endeavored to circumvent the Christian group label, favoring to be noticed like groupings whoever remained as well Christians, containing P.O.D and Collective Soul.J. J. Thompson, Raised by Wolves: the Story of Christian Rock Roll (Toronto: ECW Press, 2000), ISBN 1-55022-421-2, pp. 206–7.

Grammy Awards of 1983 - Gospel

*Grammy Award for Best Gospel Performance, Traditional|Best Gospel Performance, Traditional
**Blackwood Brothers for I'm Following You
*Grammy Award for Best Gospel Performance, Contemporary|Best Gospel Performance, Contemporary
****Amy Grant for Age to Age**
*Grammy Award for Best Soul Gospel Performance, Traditional|Best Soul Gospel Performance, Traditional
**Al Green (musician)|Al Green for Precious Lord
*Grammy Award for Best Soul Gospel Performance, Contemporary|Best Soul Gospel Performance, Contemporary
**Al Green for Higher Plane
*Grammy Award for Best Inspirational Performance|Best Inspirational Performance
**Barbara Mandrell for He Set My Life to Music

Robert Palmer (singer) - 1974–1984: Early solo career

Island Records signed Palmer to a unaccompanied transact in 1974. His foremost unaccompanied collection Sneakin' Sally Through the Alley recorded in New Orleans, Louisiana in 1974, was deeply affected by the tunes of Little Feat and the jazz combination of The Meters whoever acted as supporting group alongside with producer/guitarist Lowell George of Little Feat. Although stillborn in the UK, either the collection and sole extended the Top 100 in the US. Notably, Sailin' Shoes (the album's foremost track), Palmer's own Hey Julia and the Allen Toussaint–penned name trail take nearly the similar pace, and remained wrapped on the collection like a set of 3 related works short of a stop amid them.

After moving with his spouse to New York City, Palmer disseminated Pressure Drop (album)|Pressure Drop, designated for the cover variant of the reggae hit by Toots the Maytals, in November 1975 (featuring Motown Records|Motown bassist James Jamerson). An collection pervaded with his concerns in reggae and rock tunes, it was marked for its cover handcraft of a naked female on the brink of a terrace, somewhat compared to whatever monetarily prosperous tunes. He visited with Little Feat to advance the collection.

However, with the letdown of continuation collection Some People Can Do What They Like (album)|Some People Can Do What They Like, Palmer determined to turn to Nassau, Bahamas, immediately athwart the road as of Compass Point Studios.

In 1978, he disseminated Double Fun, a gathering of Caribbean-influenced rock, containing a cover version|cover of You Really Got Me. The collection extended the Top 50 on the US Billboard (magazine)|Billboard graph and netted a Top 20 sole with the Andy Fraser–penned Every Kinda People. The tune has been veiled by different creators containing Chaka Demus and Pliers, Randy Crawford and Amy Grant. It extended No. 16 on the Billboard Hot 100.

Palmer's following collection was an creative retreat, focussing on unadulterated rock. 1979's Secrets (Robert Palmer album)|Secrets created his second Top 20 sole with Moon Martin's Bad Case of Loving You (Doctor, Doctor). The No. 14 hit as well gave Palmer his foremost Billboard Hot 100-year finish graph hit.

The 1980s saw Palmer notice an expanding quantity of profit-oriented triumph. The collection Clues (Robert Palmer album)|Clues, created by Palmer and presenting Chris Frantz and Gary Numan, created strikes on either aspects of the Atlantic Ocean|Atlantic, foremost with the radio-friendly sole Johnny and Mary and then Looking for Clues. Catchy tunes recordings corresponding the synth pop stylings of New wave music|new wave gave him a lot required subjection to a junior public. The triumph was redone with the 1982 EP discharge of Some Guys Have All the Luck.

In April 1983 Pride (Robert Palmer album)|Pride was disseminated, that not like monetarily prosperous as Clues did characteristic the name tune and Palmer's cover of The System (band)|The System's You Are in My System, with The System's David Frank (music)|David Frank donating keyboard traces to the last one tune. On 31 May 1983, Palmer's musical performance at the Hammersmith Palais was recorded and transmit on BBC Radio 1.[http://www.yourwaytomusic.com/new-robert-palmer-live-bbc-concert-cd/ New Robert Palimer Live BBC Concert CD] Your Way To Music. Retrieved 19 April 2012 On 23 July 1983, Palmer accomplished at Duran Duran's almsgiving musical performance at Aston Villa football game terrain 1983|Duran Duran's almsgiving musical performance at Aston Villa football game terrain wherever he hit up relationships with participants of Duran Duran that ought to fruit the Supergroup (music)|supergroup Power Station (band)|Power Station.

Amy Grant - Discography

*** 1977: Amy Grant (album)|Amy Grant**
* 1979: My Father's Eyes (album)|My Father's Eyes
* 1980: Never Alone
* 1982: Age to Age
*** 1984: Straight Ahead (Amy Grant album)|Straight Ahead**
* 1985: Unguarded
*** 1988: Lead Me On (Amy Grant album)|Lead Me On**
* 1991: Heart in Motion
*** 1994: House of Love (Amy Grant album)|House of Love**
*** 1997: Behind the Eyes (Amy Grant album)|Behind the Eyes**
* 2002: Legacy... Hymns and Faith
*** 2003: Simple Things (Amy Grant album)|Simple Things**
* 2005: Rock of Ages... Hymns and Faith
* 2010: Somewhere Down the Road (album)|Somewhere Down the Road
* 2013: How Mercy Looks as of Here

Hee-Haw - Guest appearances

Hee Haw highlighted at minimum 2, and occasionally 3 either 4, visitor famous persons every one 7 days. While nearly all of the visitor stars remained of course region tunes creators, a ample span of different well known leading lights remained highlighted. Those creating visitor emergences contained, however remained not restricted to:
Alabama (band)|Alabama,
Atlanta (band)|Atlanta,
Buddy Alan,
The Aldridge Sisters,
Jed Allan,
Rex Allen,
Paul Anka,
Bill Anderson (singer)|Bill Anderson,
John Anderson (musician)|John Anderson,
Lynn Anderson,
Garner Ted Armstrong,
Eddy Arnold,
Chet Atkins,
Gene Autry,
Hoyt Axton,
Baillie the Boys,
Razzy Bailey,
Butch Baker,
Moe Bandy,

Ava Barber,
Billy Barty,
Molly Bee,
Johnny Bench,
Matraca Berg,
Byron Berline,
Amanda Blake,
Suzy Bogguss,
Randy Boone,
Tony Booth (musician)|Tony Booth,
actor Ernest Borgnine,
former ace football game participant and present FOX NFL Sunday co-host Terry Bradshaw,
comedian Foster Brooks,
Garth Brooks,
Brooks Dunn,
the Bellamy Brothers,
Clarence Gatemouth Brown,
Family Brown,
Jim Ed Brown,
Marty Brown (singer)|Marty Brown,
T. Graham Brown,
The Buckaroos (Buck Owens' band),
Kenneth C. Burns|Jethro Burns,
Johnny Bush,
comedianne Ruth Buzzi,
West Virginia senate member Robert Byrd,
Glen Campbell,
Eric Carmen,
Billy Carter,
June Carter,
Lionel Cartwright,
Johnny Cash,
Bill Caswell,
Ray Charles,
Don Cherry (singer/golfer)|Don Cherry,
comedian Jerry Clower,
Mark Collie,
Jessi Colter,
John Conlee,
David L Cook,
Helen Cornelius,
Beverly Cotten-Dillard,

Billy Crash Craddock,
Floyd Cramer,
Rob Crosby,
Scatman Crothers,
Vic Damone,
Charlie Daniels,
Dave Sugar,
Desert Rose Band,
Gail Davies,
Danny Davis (country musician)|Danny Davis,
Linda Davis,
singer/actor Sammy Davis, Jr.,
Skeeter Davis,
Billy Dean,
pro baseball game participant and reviewer Dizzy Dean,
Jimmy Dean,
Diamond Rio,
Dillard Clark,
The Dillards,
Al Downing (musician)|Al Downing,
Johnny Duncan (country singer)|Johnny Duncan,
Connie Eaton,
Dale Evans,
Exile (American band)|Exile,
Barbara Fairchild,
Donna Fargo,
pool participant Minnesota Fats,
Freddy Fender,
Lester Flatt,
Bela Fleck,
The Flying Burrito Brothers,
Eugene Fodor (violinist)|Eugene Fodor,
Tennessee Ernie Ford,
The Forester Sisters,
Janie Fricke,
David Frizzell,
Larry Gatlin,
Crystal Gayle,
Will Geer,
Don Gibson,
TV character Kathie Lee Gifford,
Vince Gill,
Mickey Gilley,

Johnny Gimble,
Tompall The Glaser Brothers|The Glaser Brothers,
George Gobel,
Southern canon quartette Gold City,
Bobby Goldsboro,
Billy Grammer,
Amy Grant,
Lee Greenwood,
Clinton Gregory,
Lewis Grizzard,
Oscar the Grouch,
Merle Haggard,
Gus Hardin,
Phil Harris,
Freddie Hart (musician)|Freddie Hart,
John Hartford,
Tom T. Hall,
Dick Haynes,
Roy Head,
Hugh Hefner,
John Hiatt,
Highway 101,
Becky Hobbs,
David Holt (musician)|David Holt,
David Houston (singer)|David Houston,
David Huddleston,
Tommy Hunter,
Southern canon cluster The Inspirations,
Alan Jackson,
Wanda Jackson,
Jana Jae,
Sonny James,
Waylon Jennings,
Jim and Jesse|Jim Jesse,
George Jones,
The Judds,
Kieran Kane,
Stan Kann,
The Kendalls,
Hal Ketchum,
Merle Kilgore,
Alan King (comedian)|Alan King,
Alison Krauss,

k.d. Lang,
pro baseball game administrator Tommy Lasorda,
Brenda Lee,
Dickey Lee,
Johnny Lee (singer)|Johnny Lee,
Robin Lee,
Jerry Lee Lewis,
Lloyd Lindroth,
George Lindsey,
LaWanda Lindsey,
Eddie London,
Trini Lopez,
Kenny Lovelace,
Lyle Lovett,
Loretta Lynn,
Shelby Lynne,
Larry Mahan,
Barbara Mandrell,
Louise Mandrell,
Mickey Mantle,
Kathy Mattea,
C. W. McCall,
Charly McClain,
O. B. McClinton,
Mel McDaniel,
Pake McEntire,
Reba McEntire,
The McGuire Sisters,
Catherine McKinnon,
TV character Ed McMahon,
Terry McMillan (musician)|Terry McMillan,
actress Ethel Merman,
Jody Miller,
Roger Miller,
the Million Dollar Band (country tunes group)|Million Dollar Band,
Mission Mountain Wood Band,
Ronnie Milsap,
Bill Monroe,
Lorrie Morgan,
Gary Morris,
Dude Mowrey,
comedian Gary Mule Deer,
pro baseball game participant Stan Musial,

Willie Nelson,
actor Leslie Nielsen,
The Nitty Gritty Dirt Band,
The Oak Ridge Boys (including the time once they remained nevertheless a canon cluster, beforehand Joe Bonsall grew to be a member),
Mark O'Connor,
Marie Osmond,
Tommy Overstreet,
Patti Page,
Dolly Parton,
Stella Parton,
Johnny Paycheck,
Carl Perkins,
TV character Regis Philbin,
Vernon Presley (Elvis Presley|Elvis' father),
Ray Price (musician)|Ray Price,
Charley Pride,
Ronnie Prophet,
Jeanne Pruett,
Eddie Rabbitt,
Boots Randolph,
Wayne Raney,
Eddy Raven,
Susan Raye,
Shotgun Red,
Jerry Reed,
The Remingtons,
Charlie Rich,
Riders in the Sky (band)|Riders in the Sky,
Jeannie C. Riley,
John Ritter (actor and boy of Tex Ritter),
Marty Robbins,
TV missionary Oral Roberts,
Dale Robertson,
Johnny Rodriguez,
Linda Ronstadt,
Kenny Rogers,
Roy Rogers,
John Schneider (screen actor)|John Schneider,
TV character Willard Scott,
Doc Severinson,
Victoria Shaw (singer)|Victoria Shaw,
Jean Shepard,

T. G. Sheppard,
actor Sonny Shroyer,
Ricky Skaggs,
Cal Smith,
Connie Smith,
Margo Smith,
Sons of the Pioneers,
Billie Jo Spears,
Jim Stafford,
Joe Stampley,
Kenny Starr,
The Statler Brothers,
Keith Stegall,
Skip Stephenson,
Ray Stevens,
Roni Stoneman,
George Strait,
Sweethearts of the Rodeo,
Sylvia (singer)|Sylvia,
Dub Taylor,
Les Taylor (singer)|Les Taylor,
comedian Rip Taylor,
B.J. Thomas,
Hank Thompson (musician)|Hank Thompson,
Sue Thompson,
Mel Tillis,
Pam Tillis,
Aaron Tippin,
Diana Trask,
Merle Travis,
Randy Travis,
Buck Trent,
Travis Tritt,
Ernest Tubb,
Tanya Tucker,
Mary Lou Turner,
Conway Twitty,
Donna Ulisse,
Conny Van Dyke,
Bobby Vinton,
Steve Wariner,
former NASCAR race automobile driver and present NASCAR reviewer Darrel Waltrip,

B. B. Watson,
Gene Watson,
actor Dennis Weaver,
Kitty Wells,
Dottie West,
Shelly West,
former Dallas Cowboys field general Danny White,
The Whites,
Boxcar Willie,
Don Williams,
Leona Williams,
Paul Williams (songwriter)|Paul Williams,
Hank Williams, Jr.,
Sheb Wooley,
Tom Wopat,
Tammy Wynette,
Dwight Yoakam,
Faron Young,
Henny Youngman, and
Red Zellner, alongside with countless slighter familiar creators and youthful seeking artists. Also, some blocking groupings often accomplished on the show, and sometimes the show highlighted kid singers whoever ought to accomplish highest region tunes of the day.

In extension to holds Buck Owens and Roy Clark, whoever ought to accomplish at minimum one tune every one 7 days, additional cast members—such as Gunilla Hutton, Misty Rowe, Victoria Hallman, and Diana Goodman—would sometimes accomplish a tune on the show; and the show ought to nearly on every relevant occasion open with a tune accomplished by the whole cast.

Lovullo as well has produced the assert the show offered what remained, in actuality, the foremost melodic recordings.Lovullo, Sam, and Mark Eliot, Life in the Kornfield: My 25 Years at Hee Haw, Boulevard Books, New York, 1996, p. 34. ISBN 1-57297-028-6 Lovullo indicated his recordings remained conceptualized by experiencing the show's workforce proceed to closeby bucolic sections and feature creatures and agriculturists, beforehand correcting the shots to appropriate the plot line of a specific tune. The audiovisual matter was a real achievable manufacture article for the show, he authored. It presented depiction narratives for tunes. However, a few of our visitors sensed the recordings took awareness off as of their live executions, that they expected ought to advance record selling. If they had a hit tune, they did not desire to play it under funny Barnyard shots. The concept's varied response finally written an finish to the audiovisual idea on Hee Haw. However, some of co-host Owens' tunes – containing Tall, Dark Stranger, Big in Vegas and I Wouldn't

Live in New York City (If They Gave Me the Whole Dang Town) – screened on the serials and have subsequently screened on Great American Country and Country Music Television|CMT as piece of their timeless region tunes program design blocks.

A set of an inside of a shed was applied like the principal stage for nearly all of the melodic executions as of the show's opening till the first public appearance of the Hee Haw Honky Tonk sketch in the first 1980s. Afterwards, the Hee Haw Honky Tonk set ought to service like the principal stage for the respite of the series' run. Other surroundings for the melodic executions all over the series' run contained a hayrick (where the whole cast accomplished songs), the exisiting area of a Victorian architecture|Victorian home, the fore gallery and grass of the Samuel B. Sternwheeler home, and a Grist factory (where Roy Clark accomplished numerous of his tunes in earliest seasons).

Elvis Presley was a fan of Hee Haw and desired to emerge like a visitor on the programme in the 1970s, however his administrator, Colonel Tom Parker, ought to not permit him to undertake thus. A alike state of affairs happened once Elvis' pal Johnny Cash questioned Presley to emerge on The Johnny Cash Show (TV series)|his show. Two of the Hee Haw Honeys dated Presley: Linda Thompson in the first 1970s and Diana Goodman soon later. Shortly following Presley's demise, his dad, Vernon Presley, produced an emergence on the show and compensated accolade to his belated boy, considering in what way a lot he relished ogleing the show.

Sheb Wooley, one of the first cast participants, authored the show's subject tune. After shooting the opening 13 chapters, additional non-amateur forcefully requests triggered him to leave the show, however he restored as of time to time as a visitor.

Loretta Lynn was the foremost visitor star of Hee Haw and produced further visitor emergences compared to whatever different creator. She as well joint hosted the show further compared to whatever different visitor co-host and consequently shows onto further of the DVD deliverances for trade deal compared to whatever different visitor star.

From 1990–92, region Superstar Garth Brooks emerged on the show 4 periods. In 1992, maker Sam Lovullo attempted without success to interaction Brooks since he desired him for the ultimate show. Brooks startled Lovullo by displaying up final minute, set to Don his overalls and accomplish for the ultimate chapter.Martin, Jeff [http://thislandpress.com/01/15/2011/return-to-kornfield-kounty-why-hee-haw-still-matters/], This Land, January 2011, entered July 6, 2011.

El Shaddai (song)

'El Shaddai' (sometimes designed El-Shaddai) is a Contemporary Christian tunes tune. It was authored by Michael Card and John Thompson, utilizing straight states as of sacred writing as their stimulation, and recorded by Michael Card on his 1981 first public appearance collection, Legacy. However, it is further normally related with the vocalist Amy Grant, whoever recorded it on her 1982 platinum collection Age to Age.

The name appears as of a Names of God in Judaism|Judaic designation of God, normally interpreted as God Almighty (see El Shaddai). Approximately fifty per cent the words of the refrain|chorus are in the Hebrew lingo, that is somewhat uncommon for a Contemporary Christian tune. The transcriptioning was in the manner of a execution ballad, however the tune was afterward issued in a few hymnbooksAmong other ones, The United Methodist Hymnal issues it like no. 123 and is sometimes sung congregationally.

The tune was a hit sole (music)|single for Grant, arriving at the top of the Billboard magazine|Billboard Christian graph. El Shaddai gained Song of the Year and Card gained Songwriter of the Year at the 1983 GMA Dove Awards. It was as well designated one of the Songs of the Century by the RIAA in 2001.

Grant has recorded at minimum 3 dissimilar workshop adaptations, and one limited version:
*The first Age To Age variant is firstly accomplished on keyboard instrument, with Harp and thread addition. Drums do not emerge in this variant till the exciting 3rd chorus. This is the variant applied on nearly all collections.
**Grant as well integrated a part of the tune (similar to the Age to Age interpretation, however somewhat further uptempo) in to her Ageless Medley promotional discharge. The potpourri was designated for the Age to Age collection, that in turn took its designation as of the words of El Shaddai.
***Before disseminating her collection Behind the Eyes (Amy Grant album)|Behind the Eyes in 1997, Grant disseminated a CD sole of Takes a Little Time (Amy Grant song)|Takes a Little Time; the B-side was a recently recorded variant of El Shaddai. This variant is noteworthy for the important fiddle addition applied all over the transcriptioning. This transcriptioning has not ever been produced accessible on whatever collection either compiling.**
*Grant recorded one other spic-and-span variant of the tune for her 2005 collection Rock of Ages...Hymns and Faith. This variant is further in a light pop manner, with auditory stringed instrument and drums all over, and attributes accord voices and auditory stringed instrument unaccompanied by Grant's spouse, Vince Gill. This variant is contained within the WOW Worship: Aqua compiling.

El Shaddai has been cover version|covered by numerous modern Christian and Gospel music|gospel transcriptioning creators, containing Pat Boone, The Winans|Winans Phase 2 and Eden's Bridge, and Michael Card re-recorded the tune for his 1994 compiling, Joy in the Journey. There as well subsist interpreted adaptations that roll into one Hebrew with different lingos.

Bekka Bramlett - As a backing vocalist

* Delaney Bramlett – Mobius Strip (1973)
* Belinda Carlisle – Runaway Horses (album)|Runaway Horses (1989)
* Warrant – Dirty Rotten Filthy Stinking Rich (1989)
* Richie Sambora – Stranger in This Town (1991)
* Belinda Carlisle – Her Greatest Hits (1992)
* Faster Pussycat – Whipped! (1992)
* Mitch Malloy – Mitch Malloy (1992)
* Joe Cocker – Have a Little Faith (1994)
* Agnes Stone – Agnes Stone (1994)
* Gregg Wright's Left Hook – Round One (1995)
* Vince Gill – High Lonesome Sound (1996)
* Bad Company – Stories Told and Untold (1996)
* Iris DeMent – The Way I Should (1996)
* Delbert McClinton – One Of The Fortunate Few (1997)
* Jonny Lang – Lie To Me (1997)
* Hank Thompson – Hank Thompson and Friends (1997)
* Bryan White – The Right Place (1997)
* Kenny Rogers – Across My Heart (1997)
* Billy Joel- On Tour (1998)
* Jim Horn – The Hit List (1998)
* Paul Craft – Brother Jukebox (1998)
* Buddy Guy – Heavy Love (1998)
* Jonny Lang – Wander This World (1998)
* Travis Tritt – No More Looking Over My Shoulder (1998)
* Delaney Bramlett – Sounds From Home (1998)
* Faith Hill – Faith (1998)
* The Why Store - Two Beasts (1998)
* Rita Coolidge – Thinkin' About You (1998)
* Faith Hill – Live Will Always Win [Australia Bonus Track] (1999)
* Jason Sellers – Matter of Time (1999)
* Faith Hill – Breathe (1999)
* Michael Peterson – Being Human (1999)
* Claudia Church – Claudia Church (1999)
* Flaco Jimenez – Sleepytown (2000)

* Mark Selby – More Storms Comin' (2000)
* Jamie O'Neal – Shiver (2000)
* Bryan White – Greatest Hits (2000)
* Sonya Isaacs – Sonya Isaacs (2000)
* Lee Ann Womack – I Hope You Dance (2000)
* Billy Burnette – Are You With Me Baby (2000)
* Luke Reed – Corridos (2000)
* Steve Wariner – Faith In You (2000)
* Vince Gill – Let's Make Sure We Kiss Goodbye (2000)
* Jewel – This Way (2001)
* Derailers – Here Come The Derailers (2001)
* Faith Hill – There You'll Be: The Best Of Faith Hill (2001)
* Dwight Yoakam – South Of Heaven, West Of Hell (2001)
* Hall Ketchum – Lucky Man (2001)
* Rick Ferrell – Different Point Of View (2001)
* Bob DiPiero – Laugh (2001)
* T Graham Brown – Lives (2001)
* Kelly Minter – Good Day (2001)
* Todd Sharp – Walking All The Way (2001)
* Delbert McClinton – Nothing Personal (2001)
* Jessica Andrews – Who I Am (2001)
* Israel New Breed – Real (2002)
* Faith Hill – Cry (2002)
* Dwight Yoakam – Reprise Please Baby: The Warner Bros. Years (2002)
* Brooks Dunn – It Wouldn't Be Christmas Without You (2002)
* Tanya Tucker – Tanya (2002)
* Delbert McClinton – Room To Breathe (2002)
* Montgomery Gentry – My Town (2002)
* Shannon Lawson – Chase The Sun (2002)
* Billy Ray Cyrus – Time Flies (2002)
* **Amy Grant – Legacy...Hymns Faith (2002)**
* Delaney Bramlett – Sweet Inspiration (2002)
* Jim Lauderdale – Hummingbirds (2002)
* Ashley Cleveland – Second Skin (2002)
* Billy Ray Cyrus – Other Side (2003)
* The Mavericks – The Mavericks (2003)
* Wynonna – What The World Needs Now Is Love (2003)
* Brooks Dunn – Red Dirt Road (2003)
* Etta James – Let's Roll (2003)
* Marcel – You, Me, and the Windshield (2003)
* Jeffrey Steele – Gold, Platinum, Chrome and Steele (2003)
* Jessica Andrews – Now (2003)
* Billy Gilman – Music Through Heartsongs: Songs Based On The Poems Of Mattie

J.T. Stepanek (2003)
* Deanna Carter – I'm Just A Girl (2003)
* Vince Gill – Next Big Thing (2003)
* Andy Griggs – This I Gotta See (2004)
* Jimmy Buffett – License To Chill (2004)
* Brooks Dunn – Greatest Hits Collection, Vol. 2 (2004)
* Jeffrey Steele – Outlaw (2004)
* Beth Nielsen – Chapman Look (2004)
* Al Anderson – After Hours (2004)
* Montgomery Gentry – You Do Your Thing (2004)
* Curtis Salgado – Strong Suspicion (2004)
* James Otto – Days Of Our Lives (2004)
* Lorrie Morgan – Show Me How
* Brooks Dunn – Very Best Of Brooks Dunn (2004)
* Warrant – Dirty Rotten Filthy Stinking Rich [Expanded] (2004)
* Montgomery Gentry – Something To Be Proud Of: The Best Of 1999–2005 (2005)
* Trisha Yearwood – Jasper County (2005)
* Jamie Oldaker – Mad Dogs Okies (2005)
* Delbert McClinton – Cost of Living (2005)
* Neal McCoy – That's Life (2005)
* Bart Millard – Hymned No. (2005)
* Faith Hill – Fireflies (2005)
* Shawn Jones – All In Good Time (2005)
* Van Zant – Get Right With The Man (2005)
*** Amy Grant – Rock of Ages...Hymns Faith (2005)**
* Jo Dee Messina – Delicious Surprise (2005)
* Jamie O'Neal – Brave (2005)
* Hacienda Brothers – Hacienda Brothers (2005)
* 3 Doors Down – Seventeen Days (2005)
* LeAnn Rimes – This Woman (2005)
* Spady Branan – The Long Way Around and Other Short Stories (2006)
* Montgomery Gentry – Some People Change (2006)
* Vince Gill – These Days (2006)
* Bob Seger – Face The Promise (2006)
* Sam Moore – Overnight Sensational (2006)
* Trace Adkins – Dangerous Man (2006)
* Eliot Morris – What's Mine Is Yours (2006)
* Albert Lee – Road Runner (2006)
* Bonnie Bramlett – Roots, Blues, Jazz (2006)
* Sara Groves – Tell Me What You Know (2007)
* Betty Harris – Intuition (2007)
* Faith Hill – Hits (2007)
* Bill Wence – Songs as of the Rocky Fork Tavern (2007)

* Lori McKenna – Unglamorous (2007)
* Bryan White – Greatest Hits (2007)
* Kenny Chesney – Just Who I Am: Poets Pirates (2007)
* Mark McKinney – Get It On (2007)
* Buddy Guy – Skin Deep (Buddy Guy album)|Skin Deep (2008)
* John Oates – 1000 Miles Of Life (2008)
* Robert Plant – Band Of Joy (2010)
* Bonnie Tyler – Rocks and Honey (2013)

Vonda Shepard - Biography

Vonda Shepard was born in New York however her kin moved to California once she was a kid. She played keyboard instrument as of an early age. Her dad is Richmond Shepard, a mimic and ad-lib performer. Vonda has 3 sisters: Armina, Rosetta (now Brianna) and Luana.[http://www.imdb.com/name/nm0005423/bio IMDb Trivia information]

After carrying out like a supporting vocalist for numerous annums she was finally specified her own transcriptioning agreement. Shepard's foremost graph emergence was in 1987 once she recorded a duo with Dan Hill allowed Can't We Try. Before this she attempted out for the part of Michael J. Fox|Michael J. Fox's female sibling in Light of Day however missed the part to Joan Jett. She was as well prepared to chant on Peter Cetera|Peter Cetera's duo The Next Time I Fall however he selected Amy Grant in lieu. She disseminated her foremost self-titled collection in 1989 with itty-bitty fanfare. The collection did return one graph sole, Don't Cry Ilene, a mid-tempo, piano-driven jazz-RB flavored tune transacting with the break up of a connection amid a black female and a white individual, occurring as of grown-up peer force. The trail is sung as of the outlook of the woman's white feminine pal, whoever harbors a wish to have the individual for herself, however retains her space out of regard for her pal. The tune reached its highest point at Number 17 on the Billboard Hot Adult Contemporary graph and remained on the graphs for 12 7-day periods. [http://www.billboard.com/charts/1990-03-03/adult-contemporary Billboard graph information]

After her 3rd collection, Shepard was signed up to emerge on Ally McBeal following being marked by the show's maker David E. Kelley. While on the show she recorded 2 complete sound recording collections and was highlighted onto 2 additional Ally McBeal collections. The tunes Shepard recorded for Ally McBeal sound recording collections remained mostly covers of aged tunes with words that correspond what was occurring in the name character's existence on-screen. However, the album's largest hit sole, Searchin' My Soul was an first wrote by Shepard and

Paul Gordon. Since materializing in the show, Shepard has disseminated 2 further workshop collections and a live collection.

Shepard has been wedded to tunes maker Mitchell Froom eversince 2004; they had their foremost kid, Jack Froom, on 15 April 2006. She is as well the step-mother to Froom's girl, Ruby, as of his wedding to Suzanne Vega.

Shepard not long ago presented voices on the result by James Newton Howard for the 2010 feature Love and Other Drugs, leading Jake Gyllenhaal and Anne Hathaway.

Behind the Eyes (Amy Grant album)

'Behind the Eyes' is the 15th collection by Contemporary Christian music|Christian tunes and pop tunes vocalist Amy Grant, disseminated within 1997 (see 1997 in music).

Issued nearby the conclusion of Grant's wedding to Christian singer-songwriter Gary Chapman (musician)|Gary Chapman, numerous of the tunes on Behind the Eyes reproduce Grant's fights in her wedding and altogether connect to a subject of hopefulness. Upon its discharge, it proceeded to No.2 on Billboard (magazine)|Billboard's Christian collections graph and No.8 on the Billboard 200|Billboard 200. Meanwhile, the foremost sole as of the collection, Takes a Little Time, was a Top Five Adult Contemporary hit and a Top Thirty pop graph sole. Like I Love You and I Will Be Your Friend as well extended the Adult Contemporary graph, at No.10 and No.27, correspondingly. The CD was as well disseminated within a restricted 2 CD variant (with the second CD named, 'More Music From Behind the Eyes').

In 2007, Behind the Eyes was reissued and digitally remastered by Grant's spic-and-span record label, EMI/Sparrow Records, alongside with 13 additional Amy Grant collections. The remastered issue is tagged with a Digitally Remastered emblem in the 'gutter' on the CD fore.[http://www.sparrowrecords.com/news/news_detail_page.aspx?id=527739tid=227 Sparrow Records News] Because of Grant's transact with her foregoing label, Word Records, the remastered versions of Behind the Eyes and A Christmas to Remember remained not traded in Contemporary Christian Music|Christian Music retail traders such like Family Christian Stores either Lifeway Christian Resources till 2009. Until that time, Word Records sustained to disperse these

names to Christian retail traders in the first, non-remastered versions when EMI dispersed the remastered versions to nearly all chief retail traders. The 12 still existing remastered versions are dispersed by EMI to altogether US retail traders, either Christian and nonreligious.[http://www.emicmg.com/press/pressRelease.aspx?id=529387 Welcome to EMICMG.com]

The collection was recorded at No.44 in the 2001 publication, CCM Presents: The 100 Greatest Albums in Christian Music and was Grant's nearly all with success graphing collection, arriving at No.8 on the Billboard 200|Billboard 200, contrasted with Heart In Motion, that extended No.10, and House of Love (Amy Grant album)|House of Love that extended No.13.

Samantha Phillips - Career

Phillips has visitor hosted and emerged as a fame visitor either specialist on countless exhibits, containing CBS' The Late Late Show (CBS TV series)|The Late Late Show with Craig Kilborn, FX Network, The Howard Stern Show, The Joan Rivers Show, The Jenny Jones Show|Jenny Jones, The Maury Povich Show, Hard Copy, Inside Edition, Extra (TV series)|Extra, Entertainment To-night, Undateable (VH1), The Doctors (CBS), Red Eye (Fox News Channel), Strictly Sex with Dr. Drew (Discovery Health Channel), and HBO. She has as well been cast in tunes recordings, containing ones for Weird Al Yankovic, Van Halen, Amy Grant, Mötley Crüe, Simply Red, Scorpions (band)|Scorpions, The Doobie Brothers, Dave Koz, Iron Maiden and Alice Cooper, to designation a limited. Phillips was picked Penthouse Pet for List of Penthouse Pets|June 1993.

Between 1998 and 2001, Phillips was a correspondent for Sexcetera on Playboy TV.

She has emerged in films such like Love Potion (1987), Deceit (1989 film)|Deceit (1989), Phantasm II (1988), Angel 4: Undercover (1993), Sexual Malice (1994) and Fallen Angel (1997), Weekend at Bernie's II (1993), Spy Hard (1996) and Rescue Me (1993) and the N.Y. Independent Film Festival prize victor Just for the Time Be-ing (2000) amid different features. Phillips is as well the maker of the Busty Cops serials of films (Busty Cops 1, Busty Cops 2, Alabama Jones and The Busty Cru-sade, Busty Cops Protect and Serve), and featured in Showtime's Hot Springs Ho-tel.[http://www.tv.com/shows/hot-springs-hotel/episodes/ TV.com Hot Springs Hotel]

In 2001 Phillips hosted Men Are From Mars, Women Are From Venus a national forenoon address show. The idea was founded on the best-seller by John Gray (U.S. Author)|John Gray and set out to survey the inborn dissimilarities amid males and females, in fore of a live public.

In 2005, she hosted chapters of Xtreme Fakeovers[http://www.imdb.com/title/tt0455898/fullcredits#cast Xtreme Fakeovers: cast] a actuality show, that merges the components of complete form makeovers and concealed camera TV. Phillips hosted KAMP-FM|97.1 The FM Talk Station/KLSX broadcast address show The Single Life, a show about navigating and extanting dating existence in Los Angeles, as of 2004-2009.

After KAMP-FM|97.1 The FM Talk Station/KLSX shifted to a Top 40 setup within February 2009, Phillips and her co-host Chris Leary branched out in to dissimilar media. The Single Life TV show debuted on MavTV in May 2009, concentrating on frank address about intercourse and dating.

In June 2009, Phillips co-created HotTalkLA.com,[http://hottalkla.com HotTalkLA.com] an world wide web broadcast facility, with Jack Sullivan, Ron Escarsega, and Rich Boerner.[http://www.allaccess.com/news-talk-sports/10-questions/archive/7417/10-questions-with-sam-phillips Allaccess.com] She is Hot Talk LA's Executive Producer and VP.[http://www.hottalkla.com/htla/index.php?option=com_contentview=articleid=670Itemid=245 Hottalkla.com]

As of 2010 Phillips Weblogs for LA Weekly on the web in their After Dark LA part. Her weblog The Single Life[http://blogs.laweekly.com/afterdark/author.php?author_id=2328 The Single Life] centers on intercourse, dating and connection guidance. Phillips as well Weblogs for DigN2it on the web.[http://dign2it.com/mag/2010/the-single-life-sex-tips-to-spice-up-your-love-life-for-2011 Dign2it.com]

Minnie Pearl - Final years

Pearl endured a important stroke in June 1991, taking her carrying out vocation to an finish. After the stroke she existed in a Nashville tending home wherever she experienced recurrent calls as of region tunes business numbers, containing Chely Wright, Vince Gill and Amy Grant. Her demise on March 4, 1996, at the age of 83, was ascribed to difficulties as of one other stroke. She is entombed at Mount Hope Cemetery (Franklin, Tennessee)|Mount Hope Cemetery in Franklin, Tennessee.

Lucky One (song) - Official versions

*** Original collection variant (4:11), accessible on the House of Love (Amy Grant album)|House Of Love album**
* Remix, accessible on the 2004 CD Greatest Hits 1986-2004

* The Lucky Street mix
* The A/C Rhythm mixture [A.k.a. Martyn Phillips mix]
* Eric Kupper|Kupper Radio Mix
* Churban Mix
* **Live variant, (live musical performance transcriptioning as of the 2006 Time Again...Amy Grant Live album)**

Clare Fischer - Later years: jazz inspiration and pop arranger

Since 1985 Fischer authored symphonical plans for pop creator Prince (musician)|Prince. Some emerged on Prince's collections and have been applied aimed at his films Under the Cherry Moon (Fischer's foremost screen credit), Graffiti Bridge (film)|Graffiti Bridge and in Spike Lee's Girl 6. One of Fischer's Prince plans was as well applied within a reconsidered shape for the film Batman (1989 film)|Batman. Prince's December 2005 sole Te Amo Corazon, a mid-tempo Latin jazz trail, highlighted thread plans by Fischer.

More not long ago, as a jazz teacher, Fischer accomplished unaccompanied keyboard instrument musical performances and directed clinics and principal groups in colleges and tunes conservatories in Europe and all over the United States. In 1995 Just Me appeared out, a Concord Jazz CD with Fischer on unaccompanied keyboard instrument. Featuring his Latin-jazz cluster and 6 singers, at the moment referenced to like Clare Fischer Friends, a JVC Music CD was disseminated within 1997 named Rockin' In Rhythm.

Two bestowed Dutch jazz pianists, Cor Bakker and Bert van Den Brink, recorded the tribute DeClared (1993) that holds 9 Fischer compositions. Five annums afterward recordings produced in 1991 and 1997 with The Netherlands Metropole Orchestra guided by Rob Pronk and Vince Mendoza appeared out like The Latin Side. Another noteworthy new CD with Clare is a re-issue of Art Pepper's Tokyo Debut on Galaxy (1995).

Fischer sustained to record for Prince and numerous different famous creators containing Michael Jackson beforehand his demise, Amy Grant, Brazilian creator João Gilberto (João), Paula Abdul, Natalie Cole and further not long ago Chaka Khan and Branford Marsalis.

With his profit-oriented work Fischer funded a expensive group of 20 brass tools, named Clare Fischer's Jazz Corps. The recordings of this group hold an absorbing plan of Antonio Carlos Jobim's Corcovado (song)|Corcovado. The demise of my pal Antonio Carlos Jobim|Tom Jobim has influenced myself intensly. Like myself he was

68, and I am nevertheless living. After he passed away I had a dream in that I was managing his 'Corcovado'. Only it was not a usual variant, there remained those vocal countermelodies in the deep-toned. When I awoke I authored down what I had dreamed. It grew to be Jobim's In Memoriam, a bit I named 'Corcovado Fúnebre.'

One of Fischer's final programs in his personal designation was a transcriptioning with Brazilian guitar player Hélio Delmiro named Symbiosis that has been disseminated on a Clare Fischer Productions transcriptioning as has his Clare Fischer's Jazz Corps transcriptioning.

In December 1999, Michigan State University School of Music discussed an Honorary Doctorate of Fine Arts Degree on Fischer in acknowledgment of his inventiveness and distinction as a jazz melodist, organizer and performing artist.

On October 22, 2009, Manhattan School of Music#Instrumental carrying out ensembles|Manhattan School of Music's Concert Jazz Band, under the management of Justin DiCoccio, celebrated 2 Clare Fischer anniversaries - either his 81st anniversary and the 40th day of remembrance of the discharge of his well-regarded great group LP, Thesaurus (Clare Fischer album)|Thesaurus - with a musical performance whose programme decided with 5 successive plans culled as of that collection. FIttingly, the five-tune order either started and finished, a lot like the collection its normal self, with The Duke and Upper Manhattan Medical Group, correspondingly,[http://www.worldcat.org/oclc/498385998 (Musical CD, 2009)]. Worldcat. Retrieved 2013-04-20. Fischer's saccolade to his twin jazz inspirations, Duke Ellington and Billy Strayhorn. Sadly, Dr. Fischer might not be at the tribute; ensuing a health crisis on the flying home as of a kin reunification in Michigan the foregoing annum, the kin had determined that air journey was simply also stressful. Email communication with Donna Fischer. May 8, 2013.

List of artists who reached number one in the United States - G

*Peter Gabriel (1)
*Art Garfunkel (see Simon and Garfunkel)
*Marvin Gaye (3)
*Gloria Gaynor (1)
*The J. Geils Band (1)
*Genesis (band)|Genesis (1)
*Bobbie Gentry (1)
*Andy Gibb (3)
*Georgia Gibbs (1)°
*Deborah Gibson|Debbie Gibson (2)

*Nick Gilder (1)
*Jimmy Gilmer|Jimmy Gilmer the Fireballs (1)
*Big Gipp|Gipp (1)
*Bobby Goldsboro (1)
*GoonRock (1)
*Lesley Gore (1)
*Gotye (1)
*Charlie Gracie (1)°
*Grand Funk Railroad (2)
***Amy Grant (2)**
*Gogi Grant (1)°
*Al Green (musician)|Al Green (1)
*Lorne Greene (1)
*The Guess Who (1)
*Guns N' Roses (1)

I Will Remember You (Amy Grant song) - Promotional CD Single

On back aspect of CD card sleeve

Track List:

1. Rhythm Remix* 5:06

2. Album Remix* 5:06

3. Album Version+ 5:00

FOR PROMOTIONAL USE ONLY - NOT FOR SALE

+Produced by Michael Omartian for Rhema Productions Executive Producers Amy Grant and Michael Blanton *Additional Production and Remix by Daniel Abraham for White Falcon Productions Keyboards: Peter Schwartz Overdub Engineer: Rick Van Benshoten Executive Producers for the Remixes: Mark Mazzetti Written by Amy Grant/Gary Chapman/Keith Thomas Published by Age To Age Music, Inc./Riverstone Music, Inc./Edward Grant,Inc./Yellow Elephant Music, Inc. (ASCAP), ADM. By Reunion Music Group Inc.75021 7339 2

Medley (music) - Other medleys

* The Grateful Dead played numerous covers as well like their personal tunes as medleys, nearly all especially in the live positioning. Examples contain a potpourri of their covers of Not Fade Away (song)|Not Fade Away and Goin' Down The Road Feelin' Bad and a potpourri of their first China Cat Sunflower with a cover of I Know You Rider. Some of their first tunes remained authored like either coherently accomplished as medleys, such like Help on the Way When|date=July 2011 disseminated a potpourri on their latest collection Bloody hole of terror. It is the final tune on the collection allowed Hell-O Medley that is their whole foremost collection in to one
* Kumikyoku Nico Nico Douga by Shimo (2007)
* Acoustic Medley by Bob Marley
* Don't Pull Your Love (Sean Maguire song)|Don't Pull Your Love/Then You Can Tell Me Goodbye by Glen Campbell (1976)
* Over the Rainbow / What a Wonderful World potpourri (1993) disseminated by Israel Kamakawiwo'ole
* Ballet for a Girl in Buchannon (1970) as of Chicago's duple collection Chicago II
* The Abbey Road Medley (1969) by The Beatles; the exciting potpourri that final for 10 minutes and 3 seconds (beginning with You Never Give Me Your Money and ending with She Came in Through the Bathroom Window) that bears up a major part of aspect 2 of the first LP.
* The Abbey Road#Track listing|Golden Slumbers Medley (1969); this potpourri that appears following the 10-minute prolonged Abbey Road potpourri. It starts with Golden Slumbers and surmises with The End (The Beatles song)|The End. (the finishing trail of the album; notwithstanding the cause that Her Majesty (song)|Her Majesty is the final trail to be played on the album)
* Beatles Medley by Tommy Emmanuel
* My Generation by The Who as of their collection Live at Leeds (1970)
* Disco Gold (1978) collection by Biddu
* Death Mix (1983) collection by Afrika Bambaataa
* **Ageless Medley (EP) (1983) by Amy Grant.**
* Maine Pyar Kiya#Songs|Antakshari (1989) by Lata Mangeshkar and S. P. Balasubrahmanyam for the feature Maine Pyar Kiya, founded on the Antakshari game.
* The Grease Megamix (1991) by John Travolta and Olivia Newton-John.
* Purple Medley (1995) by Prince (musician)|Prince.
* Never Too Far/Hero Medley (2001) by Mariah Carey.
* Medley (Five Iron Frenzy song)|Medley (2003) by Five Iron Frenzy as of their live collection The End Is Here.
* Weird Al Yankovic has had a List of Weird Al Yankovic polka medleys|polka potpourri on nearly all of his collections. Most frequently, Yankovic's polka medleys characteristic snippets of hit tunes that are well-liked at the time he records an collection, although he occasionally selects tunes of a alike category (and in one instance, dissimilar tunes recorded by a sole group) for a themed potpourri.
** Polkas on 45 (1984) as of his collection In 3-D.
** Hooked on Polkas (1985) as of his collection Dare to be Stupid.

** Polka Party! (1986) as of his collection Polka Party!.
** The Hot Rocks Polka (1989), a potpourri of The Rolling Stones tunes, as of his collection UHF - Original Motion Picture Soundtrack and Other Stuff|UHF.
** Polka Your Eyes Out (1992) as of his collection Off the Deep End.
** The Alternative Polka (1996) as of his collection Bad Hair Day.
** Polka Power (1999) as of his collection Running With Scissors (album)|Running With Scissors.
** Angry White Boy Polka (2003) as of his collection Poodle Hat.
** Polkarama! (2006) as of his collection Straight Outta Lynwood.
** Polka Face (2011) as of his collection Alpocalypse.
* The Queen Is Dead by The Smiths.
* Instrumedley (2002) by Dream Theater as of their live collection Live at Budokan (Dream Theater)|Live at Budokan. Dream Theater often does medleys of different groups live. In different medleys, Dream Theater has veiled functions by Pink Floyd, Yes (band)|Yes, Genesis (band)|Genesis, Iron Maiden, Metallica, Led Zeppelin, Journey (band)|Journey, Elton John, Queen (band)|Queen, Kansas (band)|Kansas, and Dixie Dregs, sometimes utilizing a few of their personal work to level the change amid groups.
* Imma Be Rocking That Body is a tunes audiovisual by The Black Eyed Peas, presenting 2 of their selects Imma Be and Rock That Body.
* Green Day authored 2 medleys on their praised American Idiot (2004) collection – Jesus of Suburbia and Homecoming. The erstwhile was disseminated like a sole and was contemplated one of their finest functions at any time.
* Metallica did a potpourri of Mercyful Fate tunes on their collection Garage Inc.
* Metallica did a potpourri of A National Acrobat and Sabbra Cadabra of Black Sabbath on their 1998 covers collection Garage Inc.
* Metallica did a potpourri of Orion, To Live Is to Die, and The Call of Ktulu (all devised firstly by belated bassist Cliff Burton) at 1993 musical performances. These remained altogether tunes that remained seldom either not ever played live.
* Metallica did a potpourri of tunes as of the 1988 collection ...And Justice for All (album)|...And Justice for All when on journey as of 1991 to 1993. The potpourri was named the Justice Medley and contained bits of Eye of the Beholder (song)|Eye of the Beholder, Blackened (song)|Blackened, The Frayed Ends of Sanity and ...And Justice for All (song)|...And Justice for All.
* Metallica accomplished a potpourri of Ride The Lightning, No Remorse, Hit The Lights, The Four Horsemen, Seek And Destroy and Fight Fire With Fire. This was named the Kill/Ride potpourri and may be noticed onto the Cunning Stunts (video) DVD.
* Black Sabbath accomplished a potpourri on their collection Past Lives (Black Sabbath album)|Past Lives, containing of Wicked World (Black Sabbath song)|Wicked World, Black Sabbath, Vol 4|Supernaut, Sometimes I'm Happy, and Into the Void (Black Sabbath song)|Into the Void, alongside with a stringed instrument and drum unaccompanied.

* Black Sabbath accomplished a potpourri of Heaven and Hell (Black Sabbath song)|Heaven and Hell, Sign of the Southern Cross and Paranoid (Black Sabbath song)|Paranoid live throughout the transcriptioning of the Live Evil (Black Sabbath album)|Live Evil collection, presenting stringed instrument unaccompanied and extra words.
* Bon Jovi must as well do a great deal of medleys throughout live musical performances normally Bad Medicine and a cover tune Shout either Pretty Woman. They as well tend to play I'll Sleep When Im Dead with Jumping Jack Flash either Papa was a Rolling Stone.
* Meat Loaf has accomplished numerous medleys live throughout his vocation. Most noteworthy is throughout his visits as of 1987 to 1992 he'd do a Rock Roll Medley as a climax that ought to contain Johnny B. Goode, Jailhouse Rock (song)|Jail House Rock, Slow Down (Larry Williams song)|Slow Down, Blue Suede Shoes, Roll Over Beethoven, and Around And Around. A variant of this potpourri was disseminated on Live at Wembley (Meat Loaf album)|Live at Wembley collection, that omits Roll Over BEethoven and Around And Around. During his 2011 Guilty Pleasures Tour he did medleys of Hot Patootie / The Time Warp and Boneyard/ Freebird/ All Revved Up With No Place To Go. Meat Loaf's as well completed Medleys of his strikes on exhibits such like Wetten, dass..? and at the 2011 AFL Grand Final. In 1994 it was not unusual for Meat Loaf to finish his exhibits with a potpourri of simply Johnny B. Goode and Roll Over Beethoven. During his 2008 journey, a commonplace climax to Meat Loaf's set comprised of a potpourri that contained Roadhouse Blues / Why Don't We Do It in the Road?.
* Rage Prague Symphonic Orchestra – Medley – Don`t Fear the Winter (instrumental), Black in Mind, Firestorm (instrumental), Send by the Devil, Lost in the Ice (instrumental)
* Die Ärzte frequently do medleys on their musical performances. Zu spat (Hit Summer Mix '88)|One potpourri was as well disseminated like a sole.
* UK Pianist Colin Keyes accomplished his 'TV Themes Medley' on his foremost collection 'The Magic of Piano', containing of organized adaptations of the subjects as of Cheers, L.A. Law and Cagney Lacey.
* Emerson, Lake Palmer – Tarkus Medley
* The Who at Super Bowl xlii
* Goodbye, My Coney Island Baby-1948 by Les Applegate. The small tunes Coney Island Baby and We All Fall remained foremost rolled into one as a potpourri by Les Applegate in 1924 for the melodic farce No, No, Nanette.
* Children of Bodom did a potpourri of Bodom following Midnight and Bodom Beach Terror on their live collection Stockholm Knockout Live.
* Paula Abdul's 1990 Medley Mix (a potpourri of her foremost 6 singles) was well-liked in 1990 as of her Shut Up and Dance – The Mixes collection. It was as well applied within a TV advertisement by L.A. Gear.
* Thank ABBA for the Music – a 1999 British almsgiving sole created by Pete Waterman. It highlighted 4 ABBA tunes veiled by Tina Cousins, Billie Piper, Steps

(group)|Steps, and girl-groups Cleopatra and B*Witched.
* Beyoncé did a Destiny's Child potpourri blanketing nearly all of Destiny's Child well-liked tunes throughout her international journey The Beyoncé Experience in 2007.
* George Michael accomplished a potpourri of Papa Was a Rollin' Stone and Killer (Adamski song)|Killer in 1992.
* Guns N' Roses did a potpourri of their personal tune Patience (Guns N' Roses song)|Patience and John Lennon's Imagine (song)|Imagine in 1993. It was unplugged variant.
* Brain Stew/Jaded (Green Day)|Jaded, a potpourri of 2 tunes as of the collection Insomniac (Green Day album)|Insomniac by Green Day. Are We the Waiting and St. Jimmy as of the American Idiot collection may as well be contemplated a potpourri.
* Sabaton (band) produced a potpourri of their 2 tracks: Metal Machine and Metal Crüe. It's solely played throughout live gigs.
* Foo Fighters does a few medleys live, presenting tunes like Head Like a Hole by Nine Inch Nails, How You Remind Me by Nickelback, Immigrant Song by Led Zeppelin, alongside with different as of groups like Soundgarden, The White Stripes and obscure (band)|Blur.
* FOX TV Series Glee (TV series)|Glee has completed a potpourri as of Journey (band)|Journey, crooning Faithfully, a Mash-up of Any Way You Want It and Lovin' Touchin' Squeezin', and Don't Stop Believing.
* Kanye West did a potpourri, holding his entire record designated My Beautiful Dark Twisted Memory, that was recorded in to the most heroic tunes recordings of altogether time.
* Michael Jackson did, in altogether his society visits, a potpourri of the biggest strikes of the Jackson 5, with the songs: I Want You Back, The Love You Save and I'll Be There (The Jackson 5 song)|I'll Be There
* At the WWE pay-per-view happening WrestleMania XXV, Kid Rock accomplished a live potpourri of his tunes Bawitdaba, So Hott, All Summer Long (Kid Rock song)|All Summer Long, Rock N Roll Jesus (song)|Rock N Roll Jesus, and Cowboy (song)|Cowboy.
* David Bowie – Sweet Thing – Candidate – Sweet Thing (reprise)
* Paul Williams – Give A Little Love is a type of medley/reprise of Bad Guys (changed to Good Guys) and Give A Little Love
* Anniversary Waltz (1989) by Status Quo
* Lady Gaga accomplished a potpourri of Heavy Metal Lover, Marry The Night and Born This Way at the New Year's Eve fete of 2011.
*Justin Timberlake Featuring T.I. Carrying out Medley: Let Me Talk To You/My Love. (C) 2006 Zomba Recording, LLC
*Whenever Heartbreaker (Led Zeppelin song)|Heartbreaker by Led Zeppelin plays on the broadcast, it's normally piece of a potpourri with Living Loving Maid (She's Just a Woman).
* Toto did 2 medleys in 2003. Journey, foremost one consits of: Girl Goodbye,

Goodbye Elenore, Child's Anthem and I'll Supply The Love. Second one includes: Waiting For Your Love, Georgy Porgy, Lion, Hydra, English Eyes and Till The End
* Linkin Park - Ballad Medley is a potpourri of Shadow of the Day, Leave Out All The Rest and Iridescent (song) and is played at live executions (never been recorded in a stuido)
* A Perfect Circle accomplished a live potpourri of The Cure's Lovesong (The Cure song)|Lovesong and Ozzy Osbourne's Diary of A Madman.
* Laura Marling accomplished a live potpourri of 2 of her tunes, Don't Ask Me Why and Salinas.
* Metallica recorded a potpourri named Ronnie Rising for This Is Your Life, a accolade collection for Ronnie James Dio. The potpourri is produced up of the tunes A Light in the Black, Stargazer (Rainbow song)|Stargazer, and Tarot Woman, that are altogether traces as of Rising (Rainbow album)|Rising, the second collection Dio recorded as the head singer for Rainbow (English band)|Rainbow, therefore the designation of the tune.

1984 in music - Release Date Unknown

*Change Your Mind – Raffaele Riefoli|Raf
*Aimless Love – John Prine
*All the Rage (album)|All the Rage – General Public
*Animotion (album)|Animotion - Animotion
*The Art of Defense – Nona Hendryx
*Back and Forth (album)|Back and Forth – Skinny Puppy
*Born in Captivity – Roy Harper
*Box of Frogs – Box of Frogs
*Can't Wait All Night – Juice Newton
*Caribbean Sunset – John Cale
*Centipede (album)|Centipede – Rebbie Jackson
*Cinema (Elaine Paige album)|Cinema – Elaine Paige
*Climate of Hunter – Scott Walker (singer)|Scott Walker
*Country Boy – Ricky Skaggs
*Dali (Dalida album)|Dali – Dalida
*A Dancing Foot and a Praying Knee Don't Belong on the Same Leg – Scattered Order
*Dancin' on the Edge – Lita Ford
*E2-E4 – Manuel Göttsching
*Eat My Fuc - GG Allin
*EB 84 – The Everly Brothers
*Every Man Has a Woman – Various Artists – Yoko Ono tribute
*Fans (Malcolm McLaren album)|Fans – Malcolm McLaren
*Folk of the 80s (Part III) – Men Without Hats

*Fried (album)|Fried – Julian Cope
*Glorious Results of a Misspent Youth – Joan Jett and the Blackhearts
*Gone Fishin' (Flipper album)|Gone Fishin' – Flipper (band)|Flipper
*The Grapes of Wrath (album)|The Grapes of Wrath – The Grapes of Wrath (band)|The Grapes of Wrath
*Greatest Hits – Juice Newton
*Greatest Love Classics - Andy Williams
*Guardian Angel – The Shadows
*Heart Don't Lie – La Toya Jackson
*Heart Over Mind (Anne Murray album)|Heart Over Mind – Anne Murray
*Heavy Heart (album)|Heavy Heart – Carla Bley
*Hits out of Hell – Meat Loaf
*Horizen – Jade Warrior (band)|Jade Warrior
*How Will the Wolf Survive? – Los Lobos
*I Often Dream of Trains – Robyn Hitchcock
*If the Price is Right – Bonnie Pointer
*Inside the Fire (Rita Coolidge album)|Inside the Fire – Rita Coolidge
*Intellectuals Are The Shoeshine Boys Of The Ruling Elite – Killdozer (band)|Killdozer
*It's All in the Game (Merle Haggard album)|It's All in the Game – Merle Haggard
*The Las Vegas Story (album)|The Las Vegas Story – The Gun Club
*John Parr (album)|John Parr – John Parr (debut)
*Knights of the New Thunder – TNT (band)|TNT
*Legend (Robin of Sherwood soundtrack)|Legend – Clannad (soundtrack)
*Lights Out (Peter Wolf album)|Lights Out – Peter Wolf (debut)
*Live at the Inferno – Raven (band)|Raven
*Mama – Becket

*Mast Nazren -Ecstatic Glances Live in London, 1984 – Ghulam Ali (Ghazal singer)|Ghulam Ali
*Meat Puppets II – Meat Puppets
*Meeting in the Ladies Room – Klymaxx
*Moving (The Raincoats album)|Moving – The Raincoats
*Music as of 'Cal' – Mark Knopfler – Soundtrack
*Nave Maria – Tom Zé
*Neil's Heavy Concept Album – Nigel Planer
*1984 – Ebiet G. Ade
*No Brakes – John Waite
*No Kinda Dancer – Robert Earl Keen
*Opium (KMFDM album)|Opium – KMFDM (debut)
*Optimystique – Yanni
*Overkill (EP) – Overkill (band)|Overkill
*The Politics of Time – Minutemen (band)|Minutemen

*Primitive – Neil Diamond
*Projects in the Jungle – Pantera
*Pulling Rabbits Out of a Hat – Sparks (band)|Sparks
*Reflexiones (José José album)|Reflexiones – José José
*Read My Lips – Fee Waybill
*Remote Luxury (album)|Remote Luxury – The Church (band)|The Church
*Riders in the Sky, Live – Riders in the Sky (band)|Riders in the Sky
*Rita Mitsouko (album)|Rita Mitsouko – Rita Mitsouko
*The Rock Connection – Cliff Richard
*Seasons – Dion DiMucci
*See You in Hell (album)|See You in Hell – Grim Reaper (debut)
*Sonic Death – Sonic Youth
*The Splendour of Fear – Felt (band)|Felt
*Starchild – Teena Marie
***Straight Ahead (Amy Grant album)|Straight Ahead – Amy Grant**
*The Strange Idols Pattern and Other Short Stories – Felt
*Tapdancin' Bats – NRBQ
*Team Goon – D.I. (band)|D.I. (EP)
*Tocsin (album)|Tocsin – Xmal Deutschland
*Toyah! Toyah! Toyah! (compilation)|Toyah! Toyah! Toyah! – Toyah (band)|Toyah
*United States Live – Laurie Anderson – Live
*The Voice (Bobby McFerrin album)|The Voice – Bobby McFerrin
*Youth Anthems for the New Order – Reagan Youth
*Walking in the Shadow of the Big Man – Guadalcanal Diary (band)|Guadalcanal Diary
*Walpurgis Night (Stormwitch album)|Walpurgis Night – Stormwitch
*We Hate You South African Bastards! - Microdisney
*When In Rome Do As The Vandals – The Vandals
*Who's Afraid of the Art of Noise? – Art of Noise
*Wired to the Moon – Chris Rea
*Without a Song (album)|Without a Song – Willie Nelson
*Wonderful World - Telex (band)|Telex
*Work Resumed on the Tower – News as of Babel
*World Shut Your Mouth (album)|World Shut Your Mouth – Julian Cope
*You're Gettin' Even While I'm Gettin' Odd – The J. Geils Band (final album)

1986 in music - Notable hits

*Absolute Beginners (David Bowie song)|Absolute Beginners – David Bowie
*Addicted To Love (song)|Addicted To Love – Robert Palmer (singer)|Robert Palmer
*All Cried Out – LisaLisa Cult Jam
*All I Ask of You – Cliff Richard and Sarah Brightman

*All I Need Is a Miracle – Mike + The Mechanics
*All The Things She Said – Simple Minds
*Amanda (Boston song)|Amanda – Boston (band)|Boston
*Baby Love – Regina Richards
*Bad Boy (Miami Sound Machine song)|Bad Boy – Miami Sound Machine
*Be Good to Yourself - Journey (band)|Journey
*Best of Both Worlds – Van Halen
*Breakout (Swing Out Sister song)|Breakout – Swing Out Sister
*Bigmouth Strikes Again- The Smiths
*Big Time (Peter Gabriel song)|Big Time – Peter Gabriel
*Bizarre Love Triangle – New Order
*Brother Louie (Modern Talking song)|Brother Louie – Modern Talking
*Friends and Lovers (song)|Both to Each Other (Friends and Lovers) – Juice Newton and Eddie Rabbitt
*Calling America – Electric Light Orchestra
*Can't Wait Another Minute – Five Star
*Candy (Cameo song)|Candy – Cameo (band)|Cameo
*Capitaine abandonné – Gold (band)|Gold
*The Captain of Her Heart – Double (band)|Double (released in 1985)
*Chain Reaction (song)|Chain Reaction – Diana Ross
*Cheap Love – Juice Newton
*Coming Around Again (song)|Coming Around Again – Carly Simon (released in UK in 1987)
*Conga (song)|Conga – Miami Sound Machine
*Crush on You – The Jets (band)|The Jets
*Dancing in the Dark – The Shadows
*Dancing on the Ceiling (song)|Dancing on the Ceiling – Lionel Richie
*Danger Zone (Top Gun song)|Danger Zone – Kenny Loggins
*Digging Your Scene – The Blow Monkeys
*Don't Forget Me (When I'm Gone) – Glass Tiger
*Don't Stand So Close to Me '86#1986 sole release|Don't Stand So Close to Me '86 – The Police
*Dreams (Van Halen song)|Dreams – Van Halen
*Dreamtime – Daryl Hall
*The Edge of Heaven – Wham!
*En Rouge et Noir – Jeanne Mas
*Ève lève-toi – Julie Pietri
*Everybody Have Fun Tonight – Wang Chung (band)|Wang Chung
*The Final Countdown (song)|The Final Countdown – Europe (band)|Europe
*Flash (Stéphanie song)|Flash – Princess Stéphanie of Monaco
*For America – Jackson Browne
*For America – Red Box (band)|Red Box
*Freedom Overspill – Steve Winwood

*Friends and Lovers (song)|Friends and Lovers – Gloria Loring and Carl Anderson (singer)|Carl Anderson
**also recorded as Both to Each Other by region tunes creators Juice Newton and Eddie Rabbitt
*French Kissin' In The USA – Debbie Harry
*Girl Can't Help It (song)|Girl Can't Help It - Journey (band)|Journey
*Glory of Love – Peter Cetera
*Go Home (song)|Go Home – Stevie Wonder
*The Greatest Love of All – Whitney Houston
*Harlem Shuffle – The Rolling Stones
*Heartache All Over The World – Elton John
*Heartbeat – Don Johnson
*Hey, You! – Glen Milstead|Divine
*He's Back (The Man Behind the Mask) – Alice Cooper
*Higher Love – Steve Winwood
*Hip to Be Square – Huey Lewis and the News
*Holding Back the Years – Simply Red (originally disseminated within 1985, however flopped)
*How Will I Know – Whitney Houston
*Hymn To Her – The Pretenders
*I Can Prove It – Phil Fearon
*I Want to Wake Up with You – Boris Gardiner
*Invisible Touch (song)|Invisible Touch – Genesis (band)|Genesis
*If She Knew What She Wants – The Bangles
*In Too Deep (Genesis song)|In Too Deep – Genesis (band)|Genesis
*Is It a Crime? – Sade Adu|Sade
*Jumpin' Jack Flash – Aretha Franklin
*A Kind of Magic (song)|A Kind of Magic – Queen (band)|Queen
*Keep Your Hands to Yourself — The Georgia Satellites
*Kiss (Prince song)|Kiss – Prince (musician)|Prince and the Revolution
*Kyrie (song)|Kyrie – Mr. Mister
*La puerta de Alcalá – Ana Belén and Víctor Manuel
*The Lady in Red (Chris de Burgh song)|The Lady in Red – Chris de Burgh
*Land of Confusion – Genesis (band)|Genesis
*Le Sixième Jour – Dalida
*Les Bêtises – Sabine Paturel
*Les Démons de minuit – Images
*Libertine (song)|Libertine – Mylène Farmer
*Little Baby – Divine (Glen Milstead)|Divine
*Live to Tell – Madonna (entertainer)|Madonna
*Living in America (song)|Living In America – James Brown (musician)|James Brown
*Living Doll (song)|Living Doll – Cliff Richard and The Young Ones (TV series)|The

Young Ones presenting Hank Marvin|Hank B. Marvin
*Livin' On a Prayer – Bon Jovi
*Locked In (song)|Locked In – Judas Priest
*Love Touch – Rod Stewart
*Love Walks In – Van Halen
*Lessons in Love (song)|Lessons in Love – Level 42
*Mad About You (Belinda Carlisle song)|Mad About You – Belinda Carlisle
*Manic Monday – The Bangles
*Master of Puppets (song)|Master of Puppets – Metallica
*A Matter of Trust – Billy Joel
*Modern Woman – Billy Joel
*Moonlight Shadow – The Shadows
*Mountains (Prince song)|Mountains – Prince (musician)|Prince
*Move Away – Culture Club
*My Hometown – Bruce Springsteen
*Nasty (song)|Nasty – Janet Jackson
*Never as Good like the First Time – Sade Adu|Sade
***The Next Time I Fall – Peter Cetera and Amy Grant**
*Nikita (song)|Nikita – Elton John
*No Lies – Noiseworks
*No One Is To Blame – Howard Jones (musician)|Howard Jones
*No More I Love You's – The Lover Speaks
*Notorious (song)|Notorious – Duran Duran
*Now and Forever (You and Me) - Anne Murray
*Old Flame (Juice Newton song)|Old Flame – Juice Newton
*On My Own (Patti LaBelle and Michael McDonald song)|On My Own – Patti Labelle Michael McDonald (singer)|Michael McDonald
*Open Your Heart (Madonna song)|Open Your Heart – Madonna (entertainer)|Madonna
*Opportunities (Let's Make Lots of Money) – Pet Shop Boys
*Ouragan (song)|Ouragan – Princess Stéphanie of Monaco
*Overjoyed (Stevie Wonder song)|Overjoyed – Stevie Wonder
*Papa Don't Preach – Madonna (entertainer)|Madonna
*Parce que Je little t'aime and – Dalida
*Peace Sells - Megadeth
*Pressure Down – John Farnham
*Pretty in Pink (song)|Pretty in Pink – The Psychedelic Furs
*Private Number (The Jets song)|Private Number – The Jets (band)|The Jets
*A Question of Lust – Depeche Mode
*A Question of Time – Depeche Mode
*¿A quién le importa? – Alaska (singer)|Alaska
*Raining Blood – Slayer
*Rain either Shine (song)|Rain either Shine – Five Star

*Rock Me Amadeus – Falco (musician)|Falco
*Rough Boy – ZZ Top
*Ruthless People – Mick Jagger
*Sara – Jefferson Airplane|Starship
*Say You Really Want Me – Kim Wilde (North American issue)
*Schoolgirl (song)|Schoolgirl – Kim Wilde
*Set Me Free – Jaki Graham
*Showing Out (Get Fresh at the Weekend) – Mel and Kim
*Silent Running (On Dangerous Ground)|Silent Running – Mike + The Mechanics
*Sing Our Own Song – UB40
*Sledgehammer (song)|Sledgehammer – Peter Gabriel
*Slice of Heaven – Dave Dobbyn
*Slow Rivers – Cliff Richard and Elton John
*Small Town – John Cougar Mellencamp
*So Far, So Good – Sheena Easton
*Sometimes (Erasure song)|Sometimes – Erasure
*Somewhere – Barbra Streisand
***Stay For Awhile – Amy Grant**
*Stimulation – Wa Wa Nee
*Stripped (song)|Stripped – Depeche Mode
*Stuck with You – Huey Lewis and the News
*Sweet Freedom (Michael McDonald song)|Sweet Freedom – Michael McDonald (singer)|Michael McDonald
*The Sweetest Taboo – Sade Adu|Sade
*System Addict – Five Star
*Take Me Home Tonight (song)|Take Me Home Tonight – Eddie Money
*Take My Breath Away – Berlin (band)|Berlin
*Taken In – Mike + The Mechanics
*That Was Then, This Is Now (song)|That Was Then, This Is Now – The Monkees
*Tender Love – Force MD's
*That's What Friends Are For – Dionne Warwick (duets with Elton John, Gladys Knight Stevie Wonder)
*The Themes as of 'EastEnders' and 'Howards Way' – The Shadows
*Teenage Frankenstein – Alice Cooper
*(There's Gonna Be) A Showdown – The Johnnys
*These Dreams - Heart (band)|Heart
*Throw Your Arms Around Me – Hunters + Collectors
*Throwing It All Away – Genesis (band)|Genesis
*Thorn in My Side – Eurythmics
*Turbo Lover – Judas Priest
*True Blue (Madonna song)|True Blue- Madonna (entertainer)|Madonna
*True Colors (song)|True Colors – Cyndi Lauper
*Twist and Shout#The Beatles' version|Twist and Shout - The Beatles

*Two People – Tina Turner
*Two Of Hearts – Stacey Q
*Typical Male – Tina Turner
*Venus (Shocking Blue song)|Venus – Bananarama
*Walk Like an Egyptian – The Bangles
*Walk This Way – Run DMC presenting Aerosmith
*War (Edwin Starr song)|War – Bruce Springsteen
*The Way It Is (song)|The Way It Is – Bruce Hornsby and the Range
*We Don't Have to Take Our Clothes Off – Jermaine Stewart
*What Have You Done for Me Lately – Janet Jackson
*What You Need (song)|What You Need – INXS
*When I Think of You – Janet Jackson
*Why Can't This Be Love – Van Halen
*Word Up! (song)|Word Up!- Cameo (band)|Cameo
*Words Get in the Way – Gloria Estefan Miami Sound Machine
*You Can Call Me Al – Paul Simon
*You Give Love a Bad Name (song)|You Give Love a Bad Name – Bon Jovi
*You Got It All – The Jets (band)|The Jets
*You Keep Me Hangin' On – Kim Wilde
*Your Love (The Outfield song)|Your Love – The Outfield
*Your Wildest Dreams – The Moody Blues

House of Love (Amy Grant album)

'House of Love' is the 14th collection by singer-songwriter Amy Grant, disseminated within 1994 (see 1994 in music).

House of Love was Amy's continuation to her quintuple-platinum 1991 discharge Heart in Motion. Although House of Love traded fewer compared to fifty per cent of what its forerunner traded, it likewise merges pop tunes with Christian principles. Lucky One was the album's largest hit at No.18 Pop and No.2 Adult Contemporary in the U.S., pursued by the name tune and a recreate of Joni Mitchell's Big Yellow Taxi. Say You'll Be Mine as well was a UK Top 50 hit. When it was disseminated within 1994, House of Love was the largest opening discharge in Christian tunes past, delivering nearly a fifty per cent million duplicates onto its foremost day only.

Copies of this collection traded in Europe, Australia, and Japan characteristic the extra trail Politics of Kissing. Some of the album's additional tracks gathered further notice afterward on once veiled by different creators. The Power (written by Tommy Sims and Judson Spence) is highlighted onto Cher's 1998 collection Believe, and

Vanessa L. Williams had an AC hit with her variant of Oh How the Years Go By.

In 2007, House of Love was reissued and digitally remastered by Grant's spic-and-span record label, EMI/Sparrow Records. The remastered issue is tagged with a Digitally Remastered emblem in the 'gutter' on the CD fore.[http://www.sparrow-records.com/news/news_detail_page.aspx?id=527739tid=227 Sparrow Records News]

What About the Love

'What About the Love' is a tune authored by Kye Fleming Janis Ian and disseminated like a 1988 sole by Contemporary Christian music|Christian tunes vocalist Amy Grant. It was disseminated like the 4th sole as of Grant's Lead Me On (Amy Grant album)|Lead Me On collection. Unlike a few of Grant's foregoing selects, this tune was disseminated to Christian broadcast solely and was not advertised to Pop music|pop either normal broadcast.

What About the Love is a down-tempo motivational tune that embraces a strange sound via the employ of keyboards, auditory guitars, and haunting context voices. The words centre about the thought that something's off beam in Heaven tonight, with every one poetry belittling a few section of society's disregard of one other section. The foremost poetry addresses preachers whoever are also concentrated on devout Legalism somewhat compared to fancy. The second poetry chats of the business world's misuse of desperation about the planet. The 3rd poetry bothers the futility that the aging perceives once the planet has determined that their usefulness is moved. Finally, the 4th poetry discovers the vocalist gazing at herself in the reflect, registering that she is no stronger compared to these she has condemned, and comparing herself to these whoever crucified Jesus Christ|Jesus. The words disclose that the eponymous fancy in the tune alludes to the fancy of God.

Touched by an Angel - Media

A publication on the serials, Touched by an Angel, was issued by Zondervan in November 1997. Written by Williams and Robin Sheets, it holds context data on a few of the narratives highlighted, serials manufacture data, fundamental particulars on the foremost fifty chapters and outlines of Downey, Reese and Dye. It as well has small tale adaptations of 4 episodes: Interview with an Angel, There, however for the Grace of God, An Unexpected Snow and Jacob's Ladder. A second publication, In the Words of Angels: Twenty Inspiring Stories as of Touched By an Angel, was issued by Fireside Books on August 28, 2001. Also authored by Williams, it gathers 20 small narratives founded on chapters as of the serials.

An acoustic sound recording, Touched by an Angel: The Album, was disseminated on November 3, 1998. The 15-track CD contains a full-length variant of the serials subject tune, Walk With You, accomplished by Della Reese and tunes by Celine Dion, Shawn Colvin, Bob Dylan, Faith Hill, Martina McBride, Amy Grant, Jaci Velasquez, The Kinleys, Wynonna and Amanda Marshall. The sound recording proceeded platinum. A second collection, Touched By an Angel: Christmas Album, was disseminated on November 9, 1999 with 13 traces of Christmas tunes. In extension to experiencing traces accomplished by Reese and Romey, it attributes tunes as of Randy Travis, Keb' Mo', Charlotte Church, Kirk Franklin, Collin Raye, Amy Grant and Donna Summer. Both collections remained disseminated by Sony Music Entertainment, the replacement to the erstwhile record division of CBS.

The Christmas Song (Chestnuts Roasting on an Open Fire) - Selective list of notable recordings

The Christmas Song has been veiled by countless creators as of a ample diversity of categories, including:
*Lisa Matassa (from her 3rd workshop collection, Somebody's Baby (2012); Video No. 1 on CMT.com throughout the 2012 break season)
*Aaliyah
*Trace Adkins
*Christina Aguilera (from her 3rd workshop collection, My Kind of Christmas (2000); No. 18 on the US Billboard Hot 100|Billboard Hot 100 selects chart; No. 22 on the Canadian RPM (magazine)|RPM Top 100 Singles chart)
*Christy Darlington (from his collection All the off beam advances, disseminated on indie label 'Whoa Oh Records' in 2003. Out of print.)
*Clay Aiken
*Darlington (band) (on the collection All the off beam advances disseminated by indie label Whoa Oh Records. Out of print.)
*Diana Ross
*Julie Andrews
*Herb Alpert
*Thomas Anders
*India.Arie and Stevie Wonder (winner of the Grammy Award for Best Pop Collaboration with Vocals in 2003)
*Aska (singer)|Aska
*Babyface (musician)|Babyface
*Francesca Battistelli

*Tony Bennett
*Polly Bergen (who chanted the tune on the December 14, 1957 showing of her NBC diversity show, The Polly Bergen Show)
*Justin Bieber and Usher (entertainer)|Usher (#58 in US, #59 in Canada) as of Bieber's collection Under the Mistletoe (2011)
*Big Bird and The Swedish Chef (A Muppet Family Christmas)
*Andrea Bocelli and Natalie Cole
*Michael Bolton
*Toni Braxton
*Garth Brooks
*James Brown
*Les Brown (bandleader)|Les Brown and his Orchestra (with Doris Day on head vocal)
*Michael Bublé (his variant, bearing close resemblances to Celine Dion's transcriptioning of the tune, extended #6 on the Adult Contemporary (chart)|Billboard Adult Contemporary graph in December 2003.)
*Kenny Burrell
*Colbie Caillat (from her 2012 Christmas collection Christmas In The Sand)
*Glen Campbell
*Royce Campbell
*The Canadian Brass (from their 1985 Christmas collection A Canadian Brass Christmas)
*The Carpenters (from their 1978 Christmas collection Christmas Portrait)
*Cascada (from their 2012 Christmas collection It's Christmas Time (album)|It's Christmas Time)
*Celtic Woman
*Christmas Songs (Nora Aunor Album)|Nora Aunor 1972
*Charice
*Chicago (band)|Chicago
*Christmas Who? (a SpongeBob Christmas out of the ordinary. SpongeBob and Patrick in a Christmas tune chant as a words ...chestnuts roasting and burns in the 3rd level beforehand the finishing of their tune.)
*June Christy - A Friendly Session, Vol. 1 (2000) with the Johnny Guarnieri Quintet
*Charlotte Church (Dream a Dream, 2000)
*Rosemary Clooney
*Natalie Cole (Including unaccompanied variant and duo with Nat King Cole)
*Bing Crosby
*Sheryl Crow (#24 in US Adult Contemporary)
*Daffy Duck
*Danny Davis (country musician)|Danny Davis and the Nashville Brass (1970)
*Sammy Davis, Jr.
*Doris Day (from her 1964 Christmas collection The Doris Day Christmas Album)
*Gavin DeGraw

*John Denver Rocky Mountain Christmas 1975
*Celine Dion (from her 1998 Christmas collection These Are Special Times)
*Vanessa Doofenshmirtz (voiced by Olivia Olson on the collection Phineas and Ferb Holiday Favorites)
*Bob Dylan
*Gloria Estefan
*Connie Francis
*Aretha Franklin
*John Gary
*Judy Garland, whoever chanted the tune in a duo with its melodist, Mel Torme, on a Christmas-themed chapter of The Judy Garland Show|her TV show in December 1963.
*Robert Goulet
*Ariana Grande and Elizabeth Gillies
*JoJo (singer)|JoJo
***Amy Grant (from her 1983 Christmas collection A Christmas Album (Amy Grant album)|A Christmas Album)**
*Cee Lo Green (from his 2012 Christmas collection Cee Lo's Magic Moment)
*Josh Groban (from his 2007 break collection, Noël (Josh Groban album)|Noël)
*Vince Guaraldi|Vince Guaraldi Trio
*Hampton String Quartet
*Eddie Higgins
*Hollyridge Strings
*Hootie and the Blowfish
*Whitney Houston
*Ramon Jacinto|Ramon RJ Jacinto (from his 1988 Christmas collection Pasko Na Naman)
*Alan Jackson (from his 2007 Christmas collection Let It Be Christmas)
*The Jackson 5
*Joni James (from her 1956 Merry Christmas as of Joni). Joni's variant changes the lyric: I'm contributing this straightforward expression, for children as of one to ninety-two to ... Children as of one to ninety-one.
*Al Jarreau
*Joe (singer)|Joe
*Wynonna Judd
*Toby Keith
*Peggy Lee
*Damien Leith (from a out of the ordinary restricted Christmas issue of his 2007 collection Where We Land)
*The Lettermen
*Demi Lovato
*Lovedrug
*The Manhattan Transfer (with Tony Bennett)

*Barry Manilow
*Aimee Mann (from her 2006 collection One More Drifter in the Snow)
*Richard Marx
*Johnny Mathis and Billy Joel as a duo, on Mathis 2013 collection Sending You a Little Christmas
*Martina McBride
*Paul McCartney (from the 2012 collections Kisses on the Bottom#Kisses on the Bottom – Complete Kisses|Kisses on the Bottom – Complete Kisses and Holidays Rule, disseminated like a sole and reached its highest point at numeral 25 on Billboard's Billboard Adult Contemporary|Adult Contemporary graph.)
*Reba McEntire
*Brian McKnight
**NSYNC
*Ricky Nelson (on the chapter of TV's The Adventures of Ozzie and Harriet named A Busy Christmas)
*Aaron Neville
*New Kids on the Block
*Des O'Connor (from a Tesco Christmas advert)
*Alexander O'Neal
*Olivia Olson (from a 2010 Christmas collection Phineas and Ferb: Holiday Favourites)
*The Partridge Family (from their 1971 Christmas collection A Partridge Family Christmas Card)
*Les Paul
*CeCe Peniston (from the 1996 Christmas collection Merry Arizona II: Desert Stars Shine at Christmas)
*Raven-Symoné
*LeAnn Rimes (on her foremost break collection What a Wonderful World (LeAnn Rimes album)|What a Wonderful World)
*Smokey Robinson and The Miracles (from their 1963 Christmas collection Christmas with The Miracles)
*Linda Ronstadt (from her 2000 Christmas collection A Merry Little Christmas (Linda Ronstadt album)|A Merry Little Christmas)
*Kenny Rogers
*SWV
*Diane Schuur (nominated for a Grammy Award for Best Jazz Vocal Performance, Female in 1990)
*Neil Sedaka (from his 2008 first-ever break collection, The Miracle of Christmas)
*She Him (from their 2011 Christmas collection A Very She Him Christmas)
*Jessica Simpson
*Frank Sinatra (including 2 recordings: a virtual duo with Nat King Cole, and an real duo with Bing Crosby)
*Tom Smith (musician)|Tom Smith (of the Editors (band)|Editors) and Agnes Obel

(on the 2011 Smith and Burrows collection, Funny Looking Angels)
*Rod Stewart (on the luxurious issue of his 2012 break collection Merry Christmas, Baby (album)|Merry Christmas, Baby)
*George Strait
*Barbra Streisand (from her 1967 collection A Christmas Album (Barbra Streisand album)|A Christmas Album)
*Donna Summer
*The Supremes (remained unreleased till their 1965 Christmas collection, Merry Christmas (The Supremes album)|Merry Christmas, was re-released in 1999 with extra tracks)
*Taeyeon|Kim Taeyeon (of the South Korean pop cluster Girls' Generation)
*Take 6
*James Taylor
*Randy Travis
*Team Rocket (voiced by Rachael Lillis, Eric Stewart and Maddie Blaustein on the collection Pokémon Christmas Bash)
*The Temptations
*Mel Tormérecorded by the author 4 periods (1954, 1961, 1966 and eventually in 1992 as piece of his collection Christmas Songs)
*Twisted Sister, on their 2006 collection A Twisted Christmas.
*Frankie Valli and the Four Seasons
*Luther Vandross
*Andy Williams
*Stevie Wonder (from his 1967 Christmas collection Someday at Christmas)
*Dwight Yoakam
*[http://www.ascap.com/ace/search.cfm?requesttimeout=300andmode=result sandsearchstr=330056569andsearch_in=iandsearch_type=exactandsearch_det=t,s,w,p,b,vandresults_pp=25andstart=1 ASCAP admission for tune displaying countless additional covers]

Stay for Awhile

'Stay for Awhile' is a 1986 sole by Christian vocalist Amy Grant, and was the foremost sole as of her collection The Collection (Amy Grant album)|The Collection. Background voices remained presented by Richard Page (musician)|Richard Page, head vocalist for Mr. Mister at the time.

Behind the Eyes

'Behind the Eyes' is the 15th collection by Contemporary Christian music|Christian tunes and pop tunes vocalist Amy Grant, disseminated within 1997 (see 1997 in music).

Issued nearby the conclusion of Grant's wedding to Christian singer-songwriter Gary Chapman (musician)|Gary Chapman, numerous of the tunes on Behind the Eyes reproduce Grant's fights in her wedding and altogether connect to a subject of hopefulness. Upon its discharge, it proceeded to No.2 on Billboard (magazine)|Billboard's Christian collections graph and No.8 on the Billboard 200|Billboard 200. Meanwhile, the foremost sole as of the collection, Takes a Little Time, was a Top Five Adult Contemporary hit and a Top Thirty pop graph sole. Like I Love You and I Will Be Your Friend as well extended the Adult Contemporary graph, at No.10 and No.27, correspondingly. The CD was as well disseminated within a restricted 2 CD variant (with the second CD named, 'More Music From Behind the Eyes').

In 2007, Behind the Eyes was reissued and digitally remastered by Grant's spic-and-span record label, EMI/Sparrow Records, alongside with 13 additional Amy Grant collections. The remastered issue is tagged with a Digitally Remastered emblem in the 'gutter' on the CD fore.[http://www.sparrowrecords.com/news/news_detail_page.aspx?id=527739tid=227 Sparrow Records News] Because of Grant's transact with her foregoing label, Word Records, the remastered versions of Behind the Eyes and A Christmas to Remember remained not traded in Contemporary Christian Music|Christian Music retail traders such like Family Christian Stores either Lifeway Christian Resources till 2009. Until that time, Word Records sustained to disperse these names to Christian retail traders in the first, non-remastered versions when EMI dispersed the remastered versions to nearly all chief retail traders. The 12 still existing remastered versions are dispersed by EMI to altogether US retail traders, either Christian and nonreligious.[http://www.emicmg.com/press/pressRelease.aspx?id=529387 Welcome to EMICMG.com]

The collection was recorded at No.44 in the 2001 publication, CCM Presents: The 100 Greatest Albums in Christian Music and was Grant's nearly all with success graphing collection, arriving at No.8 on the Billboard 200|Billboard 200, contrasted with Heart In Motion, that extended No.10, and House of Love (Amy Grant album)|House of Love that extended No.13.

28th Grammy Awards - Gospel

*Grammy Award for Best Gospel Vocal Performance, Female|Best Gospel Performance, Female
Amy Grant for Unguarded
*Grammy Award for Best Gospel Vocal Performance, Male|Best Gospel Performance, Male
**Larnelle Harris for How Excellent Is Thy Name
*Grammy Award for Best Gospel Vocal Performance by a Duo either Group, Choir either Chorus|Best Gospel Performance by a Duo either Group, Choir either Chorus
**Larnelle Harris Sandi Patty|Sandi Patti for I've Just Seen Jesus
*Grammy Award for Best Soul Gospel Performance, Female|Best Soul Gospel Performance, Female
**Shirley Caesar for Martin
*Grammy Award for Best Soul Gospel Performance, Male|Best Soul Gospel Performance, Male
**Marvin Winans for Bring Back the Days of Yea and Nay
*Grammy Award for Best Soul Gospel Performance by a Duo either Group, Choir either Chorus|Best Soul Gospel Performance by a Duo either Group, Choir either Chorus
**The Winans for Tomorrow
*Grammy Award for Best Inspirational Performance|Best Inspirational Performance
**Jennifer Holliday for Come Sunday

Chris Christian

'Chris Christian' (born on February 7, 1951) born Lon Christian Smith to JE and June Smith in Abilene, Texas, is a composer, record maker, and a record label head. His tunes have been recorded by Elvis Presley, Olivia Newton-John, Natalie Cole, Sheena Easton, The Pointer Sisters, Al Jarreau, The Carpenters, Amy Grant, Patti Austin, Dionne Warwick, America (band)|America, The Imperials, B.J. Thomas, B W Stevenson, Marilyn McCoo, Dan Peek, Cheryl Ladd, Jane Olivor, Sandi Patti, Ali Lohan, Donnie and Marie Osmond, and other ones.

As a associate of the triad of Cotton, Lloyd Christian (put alltogether by Mike Curb) in the first 1970s, he relished 2 highest 40 Billboard Hits on 20th Century Records. The cluster accomplished on Dick Clark's American Bandstand and Midnight Special. As a unaccompanied creator he accomplished on The Merv Griffin Show, Solid Gold, and was a justice on Star Search. Christian as well played stringed instrument with Chet Atkins, Jerry Reed, and the Wayne Newton group.

As a record maker, he is finest familiar for beginning Amy Grant's tunes vocation by autographing her at age 16 to his manufacture corporation and naming Myrrh Records head Stan Moser to counsel he was creating an collection on Amy as piece of a prolonged period manufacture accord Christian had signed with Myrrh Records. Christian created her foremost collection and acted as head maker for her second, passing over manufacture responsibilities to his school pal Brown Bannister.

He has created The Pointer Sisters, Patti Austin, Al Jarreau, Natalie Cole, Amy Grant, Dallas Cowboys, B J Thomas, Dan Peek, B W Stevenson, Debby Boone, Steve Archer, Bill Gaither (gospel singer)|Bill Gaither, Marilyn McCoo, Eric Champion, Ali Lohan, Pat Boone,and over 100 additional collections.

As the foremost creator signed to Boardwalk Records possessed by Neil Bogart, with Bob Gaudio (Four Seasons) making, he recorded I Want You, I Need You, that reached its highest point at #37 on the Billboard Hot 100 in November 1981 and extended the Top 10 on Billboards A/C Chart. I Want You, I Need You was a numeral one tune in a few nations external the USA. Cheryl Ladd sings back-up on the tune alongside with numerous different creators on the collection containing Christopher Cross, Nigel Olsen, Frankie Vallie, Dann Huff, Tommy Funderburk, Bill Champlin, Amy Holland, and Robbie Patton. Other creators on Boardwalk remained Ringo Starr, Joan Jett, Mike Love (Beach Boys), and Night Ranger. Robert Kardashian (the Kardashians' father) was his finest pal, administrator and was accountable for Chris autographing with Boardwalk Records.

Christian has created collections that have been proposed for 9 and gained 4 Grammy Awards. He has as well been proposed for 7 Gospel Music Association Dove Awards as an creator, composer, and maker, conquering 5. He has as well disseminated sixteen additional collections as a unaccompanied creator.

Throughout his vocation, he has authored tunes for numerous chief TV athletics happenings such like the Super Bowl, NCAA Finals, The Masters, Olympics, NFL Today, US Open, and numerous further.

In 1981, Chris started his personal label Home Sweet Home Records. On that label he created collections for White Heart, Steve Archer, Mark Heard, Dan Peek, B J Thomas, Eric Champion, Rick Riso, Luke Garrett, Marilyn McCoo and other ones.

In 1992 he set up HSH Educational Media and Executive Produced and authored the tunes for the well-liked children's serials Gerbert that screened on PBS and what is at the moment ABC Family for over 10 annums. His corporation resumes to possess and permit the Gerbert exhibits and tunes. The Gerbert TV serials gained an ACE prize for finest Pre-School Show.

Chris bought The Studios at Las Colinas in 1992 with collaborator Steve Jarchow. Ross Perot Jr. Purchased Jarchows attention in 1993. Chris and Ross bought the acreage about the Studios Complex vending their attention in the Studio and the still existing terra firma to Fox Sports Southwest in 2003.

Christian was CEO of World Digital Media Group and YMC Records, a collective endeavor by Radio Shack, Dish Network, and Sirius Radio, till May 2007.

He was inaugurated in to the West Texas Music Hall of Fame. [http://www.westexmusichof.com/artists/chrischristian.html], as well like the Christian Music Hall of Fame in 2007.[http://www.hallmuseum.com/induction.htm] Most not long ago, he joined the possession cluster of the WNBA's Tulsa Shock [http://www.wnba.com/shock/news/owners.html]

Galileo Galilei - In artistic and popular media

Galileo is alluded to some periods in the production part of the Queen (band)|Queen tune, Bohemian Rhapsody. He attributes conspicuously in the tune Galileo (Indigo Girls song)|Galileo accomplished by the Indigo Girls and Amy Grant's Galileo on her Heart in Motion collection.

Twentieth-century plays have been authored on Galileo's existence, containing Life of Galileo (1943) by the German playwright Bertolt Brecht, with a Galileo (1975 film)|film alteration (1975) of it, and Lamp At Midnight (1947) by Barrie Stavis,Stavis, Barrie. Lamp at Midnight. South Brunswick, New Jersey: A.S. Barnes, 1966. As well like the 2008 play Galileo Galilei.Lalonde, Robert. [http://www.archive.org/details/GalileoGalileivesaliusAndServetus Galileo Galilei/Vesalius and Servetus]. February 2008. ISBN 978-0-9783909-1-4.

Kim Stanley Robinson authored a discipline stories bestseller allowed Galileo's Dream (2009), in that Galileo is accompanied in to the time to come to aid settle a catastrophes of methodical philosophy; the tale advances back and ahead amid Galileo's own time and a theoretical far-off time to come, and holds a significant transact of life story data.

Galileo Galilei was not long ago picked like a principal pattern for a elevated worth collectors' coin: the €25 Euro gold and silvery commemorating small change (Austria)#2009 Coinage|International Year of Astronomy commemorating money, made in 2009. This coin as well commemorates the 400th day of remembrance of the creation of Refracting telescope#Galileo's telescope|Galileo's spyglass. The obverse exhibits a part of his picture and his spyglass. The context exhibits one of his foremost sketches of the top of the moon. In the silvery circle additional spyglasses are depicted: the Isaac Newton Telescope, the Observatory in Kremsmünster Abbey, a contemporary spyglass, a broadcast spyglass and a Space observatory|space spyglass. In 2009, the Galileoscope was as well disseminated. This is a mass-produced, low-cost instructive spyglass with comparatively elevated caliber.

’Tis So Sweet to Trust in Jesus - Amy Grant single

In 1989, Amy Grant recorded a further modern variant of the tune for a Word Records forte collection of different creators allowed Our Hymns. Word disseminated Grant’s transcriptioning as a sole to Christian broadcast to advance the collection. It was Grant’s solely broadcast sole in amid her extremely prosperous Lead Me On (Amy Grant album)|Lead Me On and Heart in Motion collections. The tune as well pronounced the foremost time that Grant disseminated a modern transcriptioning of a customary anthem to broadcast. She proceeded on to discharge some hymns to broadcast, directing up to the 2000s, once she ought to discharge 2 award-winning hymns collections with some broadcast selects as of every one.

Love Beyond Reason

‘Love Beyond Reason’ is an collection by Randy Stonehill, disseminated within 1985, on Myrrh Records.

The collection held the hit sole, I Could Never Say Goodbye, that was a duo with vocalist Amy Grant. Grant had not long ago come to be one of the largest designations in Christian tunes, and had traversed over in to the normal with her Unguarded collection.

Stonehill as well disseminated a Love Beyond Reason Video gathering in 1985 on VHS and Beta, that contained recordings of Love Beyond Reason, Until Your Love Broke Through, Hymn, You’re Loved Tonight, Still Small Voice, (from Stonehill’s Celebrate this Hearbeat album) and The Gods of Men.

Top Christian Albums - Most cumulative weeks at number one

***Amy Grant (329)**
*WOW serials (115)

*Sandi Patti (112)
*Kirk Franklin (79)
*Michael W. Smith (79)
*Carman (64)
*Steven Curtis Chapman (62)
*Casting Crowns (57)
*P.O.D. (54)
*dc Talk (53)
*Switchfoot (47)
*Petra (44)
*The Imperials (39)

Heart in Motion - Personnel

* **Amy Grant: Vocals.**
* Tom Hemby: Guitars (track 10).
* Dann Huff: Guitars (track 7).
* Gordon Kennedy (musician)|Gordon Kennedy: Guitars (tracks 7).
* Jerry McPherson Guitars (tracks 1, 2, 3).
* Donald Kirkpatrick: Guitars (tracks 4, 5, 6).
* Chris Rodriguez: Guitar, Background voices (tracks 7, 8).
* Robbie Buchanan: Bass, Keyboards, Drum Programming (track 7, 10).
* Tommy Sims: Bass (tracks 3, 7, 8).
* Blair Masters: Keyboards (track 7).
* Michael Omartian: Keyboards, Background voices, Producer, Drum Sequencing (tracks 4, 5, 6, 7, 9, 11).
* Charlie Peacock: Keyboards, Programming, Drum Programming (track 3, 7, 8, 10).
* Brian Tankersley: Synthesizer.
* Keith Thomas (producer)|Keith Thomas: Synthesizer, Bass, Drums (tracks 1 and 2), Background voices (track 1), Drum Programming.
* David Raven: Drums (track 4).
* Chris McHugh: Drums (tracks 7, 8).
* Mark Hammond: Drums, Drum Programming.
* Mark Douthit Saxophone (tracks 3 and 8)
* Sam Levine (musician)|Sam Levine Baritone Sax (track 8).
* Barry Green Trombone (track 3 and 8)
* Mike Haynes Trumpet (track 8)
* Gary Chapman (musician)|Gary Chapman: Background voices (track 4).
* Diana DeWitt: Background voices (track 4).
* Chris Eaton (British musician)|Chris Eaton: Background voices (tracks 3, 7, 8).
* Kim Fleming: Background voices (track 3).

* Vicki Hampton: Background voices (track 2).
* Ron Hemby: Background voices (tracks 1 and 2).
* Kurt Howell: Background voices (track 11).
* Donna McElroy: Background voices (tracks 1 and 2).
* Susanne Schwartz: Background voices (track 11).

Love Beyond Reason - Side one

 # I Could Never Say Goodbye (Duet With Amy Grant) – 3:34
Love Beyond Reason – 3:36
The Gods of Men – 4:12
Bells – 4:19
You're Loved Tonight – 5:47

Amy Grant - GMA Dove Awards

Inaugurated in to the GMA Gospel Music Hall of Fame in 2003
* 1983: Artist of the Year
* 1983: Pop/Contemporary Album of the Year – Age to Age
* 1983: Recorded Music Packaging – Age to Age
* 1984: Recorded Music Packaging – A Christmas Album
* 1985: Pop/Contemporary Album of the Year – Straight Ahead
* 1986: Artist of the Year
* 1986: Recorded Music Packaging – Unguarded
* 1988: Short Form Music Video of the Year – Stay For a While
* 1989: Artist of the Year
* 1989: Pop/Contemporary Album of the Year – Lead Me On
* 1989: Short Form Music Video of the Year – Lead Me On
* 1990: Country Song of the Year – Tis So Sweet to Trust in Jesus
* 1992: Song of the Year – Place in This World
* 1992: Artist of the Year
* 1994: Praise and Worship Album of the Year – Songs as of the Loft
* 1996: Special Event Album of the Year – My Utmost for His Highest
* 1998: Pop/Contemporary Album of the Year – Behind the Eyes
* 2000: Special Event Album of the Year – Streams
* 2003: Inspirational Album of the Year – Legacy...Hymns Faith
* 2003: Song of the Year – The River's Gonna Keep On Rolling
* 2006: Inspirational Album of the Year – Rock of Ages...Hymns Faith
* **2007: Long Form Music Video of the Year – Time Again...Amy Grant Live**

Brown Bannister

'Elliott Brown Bannister III' (born August 31, 1951 in Topeka, Kansas) is a Contemporary Christian music|CCM (Contemporary Christian Music) maker and composer. Bannister disseminated one collection of his personal, Talk to One Another, in 1981 on NewPax Records. It was reissued on the Reunion Records Label 5 annums afterward, presenting a recently developed transcriptioning of the album's ultimate cut, Create In Me A Clean Heart. The first NewPax variant highlighted Ed DeGarmo on the Hammond B3 Organ; the 1986 variant highlighted Amy Grant and her additionally spouse Gary Chapman (musician)|Gary Chapman on voices with him. The 1986 variant was disseminated like a radio-single and obtained modest airplay in a a few markets.

Bannister is finest familiar for his work in the acoustic designing and building, transcriptioning, and manufacture business. He created his personal autonomous label, Vireo Records, in 1991. Bannister has gained 25 Dove Awards and 14 Grammy prizes. He as well was not long ago inaugurated in to the Gospel Music Hall of Fame. He has authored numerous tunes, especially for Amy Grant. Bannister as well educated Grant in his Sunday School grade at Belmont Church of Christ.

Brown is a 1975 alumna of Abilene Christian University. His girl are Ellie Holcomb|Ellie Bannister Holcomb and Caroline Blair Bannister.

Say You'll Be Mine (Amy Grant song)

: For the sole by Steps, perceive Say You'll Be Mine (Steps song)

'Say You'll Be Mine' is a 1994 sole by Contemporary Christian music|Christian tunes vocalist Amy Grant. It was disseminated like the second sole as of the House of Love (Amy Grant album)|House of Love collection in the United Kingdom. However, dissimilar the foregoing selects as of House of Love, Say You'll Be Mine was not disseminated within the United States. On her 2004 DVD discharge, Greatest Videos 1986-2004, Grant disclosed that Say You'll Be Mine was designed as a U.S. Sole however the label tugged its discharge at the final minute. It accomplished stronger in the UK compared to its 3 forerunners, arriving at #41.

John Lloyd Taylor - Performances

John Taylor has played stringed instrument next to the Jonas Brothers as

they accomplished with Stevie Wonder, Brad Paisley, Steven Curtis Chapman, Michael W. Smith, Amy Grant, Vince Gill, Dan Aykroyd, Demi Lovato, Jordin Sparks, Jesse McCartney, Taylor Swift, and Miley Cyrus.

When Love Finds You - Track listing

#Whenever You Come Around (Vince Gill, Pete Wasner) - 4:19
#You Better Think Twice (V. Gill, Reed Nielsen) - 3:47
#Real Lady's Man (V. Gill, Carl Jackson) - 3:34
#What the Cowgirls Do (V. Gill, Nielsen) - 3:06
#When Love Finds You (song)|When Love Finds You (V. Gill, Michael Omartian) - 4:05
#If There's Anything I Can Do (V. Gill, John Jarvis) - 3:48
#South Side of Dixie (V. Gill, Delbert McClinton) - 4:15
#Maybe Tonight (V. Gill, Janis Gill) - 4:51
#Which Bridge to Cross (Which Bridge to Burn) (Bill Anderson (singer)|Bill Anderson, V. Gill) - 4:17
#If I Had My Way (V. Gill, Amy Grant) - 3:55
#Go Rest High on That Mountain (V. Gill) - 5:15

Soundstage (TV series) - Season 1: 2003

* Lyle Lovett, Randy Newman, and Mark Isham, March 2003
* Chicago (band)|Chicago, live in musical performance, June 2003 [http://www.shoppbs.org/sm-pbs-soundstage-soundstage-presents-chicago-dvd--pi-1881525.html Soundstage Presents: Chicago DVD], Shop PBS
* Michael McDonald (singer)|Michael McDonald, July 2003
* Alison Krauss and Union Station, July 2003
* Tom Petty and the Heartbreakers, July 2003
* Lucinda Williams and Kasey Chambers, July 2003
* Chris Isaak and Raul Malo, August 2003
* Trace Adkins and Travis Tritt, August 2003
* Tori Amos, August 2003
* Wilco and Sonic Youth, September 2003
* John Hiatt and the Goners, Dar Williams, Robinella|Robinella and the CCString Band, September 2003
* **Peter Cetera and Amy Grant, October 2003**
* Farm Aid 2003 at Germain Amphitheater, Columbus, OH, presenting Willie Nelson, Neil Young and Crazy Horse, John Mellencamp, Dave Matthews, Sheryl Crow, Brooks Dunn, Emmylou Harris, Los Lonely Boys, Hootie the Blowfish, Billy Bob Thornton and Trick Pony, November 2003

Mosaic: Pieces of My Life So Far - Introduction

In the book's beginning part, Grant clarifies her disinclination to record a publication and the way that guided to her authoring and produces a serials of acknowledgments. Additionally, this part holds the words to a tune that Grant authored however not ever recorded (it was recorded by Faith Hill for the Mad About You sound recording instead): Who I Am (Amy Grant song)|Who I Am.

Keith Thomas (producer) - Biographyhttp://www.keiththomas.com/about.html

Born and raised in the Atlanta residential area of Conyers, GA., Keith was crooning head for his father's canon cluster by the age of 9. His capacity as a keyboard participant guided him, when nevertheless in High School, to transcriptioning meetings in Atlanta studios. Here he appeared to the awareness of region Superstar Ronnie Milsap.

Keith repositioned to Nashville as Ronnie's foremost workforce author for Milsap's recently created issuing corporation, Ronjoy Music. Shortly afterward, Keith signed on with Word Records and started a seven-year term as their workforce author and maker. During this time, Keith created over 16 collections for different creators receiving over 20 #1 selects.

Encouraged by this triumph, Keith left Word and set up his personal issuing and manufacture corporation, Yellow Elephant Music, and started authoring and making tunes for BeBe CeCe Winans. During their 4 collection cooperation, the 3 traded over 3 million collections and had 9 highest 30 selects, 6 of that proceeded highest 10 and 2 of that proceeded #1. As a effect of this connection, BeBe CeCe received 4 Grammy prizes, an extra Grammy recommendation, and 5 Dove prizes.

In 1991, Keith traversed over in to the planet of normal pop once he teamed up with long-established pal Amy Grant to gather their foremost #1, Top 40 hit, Baby Baby (Amy Grant song)|Baby Baby. At the similar time, Keith concentrated his abilities on erstwhile Miss America, shortly to come to be global pop and film star, Vanessa L. Williams|Vanessa Williams. He authored and created 5 traces on her Comfort Zone collection containing the #1 hit, Save the Best for Last. These 2 #1 tunes with Grant and Williams received Keith Grammy recommendations for Grammy Award for Producer of the Year, Non-Classical|Producer of the Year, Grammy Award for Song of the Year|Song of the Year, and Record of the Year.

Responding to the impetus generated by this triumph, Keith obtained The Bennett

House transcriptioning compound in Franklin, TN. Twenty minutes as of inner city Nashville, The Bennett House not solely accommodates Keith's private program workshop and managerial workplaces however as well proffers external customers a 19th era transcriptioning ecosystem that is distinctive in the Nashville tunes set.

Christening the turn in to The Bennett House, Keith turned his awareness once more to Amy Grant by authoring and making for her House of Love (Amy Grant album)|House of Love collection. This collection boasted some strikes for Keith containing the tunes, Lucky One (song)|Lucky One, and the name trail, House of Love (Amy Grant song)|House of Love. Keith created the tune The Sweetest Days for Vanessa L. Williams|Vanessa Williams as well like records for James Ingram, Peabo Bryson, Deborah Cox, Regina Belle and Wendy Moten. In 1995, Keith authored and created the hit tune, I Could Fall In Love, for Selena. Selena consequently grew to be the foremost creator to place either a Spanish- and an English-language tune in the top 10 of the Hot Latin Tracks graph. I Could Fall In Love grew to be the 5th best-charting tune as of that graph in 1995 and stayed the highest-charting English-language tune for 2 annums, till Celine Dion's 1998 sole My Heart Will Go On excelled it once it reached its highest point at numeral 1.The collection, Dreaming Of You, on that I Could Fall In Love shows, has at the moment been endorsed 35x platinum. That annum Keith as well created Vanessa L. Williams|Vanessa Williams' Academy Award conquering sole, Colors of the Wind, for the Multi-platinum vending motion depiction sound recording, Pocahontas.

In 1997, Keith finished traces for Amy Grant's following collection, Behind The Eyes and Vanessa Williams' come after up collection, Next (Vanessa Williams album)|Next. He as well created records for Michael Bolton, Luther Vandross, Brian McKnight, Tamia and Puff Johnson.

In first 1998, Keith created some tunes for Vanessa L. Williams|Vanessa Williams and Jon Secada for the film, Dance with Me (film)|Dance with Me. He as well created the trail, I Do (Cherish You), for 98°'s Multi-platinum collection on Universal Records, 98° and Rising The tune was as well highlighted in the Julia Roberts/Hugh Grant amorous farce, Notting Hill. In Addition, Keith was proposed for a Grammy for Grammy Award for Producer of the Year, Non-Classical|Producer of the Year for the 40th Grammy Awards|1998 Grammy prizes.

In belated 1998, Keith serviced like the concept Producer and co-executive Producer for the multi-artist Touched By An Angel collection presenting tunes motivated by the well-liked TV serials. On this program, Keith operated with Deana Carter, Amy Grant, Faith Hill, Uncle Sam (singer)|Uncle Sam and Wynonna.

Early in 1999, Keith created the trail Precious Wings on MJJ creator Tatyana Ali for the Disney film, Fantasia 2000. During that annum he as well created traces for Yolanda Adams, Wild Orchid (band)|Wild Orchid and Vanessa L. Williams|Vanessa Williams. Keith as well created the tune, You're Where I Belong, for Trisha Yearwood for the film, Stuart Little.

In first 2000, Keith authored and created the hit tune, I Wanna Be with You (Mandy Moore song)|I Wanna Be With You, for Mandy Moore. The tune was highlighted in the Columbia Pictures feature, Center Stage (2000 film)|Center Stage.

After a 3 annum pause at the spin of the millenary, in 2005 Keith created Levosia Entertainment, with an prominence on elaborating youthful unknown aptitude. His opening finding, Jordan Pruitt, he signed with Hollywood Records, and in combination with the discharge of her first public appearance collection, No Ordinary Girl, Jordan unlocked for countless Disney backed musical performance visits, containing High School Musical: The Concert, The Cheetah Girls and Demo Lovato.

Keith following grew to be conscious of a youthful YouTube impression, Savannah Outen. Her 3 selects disseminated to Radio Disney, Goodbyes, If You Only Knew and Fighting For My Life, experienced unparalleled airplay for an autonomous label creator, double whipping out The Jonas Brothers and The High School Musical for the Dot Com Top 3 #1 placing. Under Keith's watch, Savannah's YouTube fan reply matured to 75 million YouTube perspectives with 250,000 members.

In 2009 Keith created the Grammy Award wining Heather Headley collection, Audience Of One. In 2012 Keith created the Grammy proposed group, incessantly JONES' spic-and-span collection, Musical Revival disseminated April 10th 2012 on EMI Records. He as well reconnected with Heather Headley in 2012 to make a program in combination with her head part in the stage alteration of The Body Guard, that unlocked in the UK, November of 2012. The Whitney Houston accolade advances as of the UK to Broadway in 2014.

Keith as well created the name trail and 3 extra tunes for The Voice contender, Chris
Mann's first public appearance CD, Roads on Universal Republic. Chris as well provided a astronomical execution on his foremost PBS, that screened March of 2012.

In first 2013 Keith was questioned to partake in the actuality serials Chasing Nashville on Lifetime, that tails 7 seeking creators as of West Virginia, Kentucky and North Carolina. Given Keith's trail record for recognizing and elaborating aptitude, this was a normal appropriate. 9 chapters are at the moment accessible on the web. Keith as well created and co-wrote some tunes for the sound recording.

Keith is as well a establishing associate of farfurther.com - the approaching .music approach. To learn
more, sojourn www.farfurther.com

Keith is directing the creation of Celica Westbrook, a adolescent pop-prodigy whose voices competitor even the most recognized singers of the planet. To absorb further about Celica sojourn celicawestbrook.com.

Currently Keith organizes 18 annum aged Celica Westbrook, vocalist composer Jonathan Wyndham, the Grammy proposed group foreverJONES and Dominique Jones. Www.foreverJONES.com

A Christmas To Remember

'A Christmas to Remember' is a 1999 Christmas collection by Amy Grant with the Patrick Williams Orchestra, that grew to be endorsed gold. It is her 3rd Christmas collection with a mix of a few customary Christmas song|songs however mainly originals.

In 2007, A Christmas to Remember was reissued and digitally remastered by Grant's spic-and-span record label, EMI/Sparrow Records, alongside with 13 additional Amy Grant collections. The remastered issue is tagged with a Digitally Remastered emblem in the 'gutter' on the CD fore.[http://www.sparrowrecords.com/news/news_detail_page.aspx?id=527739tid=227 Sparrow Records News] Because of Grant's transact with her foregoing label, Word Records, the remastered versions of A Christmas to Remember and Behind the Eyes (Amy Grant album)|Behind the Eyes was not traded in Contemporary Christian Music|Christian Music retail traders such like Family Christian Stores either Lifeway Christian Resources till 2009. Until 2009, Word Records sustained to disperse these names to Christian retail traders in the first, non-remastered versions when EMI dispersed the remastered versions to nearly all chief retail traders. The 12 still existing remastered versions remained dispersed by EMI to altogether US retail traders, either Christian and nonreligious.[http://www.emicmg.com/press/pressRelease.aspx?id=529387 Welcome to EMICMG.com]

An first discharge of the CD was traded solely at Target Corporation|Target Stores and highlighted a cover of The Carpenters tune Merry Christmas Dar-

ling as a concealed trail. This trail was finally re-released on Amy Grants' 2005 compiling Christmas collection My Best Christmas.

A primetime Christmas out of the ordinary named 'Amy Grant: A Christmas to Remember' screened on December 15, 1999 on CBS, ABC, 36, Vision Celestial. Special visitors contained 98 Degrees (whose vocation saw a increase following the appearance), Tony Bennett and CeCe Winans.

House of Love (Amy Grant album) - US version

 # Lucky One (song)|Lucky One (Amy Grant, Keith Thomas) – 4:11
 # Say You'll Be Mine (Amy Grant song)|Say You'll Be Mine (Amy Grant, Wayne Kirkpatrick, Keith Thomas) – 4:04
 # Whatever It Takes (Amy Grant, Gary Chapman (musician)|Gary Chapman, Keith Thomas) – 4:10
 # House of Love (Amy Grant song)|House of Love (duet with Vince Gill) (Greg Barnhill, Kenny Greenberg, Wally Wilson) – 4:38
The Power (Tommy Sims, Judson Spence) – 3:54
Oh How the Years Go By (Simon Climie, Will Jennings) – 5:12
Big Yellow Taxi (Joni Mitchell) – 3:01
 # Helping Hand (Amy Grant, Beverly Darnall, Tommy Sims) – 4:39
 # Love Has a Hold On Me (Amy Grant, Keith Thomas) – 3:55
 # Our Love (Amy Grant, Tom Hemby) – 5:08
 # Children of the World (Amy Grant, Wayne Kirkpatrick, Tommy Sims) – 5:16

Grammy Awards of 1985 - Gospel

*Grammy Award for Best Gospel Vocal Performance, Female|Best Gospel Performance, Female
****Amy Grant for Angels**
*Grammy Award for Best Gospel Vocal Performance, Male|Best Gospel Performance, Male
**Michael W. Smith for Michael W. Smith
*Grammy Award for Best Gospel Vocal Performance by a Duo either Group, Choir either Chorus|Best Gospel Performance by a Duo either Group
**Debby Boone Phil Driscoll for Keep The Flame Burning
*Grammy Award for Best Soul Gospel Performance, Female|Best Soul Gospel Performance, Female
**Shirley Caesar for Sailin'
*Grammy Award for Best Soul Gospel Performance, Male|Best Soul Gospel Performance, Male
**Andrae Crouch for Always Remember

*Grammy Award for Best Soul Gospel Performance by a Duo either Group, Choir either Chorus|Best Soul Gospel Performance by a Duo either Group
**Shirley Caesar Al Green for Sailin' on the Sea of Your Love
*Grammy Award for Best Inspirational Performance|Best Inspirational Performance
**Donna Summer for Forgive Me

These Days (Vince Gill album) - The Reason Why

The Groovy Record

#What You Don't Say (with LeAnn Rimes)
#The Reason Why (with Alison Krauss)
#The Rock of Your Love (with Bonnie Raitt)
#What You Give Away (with Sheryl Crow)
#Faint of Heart (with Diana Krall)
#Time to Carry On (with Jenny Gill)
#No Easy Way
#This Memory of You (with Trisha Yearwood)
#How Lonely Looks
#Tell Me One More Time About Jesus (with Amy Grant)
#Everything and Nothing (with Katrina Elam)
#Which Way Will You Go
#These Days

2006 Grammy Awards - Gospel music | Gospel

;Grammy Award for Best Gospel Performance|Best Gospel Performance
*'Pray-CeCe Winans'
;Grammy Award for Best Gospel Song|Best Gospel Song
*'Be Blessed-Yolanda Adams'
**'Yolanda Adams, James Harris III, Terry Lewis James 'big Jim' Wright, songwriters'
;Grammy Award for Best Pop/Contemporary Gospel Album|Best Pop/Contemporary Gospel Album
*'Lifesong-Casting Crowns'
;Grammy Award for Best Rock Gospel Album|Best Rock Gospel Album
*'Until My Heart Caves In-Audio Adrenaline'
;Grammy Award for Best Southern, Country either Bluegrass Gospel Album|Best Southern, Country either Bluegrass Gospel Album
***'Rock of Ages...Hymns Faith-Amy Grant'**
;Grammy Award for Best Traditional Soul Gospel Album|Best Traditional Soul Gospel Album

*'Psalms, Hymns Spiritual Songs-Donnie McClurkin'
;Grammy Award for Best Contemporary Soul Gospel Album|Best Contemporary Soul Gospel Album
:CeCe Winans for Purified
;Grammy Award for Best Gospel Choir either Chorus Album|Best Gospel Choir either Chorus Album
:Gladys Knight, chorus director Saints Unified Voices for One Voice

Point of Grace - Tours

* The Whole Truth Tour with Phillips, Craig Dean and Cheri Keaggy (1995)
* The Life Love Other Mysteries Tour with 4Him (1996–97)
* The Steady On Tour with out of the ordinary visitors Watermark (1998–99)
* **An Amy Grant Christmas Tour (with Michael W. Smith and The Katinas) (1999)**
* The Free To Fly Tour with out of the ordinary visitors FFH (band)|FFH (2001–02)
* The Christmastime Tour with Michael W. Smith and The Katinas (2002, 2003, 2004)
* The I Choose You Tour with Scott Krippayne and out of the ordinary visitor Charity Von (2004)
* The Winter Wonderland Tour with out of the ordinary visitor John David Webster (2005)
* The Winter Wonderland Tour with out of the ordinary visitor Scott Krippayne (2006, 2007)
* The All The World Tour with out of the ordinary visitors Selah and Michael Passons (2008)
* The Winter Wonderland Tour with out of the ordinary visitor Ronnie Freeman (2008)
* The Come Alive Tour with Mark Schultz (musician)|Mark Schultz (2009–10)

Danny Gokey - 2009–2010 : My Best Days

On September 1, 2009, Gokey signed with 19 Recordings/RCA Records Nashville|RCA Nashville, getting to be the foremost 3rd place finisher to record with 19 and the foremost masculine Idol to be signed to a chief region label. On November 19, 2009, 19 Recordings and RCA Records proclaimed the discharge of the first public appearance sole My Best Days Are Ahead of Me. Gokey's first public appearance collection, My Best Days, was disseminated on March 2, 2010. It launched on the Billboard graphs at numeral 4, and it netted Gokey the finest opening-week selling by a first public appearance region masculine in 18 annums. Gokey as well had the biggest first public appearance of digital downloads traded by whatever spic-and-span region creator at any time.[http://www.sonymusicnashville.com/press-releases/danny-gokey-makes-chart-history-debut-album Danny Gokey Makes Chart History with Debut Album!] In aid of the collection, Gokey was the beginning play on Sugarland's Incredible Machine journey that started in April.[http://www.jsonline.com/entertainment/83923832.html Gokey to journey with Sugarland] Gokey as well accomplished at region vocalist Darryl Worley's 9th yearly Tennessee River Run fete in Savannah, Tennessee alongside with different creators such like Joe Diffie and Lee Brice. The happening aided rise $200,000 for the Darryl Worley Foundation.

On October 18, 2010, Gokey received a recommendation for Best New/Breakthrough Artist at the foremost yearly American Country Awards. He disclosed in an conference disseminated on October 26, 2010, that he had not long ago recorded his personal variant of the Amy Grant tune, Tennessee Christmas, to be disseminated to region broadcast as a break sole..

On November 21, 2010, Gokey was a piece of ABC's pre-show happening at the American Music Awards.

Mosaic: Pieces of My Life So Far - Track list

Every Road
Ask Me
Turn This World Around
Thy Word
All Right
Heirlooms
 # Say Once More (from Lead Me On (Amy Grant album)|Lead Me On, not to be puzzled with Grant's tune of the similar designation as of 1980s Never Alone)
Saved by Love
 # Baby Baby (Amy Grant song)|Baby Baby
 # I Will Remember You (Amy Grant song)|I Will Remember You
 # Missing You (Amy Grant song)|Missing You
 # Lead Me On (Amy Grant song)|Lead Me On
 # House of Love (Amy Grant album)|Helping Hand
Breath of Heaven (Mary's Song)
Takes a Little Time (maxi single)|Takes a Little Time
Carry You (version as of Rock of Ages...Hymns and Faith)
 # Somewhere Down the Road (Amy Grant song)|Somewhere Down the Road
 # Excerpts as of Mosaic - Read by Amy Grant

Let the Season Take Wing

'Let the Season Take Wing' is a 1992 Christmas tunes sole by Contemporary Christian music|Christian music/Pop tunes singer-songwriter Amy Grant. The sole was disseminated solely on cartridge tape and was traded solely in Target Corporation|Target stores throughout the 1992 Christmas season. The sole was accessible gratis with whatever acquisition of Grant's 1992 Home for Christmas (Amy Grant album)|Home for Christmas collection.

The tune is alike in manner and sound to the other first compositions on Home for Christmas (Amy Grant album)|Home for Christmas and is contemplated by a few to be a 13th trail of sorts for that collection. The collection graphics for the sole shows to be as of the similar picture meeting as that for the Christmas collection. Though the tune was disseminated like a sole, AM Records did not spin a lot awareness to advancing the tune, as it was a Target unique. Target advanced the tune in lieu. This tune was authored by Robert E. Irving Kevin Quinn.

Grant operated like a representative for Target Corporation|Target on different advertising crusades and almsgiving programs throughout the 1980s, 1990s, and first 2000s. She often gives to the Target Corporation|Target House almsgiving. Grant's participation with Target encountered a few disagreement once a few in her Contemporary Christian music|Christian tunes fan center disliked of Target's alliance with Planned Parenthood.

Grant had formerly recorded a tune named Love Makes You Real for a 1989 Target Christmas TV advertisement.http://www.youtube.com/watch?v=zLRhzXFyRoQ However, that tune was not ever produced accessible aimed at trade, in Target stores either somewhere else. Grant ought to afterward discharge Target-exclusive selects to advance her 1997 collection, Behind the Eyes (Amy Grant album)|Behind the Eyes. Likewise, she disseminated a Target-exclusive issue of her 1999 break collection, A Christmas to Remember, that contained a extra track: Grant's cover of Merry Christmas, Darling.

Let the Season Take Wing has not ever been disseminated on the CD setup. When the sole was disseminated, Grant possessed a significant transact of her own tunes (a infrequency in the contemporary tunes industry) however was concurrently constituted by 2 record labels (another infrequency in the industry). AM Records dispersed her tunes to normal Pop music|pop broadcast and retail traders, when Word Records dispersed her tunes to Contemporary Christian music|Christian broadcast and retail traders. In 2007, Grant left either tags and took altogether of the tunes that she possesses herself,

as well like nearly all of the tunes nevertheless possessed by whichever AM either Word, to EMI Records. EMI took the occasion offered by their spic-and-span record transact with Amy Grant to subject spic-and-span, digitally remastered versions of the artist's collections and spic-and-span collections of her hit tunes.

It is not clear if EMI at the moment possesses Let the Season Take Wing either if the tune stays the assets of whichever AM Records either Amy Grant herself. In September 2008, EMI disseminated a spic-and-span Amy Grant break compiling allowed The Christmas Collection (Amy Grant album)|The Christmas Collection. EMI released a initial trail itemizing for that discharge in July 2008 however marked that it was not ultimate, directing to conjecture and a fan drive directed at Let the Season Take Wing materializing in remastered shape on the compiling.http://www.chordant.com/products/new_releases_detail.aspx?bid=25144bname=September+30%2c+2008+Street+Date The ultimate collection disseminated by EMI, nevertheless, did not hold the tune.

Brown Bannister - Grammy Awards

*2006: Third Day, Wherever You Are (Third Day album)|Wherever You Are - Best Pop/Contemporary Gospel Album
***2005: Amy Grant, Rock of Ages, Hymns Faith - Best Southern, Country either Bluegrass Gospel Album**
*2004: Steven Curtis Chapman, All Things New (Steven Curtis Chapman album)|All Things New - Best Pop/Contemporary Gospel Album
*2001: CeCe Winans, CeCe Winans (album)|CeCe Winans - Best Pop/Contemporary Gospel Album
*1999: Steven Curtis Chapman, Speechless (Steven Curtis Chapman album)|Speechless - Best Pop/Contemporary Gospel Album
*1994: Petra, Wake-Up Call (album)|Wake-Up Call - Best Rock Gospel Album
*1992: Bruce Carroll, Sometimes Miracles Hide - Best Southern Gospel Album
***1988: Amy Grant, Lead Me On (Amy Grant album)|Lead Me On - Best Gospel Performance, Female**
***1985: Amy Grant, Unguarded - Best Gospel Performance, Female**
***1984: Amy Grant, Angels - Best Gospel Performance, Female**
*1984: Debby Boone Phil Driscoll, Keep the Flame Burning as of Surrender (Debby Boone album)|Surrender - Best Gospel Performance By A Duo either Group
***1983: Amy Grant, Ageless Medley - Best Gospel Performance, Female**
***1982: Amy Grant, Age To Age - Best Gospel Performance, Contemporary**
*1980: Debby Boone, With My Song - Best Inspirational Performance

David Anderle

'David Anderle' is a popular record maker. He graduated as of Fairfax High School in Los Angeles in June 1955, piece of the similar advancing grade as time to come maker Shel Talmy. His manufacture acclaims contain collections for Judy Collins, Rita Coolidge, Amy Grant, Delaney and Bonnie, David Ackles, Kris Kristofferson, Aaron Neville, Chris De Burgh, Rhinoceros (band)|Rhinoceros, Ozark Mountain Daredevils, Doc Holliday (band)|Doc Holliday and the Circle Jerks. In new annums, he has come to be an established and displayed picture creator.See details of [http://billyshirefinearts.com/07Anderle/self.html Better Late Than Never exhibition], being an display of composed functions 1963-2005. Billy Shire Fine Arts, January— February 2007; www.billyshirefinearts.com. See as well David Anderle, Better Late Than Never: The Paintings of David Anderle (Last Gasp Publishing|Last Gasp, 2007, ISBN ISBN 0-86719-680-7, ISBN 978-0-86719-680-1, being a gathering of the images of David Anderle, offered like a index for his unaccompanied show at Billy Shire Fine Arts galleria.

Gary Chapman (musician) - Personal life

Chapman wedded Amy Grant on June 19, 1982. Citing irreconcilable dissimilarities, Grant recorded for annulment as of Chapman in March 1999 and the annulment was settled in June 1999.

Chapman wedded Jennifer Pittman in July 2000. Chapman and Pittman separated in 2007.

On December 22, 2008, Chapman wedded Cassie Piersol. The pair started a program named A Hymn a Week in 2010 to merit the melodic legacy left to Chapman by his father and mother. Chapman has declared that either his father and mother, whoever remained not so large municipality pastors for their whole lives, had a forceful impact in his existence and they breed the hymns in to [his] heart. Chapman's mom, Mary, passed away on December 26, 2002. His dad Terry passed away on April 12, 2009, following a long combat with Parkinson's illness and a shape of malignancy named numerous myeloma. During his final annums, he existed with Chapman and his spouse. During that time, Chapman played and chanted aged hymns at his father's side of bed. They additionally started shooting the brief past and private generally to a dissimilar anthem every one 7 days alongside with a stringed instrument and vocal execution of the work and publishing them on Facebook, on a page named A Hymn a Week.

Chapman and his spouse are included in numerous aids and organizations: Nashville Rescue Mission, Agape Animal Rescue, T.J. Martell Foundation, Make a Wish

Foundation.

Chris Eaton (UK musician)

'Christopher Neville Eaton' (born 16 September 1958 in Sedgley, Staffordshire) is a British Contemporary Christian music|Contemporary Christian singer-songwriter. Prior to his unaccompanied vocation, he was a associate of the 1980s groups Lyrix and the Mark Williamson Band.

Eaton has visited the US to advance his collections, and as well visited Europe as beginning play for Art Garfunkel in 1998. He operated on Roger Daltrey's 1987 unaccompanied collection Can't Wait to See the Movie, crooning Backing vocalist|backing voices.

Eaton authored Cliff Richard's 1990 List of UK Singles Chart Christmas numeral ones|Christmas No.1 sole Saviour's Day (song)|Saviour's Day and has as well authored tunes that have been accomplished by different CCM creators such like Amy Grant, whoever recorded a variant of Eaton's Breath of Heaven (Mary's Song)|Breath of Heaven. He as well authored some Jaci Velasquez tunes containing On My Knees and God So Loved as well like making 2 collections. Eaton wedded vocalist composer Abby Scott in May 2009.

The Prince of Egypt - Audio

The assignment of generating God's vocal was specified to Lon Bender and the group functioning with the film's tunes melodist, Hans Zimmer. The dare with that vocal was to attempt to develop it in to somewhat that had not been perceived beforehand, speaks Bender. We did a great deal of study in to the vocals that had been applied aimed at bygones Hollywood films as well like for broadcast exhibits, and we remained attempting to produce somewhat that had not ever been formerly perceived not solely as of a directing angle however as of a vocal handling angle as well. The resolution was to employ the vocal of performer Val Kilmer to propose the sort of vocal we perceive inner our own heads in our daily lives, as against to the greater compared to existence timbres with that God has been endowed in previous cinematic personifications. As a effect, in the ultimate feature, Kilmer gave vocal to Moses and God, as well, up till now the proposal is that somebody other ought to have perceived God talk to him once more in his personal vocal.

Composer and songwriter Stephen Schwartz started functioning on authoring tunes for the feature as of the real start of the film's manufacture. As the tale developed, he sustained to record tunes that ought to service to either disport and aid turn the tale alongside.composer Hans Zimmer organized and created the tunes and then finally authored the film's result. The film's result was recorded completely in London, England.

Three recordings remained disseminated concurrently for The Prince of Egypt, every one of them directed in the direction of a dissimilar mark public and one was advanced by persuasion master Rick Hendrix. While the other 2 subsequent records, the region music|country-themed The Prince of Egypt (Nashville)|Nashville sound recording and the gospel-based The Prince of Egypt (Inspirational)|Inspirational sound recording, functioned as feature saccolade, the The Prince of Egypt (soundtrack)|official The Prince of Egypt sound recording held the real tunes as of the feature. This collection merges components as of the result devised by Hans Zimmer, and feature tunes by Stephen Schwartz (composer)|Stephen Schwartz. The tunes remained whichever vocalized over by non-amateur singers (such as Salisbury Cathedral Choir), either sung by the film's vocal performers, such like Michelle Pfeiffer and Ofra Haza. Various traces by modern creators such like K-Ci JoJo and Boyz II Men remained appended, containing the Mariah Carey and Whitney Houston duo When You Believe, a Babyface (musician)|Babyface revise of the first Schwartz constitution, sung by Michelle Pfeiffer and Sally Dworsky in the feature. Amy Grant as well sings a variant of River Lullaby.

Doctor Strange - Recalled issue

Jackson Guice's cover for Doctor Strange #15 (March 1990) applied Christian tunes vocalist Amy Grant's likeness short of her authorization, directing to a objection indicating that the cover gave the emergence that she was linking with bewitchery. A US District Court sealed an out-of-court arrangement amid Grant and Marvel in first 1991, with a agreement order in that Marvel did not confess to obligation either wrongdoing.

The Veronicas - 2010–present: Third studio album 'You and Me' and other musical experiments

Writing for their 3rd workshop collection had started in December 2009, and transcriptioning started in January 2010.[http://www.theveronicas.com/content/hi-cute-kids HI CUTE KIDS]Third workshop collection. [http://twitter.com/Jessicaveronica/status/4708974751 First day of authoring for the 3rd record today] Twitter. Retrieved

2 February 2010.Third workshop collection. [http://popdirt.com/the-veronicas-begin-writing-third-album-plot-side-project/73591/ The Veronicas Begin Writing Third Album, Plot Side Project] popdirt.com. Retrieved 2 February 2010.Third workshop collection. [http://angryape.com/news/the-veronicas-give-new-album-update The Veronicas Give New Album Update] angryape.com. Retrieved 2 February 2010. The collection, that quotes effects by traditional tunes, traditional rock and Pop music|pop categories, must be their foremost discharge in over 3 annums. Jessica Origliasso declared that the collection tend to be motivated by creators The Subways, The Dead Weather, Mazzy Star, Ladytron and Peaches (musician)|Peaches. Lisa and Jessica Origliasso have depicted the collection like [...] a itty-bitty dissimilar as of [...] the final 2 records and [...] a pop record [with] dissimilar undertones.

Lending their voices somewhere else, Lisa and Jessica as well co-operated with Michael Paynter to record a tune named Love the Fall for his homonymous Extended play|EP. The tune reached its highest point at numeral 19 on the ARIA Charts. They as well disclosed in February 2011 that they had recorded supporting voices for Cherie Currie|Cherie Currie's spic-and-span collection.[http://www.theveronicas.com/news/2011/02/11/photos-studio-cherie-currie] The Veroncas Official Site Additionally The Veronicas recorded a cover variant of the tune Grown-Up Christmas List, by vocalist Amy Grant, for the Christmas compiling collection The Spirit of Christmas 2010.

Lisa as well commenced a cluster named the Dead Cool Dropouts with her pal Tyler Bryant, mainly completed utilizing GarageBand on Mac. They have disseminated an EP of tunes, those tunes are called: Write You Off, Green Eyes Make Me Blue, Blame It On Me, Shallow, Playing For Keeps, Ju Ju Ya Ya and Criminal Heart.[http://www.facebook.com/pages/Dead-Cool-Dropouts-Lisa-Marie-Tyler-Bryant/190236554353961] Outside origin with melodic proof and ties to origins of those songs[http://deadcooldropouts.tumblr.com/] The Band Tumblr
In 2013 on Instagram Tyler Bryant and Lisa Veronica relieved that they remained either in the workshop functioning on a few spic-and-span tunes.

In February 2012, they proclaimed that a discharge date for the collection was pending shortly.[http://lovetheveronicas.com/2012/02/third-album-soon/ Third Album Release Dates Coming Soon!]. LoveTheVeronicas.com (29 February 2012). LOM was tagged on their Twitter feeds as an essential expression on 15 May 2012. They as well specified the collection was for certain pending in belated 2012. Life On Mars was to be disseminated within belated 2012 however Warner Music has at the moment thrusted date back to 2013, this data was disseminated by the Daily Telegraph on 2 September.Moran, Jonathon. (2 September 2012) [http://www.dailytelegraph.com.au/entertainment/veronicas-lisa-and-jess-rocket-to-new-heights/story-e6frewyr-1226462956757 Veronicas Lisa and Jess missile to spic-and-span Heights]. The Daily Telegraph (Australia). On 2 June 2012, The Veronicas disclosed

the designation of their spic-and-span collection ought to be Life On Mars (Working name was; 'The Awakening' and they played with different names like Death On Mars and Skeleton), and that it ought to be disseminated within September either October.[http://video.perthnow.com.au/2241202907/The-Veronicas-Return Video: The Veronicas Return]. Video.perthnow.com.au (2 June 2012).
The foremost sole off the collection is named Lolita. The words tunes audiovisual was disseminated on 27 July 2012 and the formal tunes audiovisual was disseminated on 30 August.http://www.take40.com/news/32481/the-veronicas-are-coming-to-australia-this-month-with-new-song[http://twitter.com/LoveTheVs/status/220813182187474944 Twitter / LoveTheVs: The Veronicas spic-and-span sole 'Lolita']. Twitter.com.

Due to the reality of Label clash (Its not since they did not like the record, its since they have been via 3 dissimilar CEO's and 4 dissimilar AR, there has been no center athwart the committee having supervisory powers for the label.) The Veronicas are in the procedure of numerous amends to the collection. The discharge date was delayed and subject matter and subject of the collection is in the procedure of differing. The young ladies clarified by way of a UStream that the collection name might pretty perhaps change and that there are a limited plans for collection name designation shift. The young ladies as well clarified that 'Lolita' is not an formal sole advancing the spic-and-span collection It was simply a sole discharge for our Australian fans, as its been such a prolonged time eversince we have had whatsoever spic-and-span over there.

On October 26, 2013, The Veronicas proclaimed by way of their formal Facebook page that they had cut as of Warner Bros. Records.

On November 6, 2013, The Veronicas proclaimed that their approaching 3rd workshop collection tend to be named 'You and Me', with the album's head sole set to be disseminated within February 2014.

Jessy Dixon

'Jessy Dixon' (March 12, 1938 – September 26, 2011) was an United States|American canon tunes vocalist, composer, and Pianist, with triumph amid viewers athwart ethnic rules. He gathered 7 Grammy prize recommendations throughout his vocation.

Musicians with who he operated contain Paul Simon, Andrae Crouch, DeGarmo Key and nearly all not long ago Bill Gaither (gospel singer)|Bill Gaither

in the Gaither Homecoming|Homecoming serials of musical performances. He authored tunes for Amy Grant, Natalie Cole, Cher, and Diana Ross.[http://www.allmusic.com/artist/jessy-dixon-p2262/credits Allmusic credits]

Dixon was an ordained minister with Calvary Ministries International of Fort Wayne, Indiana.

1987 in music - September–October

*September 3 - Fugazi plays their foremost live show (as a three-piece; Guy Picciotto had not joined the group yet) at the Wilson Center in Washington DC.
*September 6 – Madonna (entertainer)|Madonna stops her Who's That Girl Tour in Florence, Italy.
*September 7 - Pink Floyd discharge A Momentary Lapse of Reason, their foremost collection following the retreat of and lawful combat with bassist, Roger Waters. The following journey earned about $135 million international, a total that was solely equaled by the incomes of Michael Jackson and U2 rolled into one.
*September 11 – Reggae performer Peter Tosh is killed throughout a theft in his home.
*September 12 – Michael Jackson begins the Bad World Tour, helping his Bad collection.
*September 25
Matthew Garrison Chapman is born, the foremost kid of Amy Grant and Gary Chapman (musician)|Gary Chapman. Lead Me On (Amy Grant album)|Lead Me On, Amy's 1988 collection, is indicated to have been committed to Matt.
**CBS starts an American variant of the long-running UK TV show Top of the Pops. It endures one annum.
*October 4 – microelectronic information assembling totally substitutes the aged selling journal method in assembling the UK selects and collections graph. The issue day of spic-and-span graphs is repositioned as of Tuesday to Sunday.
*October 8 – Chuck Berry collects a star on the Hollywood Walk of Fame.
*October 19 – Mötley Crüe discharge the tune You're All I Need as a sole. Its words trigger MTV to decline to play its audiovisual. Radio stations not ever play the tune whichever.
*October 30 – George Michael deliverances his foremost unaccompanied workshop collection, Faith (George Michael album)|Faith, that ought to gain the Grammy Awards of 1989|Grammy Award for collection of the annum and vend 11 million duplicates within USA only.
*October 31 -the Zorros heading on the Halloween for the final at any time show at the Crystal Ballroom (Melbourne)|Crystal Ballroom, Melbourne's principal Punk/New Wave Venue. The Crystal Ballroom has noticed nearly 10 annums of extreme melodic development. The locale has chandeliers, varnished glass Windows, Pais-

ley wallpaper and a tiled lobby.

Carter Oosterhouse - Television shows and appearances

In 2003, Oosterhouse joined TLC's serials Trading Spaces in its 4th season. In that similar annum, TLC as well appended the spin-offs Trading Spaces: Family and Trading Spaces: Boys V. Girls to their programmes, that permitted Oosterhouse the occasion to work with kids.

In 2004, Oosterhouse did an chapter of CBS Sunday Morning in New York in that he remodeled reporter Bill Geist's function with the aid of reviewer Andy Rooney.

In 2005, Oosterhouse was a donor to NBC's show Three Wishes (TV series)|Three Wishes, a primetime unscripted serials with Amy Grant, in that Oosterhouse went to see not so large municipalities athwart America to aid desires come genuine.

Oosterhouse has been highlighted like an specialist for programmes including: Rachael Ray, The Today Show, The CBS Early Show, The Oprah Winfrey Show, The View, CNN, Entertainment Tonight and Extra.

In Fall 2007, Oosterhouse started 2 spic-and-span exhibits, Carter Can, a home advancement show premiering on October 4 on HGTV, and The Inside Job, a behind-the-scenes view of Carter Can, that tend to proffer homeowners get off data, on the DIY Network.

In first 2008, a second show was appended on the HGTV net-work, Red Hot Green, with Nicole Facciuto, on that Oosterhouse promotes eco-friendly matters for earth-friendly exisiting.

Oosterhouse is the service of the spic-and-span HGTV net-work show Million Dollar Rooms, showcasing over the top and profligate attributes of a few of the most elaborately assembled residences.

Amy Grant discography

The discography of American singer-songwriter Amy Grant comprises of 14 workshop collections, one expanded play, 3 live collections, 3 Christmas col-

lections, 4 compiling collections, 6 Music video|video collections and twenty-one tunes recordings, and seventy-one Music single|singles.

Grant produced her first public appearance as a adolescent and by the 1980s had obtained celebrity in Christian tunes cheers to the tunes Father's Eyes, El Shaddai (song)|El Shaddai, and Angels (Amy Grant song)|Angels. In 1986, she had her foremost No. 1 sole on the Billboard Hot 100|Billboard Hot 100 in a duo with Peter Cetera, The Next Time I Fall. Grant was getting to be further well known in the planet of pop with such collections as Unguarded and Lead Me On (Amy Grant album)|Lead Me On. However, it was not till her eighth workshop collection Heart in Motion that Grant produced a success in to normal tunes. Heart in Motion created the hit selects Baby Baby (Amy Grant song)|Baby Baby, Every Heartbeat, That's What Love Is For and Good for Me (song)|Good for Me, altogether of that produced it in to the top 10 of the Billboard Hot 100, with the foremost 2 arriving at No. 1 and No. 2 correspondingly. It stays Grant's nearly all monetarily prosperous collection to date, experiencing been endorsed five-times platinum by the Recording Industry Association of America. A Christmas collection, Home for Christmas (Amy Grant album)|Home for Christmas, was disseminated soon later, arriving at No. 2 on the Billboard 200|Billboard 200, her biggest collection admission to date. Grant proceeded on to discharge the collections House of Love (Amy Grant album)|House of Love and Behind the Eyes (Amy Grant album)|Behind the Eyes in the mid-nineties. Her foremost full-length workshop collection of all-new matter eversince 2003, How Mercy Looks as of Here, was disseminated on May 14, 2013.

Her recordings are approximated to have traded further compared to 30 million components international, that produces her one of the most prosperous Christian transcriptioning creators.

Inspirational music - History

The category grew to be familiar like modern Christian tunes as a effect of the Jesus motion resurgence in the last one 1960s and first 1970s, Banjo, Omotayo O., and Williams, Kesha Morant . A House Divided? Christian Music in Black and White. Journal of Media Religion 10.3 (2011): 115-137. Academic Search Complete. Web. 8 Feb. 2014. And was initially named Jesus tunes.Forbes, Bruce David, and Jeffrey H. Mahan. Religion and Popular Culture In America. Berkeley, Calif: University of California Press, 2000. Ebook Collection (EBSCOhost). Web. 8 Feb. 2014. About that time, numerous youthful folks as of the sixties' counter culture avowed to trust in Jesus. Convinced of the emptiness of a way of life founded on narcotics, gratis intercourse, and revolutionary political affairs, 'hippies' grew to be 'Jesus people'.

Frame, John M. Contemporary Worship Music. Phillipsburg, NJ: PR Publishing, 1997. However there remained folks whoever sensed that Jesus was one other journey. It was throughout the 1970s Jesus motion that Christian tunes commenced to come to be an business inside its normal self. Jesus Music commenced by performing tools and crooning tunes regarding fancy and tranquility, that additionally interpreted in to fancy of God. Paul Wohlegemuth, whoever authored the publication Rethinking Church Music, indicated [the] 1970s must perceive a pronounced receipt of rock-influenced tunes in altogether degrees of kirk tunes. The rock manner tend to come to be further well known to altogether folks, its rhythmical superfluity must come to be sophisticated, and its earliest nonreligious relationships must be fewer recalled.Baker, Paul. Page 140. Contemporary Christian Music: Where it appeared as of What it is Where It's Going. Westchester, Illinois: Crossway Books, 1985. Print.

Though there remained Christian collections in the 1960s that held contemporary-sounding tunes, there remained 2 collections recorded in 1969 that are contemplated to be the foremost perfect collections of Jesus rock: Upon This Rock (Larry Norman album)|Upon This Rock (1969) by Larry Norman originally disseminated on Capitol Records,John J. Thompson, Raised by Wolves: The Story of Christian Rock Roll (2000):49. And Mylon – We Believe by Mylon LeFevre, disseminated by Cotillion, that was LeFevre's aim at mixturing canon tunes with southern rock. Unlike customary either southern canon tunes, this spic-and-span Jesus tunes was birthed out of rock music|rock and people tunes.

Pioneers of this motion as well contained Keith Green, 2nd Chapter of Acts, Benny Hester, Barry McGuire, Andrae Crouch|Andraé Crouch and the Disciples Evie (singer)|Evie, The Imperials and Love Song (band)|Love Song, amid other ones. The not so large Jesus tunes intellectual/artistic awareness had extended in to a multi-million-dollar Christian tunes industry|industry by the 1980s.By the '80s, the special-interest net-work that Jesus tunes had seeded had elaborated in to a multimullion-dollar business. Contemporary Christian tunes had its personal periodicals, broadcast stations, and prize exhibits. The Jesus motion resurgence was over: p. 10 Many CCM creators such like Benny Hester, Amy Grant, DC Talk, Michael W. Smith, Stryper, and Jars of Clay noticed Crossover (music)|crossover triumph with Top 40 normal broadcast play.

The category appeared and grew to be widespread in the 1970s and 1980s.Nantais, David. What Would Jesus Listen To? America 196.18 (2007): 22–24. Music Index. Web. 6 Feb. 2014. Beginning in July 1978, CCM Magazine started blanketing Contemporary Christian Music creators and a ample span of religious subjects till it started on the web documents in 2009.

It has definite subjects and communications beyond the tunes and their words containing Praise and reverence, persuasion, reassurance, and orison. Adedeji, Femi. Essentials of Christian Music in Contemporary Times: A Prognosis. Asia Journal of Theology 20.2 (2006): 230-240. Academic Search Complete. Web. 8 Feb. 2014. These tunes as well center on subjects of commitment, stimulation, salvation, appeasement, and reclamation. Many folks attend to modern Christian tunes for ease via hard periods. The words and communications transferred in CCM tunes are directed to evangelize and to reverence Jesus. One of the early objectives of CCM was to outspread the information of Jesus to non-Christians. In extension, modern Christian tunes as well Strengthens the persuasion of believers.

Charlie Peacock

'Charles William Ashworth' (born, August 10, 1956) stronger familiar by the stage designation 'Charlie Peacock' is an American singer-songwriter, Pianist, record maker, meeting performer and writer. While increasing up in California Peacock started performing the keyboard instrument. After finishing his teaching he created a group and started a vocation as a non-amateur performer. His collections contain the involved jazz recordings Love Press Ex-Curio and Arc of the Circle (Runway) and his newest vocal program No Man's Land (101).Tremml, Brian (2012, September 25). Album Stream: Charlie Peacock No Man's Land. Magazine. Retrieved 2012-09-29, as of [http://www.pastemagazine.com/blogs/av/2012/09/album-stream-charlie-peacock-no-mans-land.html PasteMagazine.com] Peacock has been piece of the originative group for some prosperous tunes and collections containing Amy Grant's Every Heartbeat (1991), Switchfoot's Dare You to Move (2003) and either of the The Civil Wars (band)|The Civil Wars' workshop albums—the Gold certifiedFlood, Laura (2012, September 13). Civil Wars Earn Gold Record With Barton Hollow. Paste Magazine. Retrieved 2013-08-18, as of [http://www.pastemagazine.com/articles/2012/09/civil-wars-debut-album-reaches-gold-and-two-cma-no.html PasteMagazine.com] Barton Hollow (2011) and the self-titled continuation (2013) that launched at No. 1Caulfield, Keith (2013, August 14). The Civil Wars Debut at No. 1 on Billboard 200 Albums Chart. Billboard. Retrieved 2013-08-18, as of [http://www.billboard.com/articles/news/5650663/the-civil-wars-debut-at-no-1-on-billboard-200-albums-chart Billboard.com] on the Billboard 200 collection selling graph.Administrator (2008, March 31). Interview with Charlie Peacock. Land of Broken Hearts. Retrieved 2011-02-15, as of [http://landofbrokenhearts.org/archive/2008/03/interview-with-charlie-peacock/ LandOfBrokenHearts.org]Stiernberg, Bonnie (2010, December 2). Best of What's Next: The Civil Wars. Paste Magazine. Retrieved 2011-02-15, as of [http://www.

pastemagazine.com/articles/2010/12/best-of-whats-next-the-civil-wars.html PasteMagazine.com]Jenkins, Todd S. (2006, June 23). Charlie Peacock: Exhibits Curiosity, Returns to Jazz Roots. All About Jazz. Retrieved 2011-02-15, as of [http://www.allaboutjazz.com/php/article.php?id=22052 AllAboutJazz.com]

Tommy Sims - Notable projects

***Amy Grant - Heart in Motion, House of Love (Amy Grant album)|House of Love, Behind the Eyes (Amy Grant album)|Behind the Eyes**
*Carman - The Standard (1993), R.I.O.T. (Righteous Invasion of Truth) (1996)
*Bruce Springsteen - In Concert/MTV Plugged, Streets Of Philadelphia
*Garth Brooks - The Life of Chris Gaines, Retrospective
*Michael McDonald (singer)|Michael McDonald - Michael_McDonald_discography#Studio_albums|Blue Obsession
*Kenny Loggins - It's About Time (Kenny Loggins album)|It's About Time
*Blackstreet|BlackStreet - Another Level
*Toni Braxton - The Heat
*Robert Randolph and the Family Band - ColorBlind
*Bonnie Raitt - Silver Lining, Souls Alike, I Can't Help You Now
*Kelly Clarkson - Thankful (Kelly Clarkson album)|Thankful
*Newsboys - Shine: The Hits
*Taylor Dayne - Naked Without You (album)|Naked Without You
*Natalie Grant - Deeper Life
*Michelle Williams (singer)|Michelle Williams - Do You Know (Michelle Williams album)|Do You Know
*Marvin Winans - Marvin_Winans#Discography|Alone But Not Alone
*Darwin Hobbs - Worshipper - Broken - Darwin_Hobbs#Discography|Vertical
*Israel Houghton|Israel and New Breed - Real (Israel New Breed album)|Real, The Power of One
*Jonny Lang - Fight for My Soul (2013)

Crossover (music) - Christian crossover artists

The expression crossing creator might allude to melodic artists and groupings that are Christian tunes creators, whoever numerous periods initially are advertised via List of Christian record labels|Christian record labels, broadcast stations, churches and different Christian media however whoever commence vending in normal nonreligious markets as well. Other periods, crossing creators might commence out in the normal trade however have Christian undertones either subjects if not deliberately Christian. The expression crossing over is applied to report once an creator whoever had commenced mainly in Christian markets begins getting normal triumph. Some folks might sense that the creator is exposing the kirk for celebrity either splendor, when other ones might perceive this like a significant occasion for the creator outspread the communication of their Christian faiths.

The foremost chief creator crossing was by Amy Grant, with her 1985 collection Unguarded and 1991 hit tune Baby Baby (Amy Grant song)|Baby Baby as of the highest-selling Christian collection Heart in Motion. The collections and sole remained dispersed by a Christian label however experienced weighty play on pop broadcast stations and remained chart-toppers on the Billboard graphs. Since then, numerous creators have been tagged as crossing creator notwithstanding of if they initially designed to trade to the Christian trade, nonreligious trade, either either. The most noteworthy new Christian crossing creators are Kirk Franklin, Switchfoot, The Afters, Relient K, and numerous of the creators on Tooth Nail Records such like MxPx, Underoath, Emery (band)|Emery, Lifehouse (band)|Lifehouse, Zao (band)|Zao, and Dead Poetic.

A further uncommon illustration of a cross-over creator is Katy Perry. She disseminated a itty-bitty familiar, monetarily stillborn Christian collection in 2001 under her birthing designation, Katy Hudson. She additionally proceeded on to discharge monetarily prosperous nonreligious collections in 2008, 2010, and 2013. There are nevertheless a few obvious Christian components within her nonreligious tunes, especially her afterward work, such like Who Am I Living For (2010) and By The Grace of God (2013).

Michael Card - Awards

1983 Gospel Music Association|GMA Dove Awards
:Dove Award for Songwriter of the Year|Songwriter of the Year
:Dove Award for Song of the Year|Song of the Year: El Shaddai
1988 GMA Dove Award
:Praise Worship Album of the Year: The Final Word
1994 GMA Dove Award
:Children's Music Album of the Year: Come to the Cradle
1994 Recording Industry Association of America|RIAA Certified Gold Recording
: Sleep Sound in Jesus
1997 Western Kentucky University Distinguished Alumnus http://www.wku.edu/tradition/97hoda.html

1998 National Religious Broadcasters Chairman's Award

2001 RIAA 365 Songs of the Century
: No. 26 El Shaddai, as recorded by Amy Grant
2002 Publishers Weekly Award

:Best Religion Book: Scribbling in the Sand
2002 Chicago Book Clinic Award of Excellence
2006 ECPA Christian Book Awards

Faithless Heart - 20th Anniversary Edition

In 2007, Grant had left Word Records and AM Records, the 2 tags that had supervised the first discharge of Lead Me On. That annum, her spic-and-span record label, EMI Records, reissued a spic-and-span digitally remastered issue of Lead Me On. In 2008, EMI Records|EMI once more reissued the collection, this time as a double-disc 20th Anniversary Edition. The second disc of that re-release highlighted a spic-and-span transcriptioning of Faithless Heart by Amy Grant with Michael W. Smith on the galvanic keyboard instrument. Grant depicted the spic-and-span transcriptioning as a songwriter's variant, with the tunes cleared down to additional highlight the words. The disc as well highlighted a spic-and-span start trail with Grant and Smith debating in what way to order the tune. In advancing the re-release, Grant accomplished the spic-and-span auditory variant throughout different media emergences.

Find a Way (Amy Grant song)

'Find a Way' is a 1985 sole by Contemporary Christian music|Christian tunes vocalist Amy Grant. It was disseminated like the foremost sole as of her Unguarded collection. Also, Find a Way was Grant's foremost chief sole discharge, as it was released in nonreligious outlet vents by AM Records alongside with the collection. Although the sole was disseminated within either the United States and the United Kingdom with It's Not a Song as a B-side, it solely charted in America.

Find a Way is an increased tempo, motivational tune in that Grant heartens her listener, an annoyed youthful female, to carry on and remain hopeful notwithstanding life's tryouts, since fancy must surely notice a means.

It's the Most Wonderful Time of the Year - Other recordings

*1968: Jazz Pianist Pete Jolly recorded an involved variant for Something Festive, a multi-artist break compiling of AM Records creators dispersed by BF Goodrich. Jolly re-recorded the tune in 2009 for the Mack Avenue Records compiling Jazz Yule

Love.

*1986: Johnny Mathis disseminated a variant of the tune on his 4th break collection, Christmas Eve with Johnny Mathis.

***1992: Amy Grant disseminated a variant of the tune on her second break collection, Home for Christmas (Amy Grant album)|Home for Christmas.**

*1993: Plácido Domingo, Diana Ross, and José Carreras disseminated the tune on their live break musical performance collection, Christmas in Vienna (album)|Christmas in Vienna.

*1998: Vince Gill disseminated a variant of the tune on his second break collection, Breath of Heaven: A Christmas Collection.

*1999: Garth Brooks disseminated a variant of the tune on his second break collection, Garth Brooks and the Magic of Christmas. Brooks as well until the foremost creator to graph a variant of the tune in North America, as his region recreate reached its highest point at # 56 on Billboard (magazine)|Billboard's Hot Country Songs|Hot Country Singles Tracks graph.

*1999: Kathy Troccoli recorded the tune as a duo with Andy Williams.

*2002: Plus One (band)|Plus One recorded the tune for their Christmas (Plus One album)|Christmas collection.

*2005: The Blenders disseminated a variant of the tune on their 3rd break collection, Most Wonderful Time.

*2006: Gonzo the Great and Rizzo the Rat disseminated a cover of the tune on the Muppets' break collection, The Muppets: A Green and Red Christmas.

*2007: Captain Tennille contained a variant on their collection The Secret of Christmas (album)|The Secret of Christmas, and it was disseminated like a sole the similar annum.

*2008: BarlowGirl disseminated a variant of the tune on their break collection, Home for Christmas (BarlowGirl album)|Home for Christmas.

*2008: Harry Connick, Jr. Disseminated a variant of the tune on his 3rd break collection, What a Night! A Christmas Album. This transcriptioning reached its highest point at # 9 on Billboard (magazine)|Billboard's Hot Adult Contemporary Tracks graph (the biggest graphing variant of the tune to date within the United States).[

Artist Chart History - Harry Connick, Jr.], Billboard.com

*2009: The Mormon Tabernacle Choir accomplished the tune, with visitor singer Natalie Cole, throughout their 2009 Christmas musical performance at Temple Square in Salt Lake City. This variant was contained the ensuing annum like piece of a PBS out of the ordinary of the musical performance, and was disseminated on a DVD of the musical performance as well like the CD The Most Wonderful Time of the Year (Mormon Tabernacle Choir album)|It's the Most Wonderful Time of the Year.

*2010: Celtic Thunder disseminated a cover of the tune as piece a potpourri (music)|medley with We Wish You a Merry Christmas on their break collection, Christmas.

*2010: Take 6 disseminated a variant of the tune on their break collection, The Most Wonderful Time of the Year (Take 6 album)|The Most Wonderful Time of the Year.

*2011: Paul Anka disseminated a variant of the tune on his break collection Songs of December.

*2011: Chicago (band)|Chicago disseminated a variant of the tune on their 3rd break collection, Chicago XXXIII: O Christmas Three.

*2011: Scott Weiland disseminated a variant of the tune on his break collection, The Most Wonderful Time of the Year (Scott Weiland album)|The Most Wonderful Time of the Year.

Simon Climie - Biography

Climie is the erstwhile head vocalist of the UK pop music|pop duo (music)|duo Climie Fisher, alltogether with Rob Fisher. The couple encountered once they remained either meeting performers at Abbey Road Studios. Climie Fisher had strikes in further compared to 35 areas – and numeral ones in a few – with Love Changes (Everything), that gained an Ivor Novello Award, Rise to the Occasion, This Is Me and numerous different tunes.

After leaving EMI and the ultimate Climie Fisher collection Coming in for the Kill, Climie signed to Sony's Columbia Records|Columbia record label|label as a unaccompanied (music)|solo musician|artist, disseminating an collection named Soul Inspiration in 1992.

From the mid-90s Climie extended to record producer|production, making and songwriter|writing tunes for a numeral of artistes, containing Eternal (band)|Eternal,

Louise Redknapp, B.B. King, Michael McDonald (singer)|Michael McDonald and Zucchero Fornaciari.

In Climie's foremost pair of annums like a composer, he had tunes recorded by George Michael and Aretha Franklin, Pat Benatar, Smokey Robinson and Jeff Beck, that recognized him as a world-class global aptitude. Then, on the fringes of meeting work, he did the Fairlight CMI|Fairlight program design for Scritti Politti's fabled collection Cupid Psyche.

George Michael and Aretha Franklin's sole I Knew You Were Waiting (For Me) extended numeral one international, containing in the UK Singles Chart and Billboard's Hot 100 in America. Following this, Climie sustained to have triumph with his tunes, containing You're Not Alone, that highlighted onto Amy Grant's Heart in Motion, that traded further compared to 5 million duplicates international – the biggest-selling Christian collection of altogether tme.

Climie is as well familiar for his Grammy Award-winning work as a coworker with Eric Clapton on numerous Platinum collections, containing Pilgrim (1998 album)|Pilgrim, Reptile (album)|Reptile, Riding with the King (B.B. King and Eric Clapton album)|Riding with the King, Me And Mr Johnson, Back Home and The Road to Escondido.

During this time he created Platinum collections for different creators, containing Michael McDonald's famous Motown, Motown II and Soul Speak. The last one highlighted collaborations with Stevie Wonder and Toni Braxton, when the Grammy-nominated Motown seeded the enormous US hit Ain't No Mountain High Enough.

In 2011 triumph sustained with Climie's tunes. Sara Evans was in the American region tunes graphs for further compared to 6 months with My Heart Can't Tell You No, and Chris Medina – whoever had previously extended numeral one in a numeral of areas round the planet with his foremost sole – co-operated with Climie on his second sole, One More Time, and some tunes on the collection What Are Words.

Together with U2 originator associate Larry Mullen, Jr., Climie has co-written the film result and subject for Man on the Train (2011 TriBeCa Productions film) in that Larry stars with Donald Sutherland

He proceeded on to work with Eric Clapton and make a numeral of Grammy Award-winning collections for Eric Clapton, performing like maker and co-writer. Climie as well donated keyboards and program design to Clapton's Pilgrim (1998 album)|Pilgrim.

Climie as well operated with Clapton, on Clapton and JJ Cale's collection The Road to Escondido, disseminated within 2006. Apart as of Clapton, he as well operated with erstwhile Doobie Brothers associate Michael McDonald (singer)|Michael McDonald on his Motown collections, and the other artistes recorded overhead.

His newest program is the manufacture and blending of spic-and-span Eric Clapton collection Old Sock, that shot to numeral one in the American Billboard Independent Chart in March 2013 following striking numeral 7 in the Billboard 200

John Lloyd Miller - Career

Miller has operated in nearly any facet of the feature and TV trade like a director, author and maker. He started his vocation when visiting the alumna feature manufacture programme at the USC School of Cinematic Arts#Notable SCA alumni|University of Southern California. Miller tended to USC Film School with such notables as Jay Roach, Greg Beeman and Ken Kwapis. Miller gained a Golden Reel prize alongside with Jacqueline Woolf for their work on The Big Garage directed by Greg Beeman Miller started functioning with first tunes audiovisual director Jack Cole as a author and finally as a co-director for such creators as, Bon Jovi, Steve Perry (musician)|Steve Perry, Amy Grant, Sawyer Brown and Dionne Warwick.

Miller has managed over 250 tunes recordings, containing Garth Brooks', the Dance (song)|The Dance", The Smithereens, 11 (The Smithereens album)|A Girl Like You, Eazy E and N.W.A|NWA, Easier Said compared to Dunn, Reba McEntire, What If (Reba McEntire song)|What If, Dolly Parton, Just When I Needed You Most, The Goo Goo Dolls, There You Are (Goo Goo Dolls song)|There You Are, The Fat Boys and Chubby Checker, The Fat Boys|The Twist, Billy Ray Cyrus, I Give You My Heart and Joe Cocker, You Are So Beautiful.

Miller matured up in Westfield, New Jersey and on graduation as of Westfield Senior High School, he enlisted in the United States Navy. Miller serviced onboard the USS Nitro (AE-23) as a adorned associate of X Division.

After the Navy Miller tended to Northeastern University in Boston wherever Miller received his foremost palate of manufacture by functioning as an corrector and manager for the school's TV facility. Miller graduated with merits and left for California to be at the MFA programme at the USC School of Cinematic Arts|University of Southern California.

Miller's work in tunes audiovisual has gained countless prizes, containing audiovisual of the annum prizes for Billboard Magazine, MusicRow, ACM Awards, CMA Awards, Cine|Cine Golden Eagle and Canadian Country Music Association|CCMA.

Several of John Lloyd Miller's recordings emerge in Country Music Television|CMT's Greatest Videos of All Time, containing Vince Gill, One More Last Chance, Vince Gill, Go Rest High on That Mountain, KT Oslin, '80s Ladies, George Strait, Check Yes either No, Travis Tritt, More Than You'll Ever Know, and Garth Brooks', The Dance (song)|The Dance, that is recorded like in the top 5 altogether time. A 6 time Country Music Association|CMA Award candidate, John Lloyd Miller is one of the top 10 region tunes audiovisual directors of altogether time.[http://cmaawards.cma-world.com/.../top-cma-award-nominees.pdf CMA]

In 1999 Miller co-operated with region tunes star Mark Collie to produce what finally grew to be the seriously praised, prize conquering feature, I Still Miss Someone." It was the foremost feature depiction of Johnny Cash#Portrayals|Johnny Cash. The feature gained prizes about the planet and was the solely small feature picked to be presented in the 30 Greatest Films of the Last 30 Years, next to such features as Blue Velvet (film)|Blue Velvet, Easy Rider, Pulp Fiction at the Woodstock Festival.

Miller's has managed TV exhibits for HBO, VH1 and numerous further. As a script-writer, Miller was contractiled to record a serials of 3 characteristic texts for Dove Canyon Films. They contain, Stephen Coonts#Bibliography|Saucer" an alteration of New York Times Bestseller Stephen Coonts bestseller of the similar designation, butterfly Kisses (song)|Butterfly Kisses" and St. X Prep. He is a associate of Writers Guild of America, East|WGAe.

Miller is mentioned in The Garth Factor: The Career Behind The Country's Big Boom , The Encyclopedia of Country Music,Country Music Trivia Fact Book and The Garth Brooks Scrapbook, and was a donating author to The Real Meaning of Life.

Miller is the originator of [http://www.theavsquad.com The AV Squad], his manufacture corporation in Tennessee and a co-creator of [http://beaconbaycreative.com/who-we-are Beacon Bay Creative] with workplaces in Los Angeles, Hilton Head and Nashville.

Miller is the dad of twins, Jack and Ella, and lives firstly in Brentwood, Tennessee.

Point of Grace - 1998–2000: Artistic establishment, media attention, and hiatus

Point of Grace started work on their spic-and-span collection in belated 1997/early 1998. Brown Bannister, whoever had formerly operated with such creators as Steven Curtis Chapman and Amy Grant, was accompanied on to cover manufacture responsibilities. He accompanied an exhilarating turn to the girls' tunes. They remained sensing for a further accelerating,

live group sound for this collection, and certain sufficient, there was fewer program design compared to their foregoing attempts. Chris Eaton (British musician)|Chris Eaton was as well accompanied alongside to cover the vocal manufacture for the collection, and the outcomes happy the young ladies, as the vocal plans remained long further complicated compared to beforehand. It ought to be absorbing to appertain those vocal plans on a live show positioning, and on their never-to-be-repeated musical performance dates in the spring and summertime of 1998, the young ladies previewed a few of the spic-and-span tunes, such like Jesus Is, Steady On, and Better Days. They took a stop in the mid of transcriptioning for Terry to offer birthing to her foremost kid in April.

The still existing participants emerged at the 1998 Dove Awards short of her, wherever they remained proposed for Artist of the Year, Group of the Year, and Pop/Contemporary Song of the Year for Circle Of Friends, however the cluster proceeded home empty-handed. During The Nashville Network transmit of the show, pre-show service Kathy Troccoli enlightened fans of Cole Devore Jones' birthing April 15 (a 7 days beforehand the Doves), naming him teasingly Terry and Chris's duty return.

In July 1998, a spic-and-span sole was disseminated to broadcast stations, the name tune as of the collection Steady On. A CD sole was as well disseminated to Christian book stores. There was a pop rehash and a sway rehash variant of Steady On, either Record producer|produced by Tony McAnany, as well like increased subject matter on the CD, such like brief BIOS as of the young ladies, extracts as of a spic-and-span sacred publication, a picture galleria, and different anecdotes. The collection was disseminated on August 4, 1998, and launched at No. 1 on the SoundScan selling graph, and stayed in the Top 10 for 7 successive 7-day periods. It was endorsed gold by the RIAA in 1999 and platinum in 2002. The head sole and name trail shortly extended the top of the graphs, getting to be Point of Grace's 16th successive No. 1 sole. Five further selects pursued suit, creating it a whole of 21 successive No. 1s. In October 1998, the young ladies started their foremost journey as a star. The Steady On Tour was as well the foremost time they visited with their personal group. Led by Dana Cappillino, the performers breathed spic-and-span existence in to Point of Grace's tunes. In 1999 they gained Dove Awards for Group of the Year and Enhanced CD of the Year for the Steady On CD Single. At the 1999 Grammy Awards, they remained proposed for Best Pop/Contemporary Gospel Album for Steady On. Heather as well received wedded in 1999, in the mid of the journey. They donated the tune The River for the Experiencing God collection, the tune Forever On And On for the Streams collection program, and Love Won't Leave You Now for The Mercy Project, committed to Mercy Ministries of America.

After The Steady On Tour shut in the Spring of 1999, the young ladies started work on their foremost Christmas discharge. The collection was recorded in

Nashville, Tennessee; London, England; and Montreal, Canada. Brown Bannister at one point more managed the manufacture, and AR individual Brent Bourgeois and vocal organizer Chris Eaton (British musician)|Chris Eaton remained as well accompanied back on. The ensemble, organized by Carl Marsh and Ronn Huff, was recorded at the fabled Abbey Road Studios in London. The conclusion effect was a lush, timeless gathering of break preferences and spic-and-span originals. The young ladies remained pleased of their achievement, and on September 27, 1999, A Christmas Story (album)|A Christmas Story was disseminated. The reality that Life Love Other Mysteries had simply been endorsed platinum and The Song Is Alive had simply come to be their 21st No. 1 tune captured the media's awareness at one point more, and they emerged in some media outlet vents and on exhibits such like Donny Marie (1998 TV series)|Donny Marie, ABC's The View (U.S. TV series)|The View, and The 700 Club, wherever they plugged A Christmas Story (album)|A Christmas Story and their involvement on Amy Grant's Christmas Tour. All 4 participants commenced the journey alltogether, however Terry, whoever was 9 months expectant with her second kid (another boy, Luke Marshall), left the journey midway via, leaving Heather, Shelley, and Denise to accomplish as a triad. After the journey finished, the young ladies took a year-long pause, regrouping sometimes for Women of Faith conventions and one either 2 never-to-be-repeated dates. To hold their admirers pleased till the discharge of their following workshop collection, Word Records|Word disseminated Rarities Remixes a gathering of remixed strikes as of their foremost 2 deliverances, 4 tunes as of their autonomous collection, 2 scarce traces, and a live variant of Circle Of Friends. They as well accomplished 4 tunes at the Billy Graham Crusade in Nashville, Tennessee.

Top Christian Albums - Most weeks at number one

***(85 Weeks) Age to Age - Amy Grant (1982-84)**
*(68 weeks) Morning Like This - Sandi Patti (1986-88)
***(61 weeks) Straight Ahead (Amy Grant album)|Straight Ahead - Amy Grant (1984-85)**
*(38 weeks) Free at Last (DC Talk album)|Free at Last - DC Talk (1993-94)
*(38 weeks) The Beautiful Letdown - Switchfoot (2004-05)
***(36 weeks) Unguarded - Amy Grant (1985-86) (tie)**
***(36 weeks) Lead Me On (Amy Grant album)|Lead Me On - Amy Grant (1988-89) (tie)**
*(35 weeks) You Light Up My Life: Inspirational Songs - LeAnn Rimes (1997-98) (tie)
*(35 weeks) Satellite (P.O.D. Album)|Satellite - P.O.D. (2001-02) (tie)
*(34 weeks) Revival In The Land - Carman (1989-90)

Ward-Belmont College - Notable alumnae

* Carman Barnes, writer
* Jean Faircloth, philanthropist
* Elizabeth P. Farrington, producer of the Honolulu Star-Bulletin and Delegate (United States Congress)|Congressional Delegate
* **Amy Grant, singer**
* Iris Kelso, paper correspondent and TV information correspondent
* Clare Boothe Luce, corrector and playwright
* Mary Martin, actress
* Grace Moore, singer
* Minnie Pearl (Sarah Colley Cannon), region tunes singer
* Lila Bell Wallace|Lila Acheson Wallace, joint founder of Reader's Digest

Metro Maryland Youth For Christ - Friends Of Metro Maryland Youth For Christ Fundraising Banquet

The yearly Friends of Youth For Christ Fundraising Banquet spotlights the functions and achievements of YFC/Campus Life workforce and volunteers and testimonies as of adolescents and grown-ups whoever have been definitely hit by the programmes. The feast has highlighted a diversity of praised theme speakers amid them: Multi-Grammy and Dove-Award Winning singers, songwriters and writers Vince Gill, Amy Grant and Michael W. Smith, Former U.S. Attorney General John Ashcroft, twice Emmy Award-winning communicator Deborah Norville, Olympic gymnastics gold medal winner and writer Mary Lou Retton, Former U.S. Congressman and football game protagonist J.C. Watts and world-renowned Director of Pediatric Neurosurgery at The Johns Hopkins Hospital and finest vending writer Dr. Ben Carson.

Everywhere I Go (Amy Grant song)

'Everywhere I Go' is a 1985 sole by Contemporary Christian music|Christian tunes vocalist Amy Grant. It was disseminated like the second sole as of her Unguarded collection. Unlike Find a Way (Amy Grant song)|Find a Way beforehand it and Wise Up (Amy Grant song)|Wise Up following it, the tune disappointed to reach The Billboard Hot 100. However, the tune did create the Adult Contemporary and Contemporary Christian Music|Christian tunes graphs in

the United States.

Everywhere I Go is a a little down-tempo motivational tune that attributes weighty employ of the synthesiser and a few sound results. The words commend God's in-variable occurrence in Grant's existence. In the Unguarded liner records, Grant calls the tune my own variant of Psalm 139.

When Love Finds You - Personnel

*Barry Beckett – keyboard instrument, Keyboard instrument|keyboards, synthesizer
*Stuart Duncan – fiddle
*Vince Gill – head voices, Backing vocalist|background voices, stringed instrument, mandolin
***Amy Grant – background vocals**
*John Hughey – steel guitar
*John Barlow Jarvis – keyboard instrument, keyboards, synthesizer
*Alison Krauss – context vocals
*Patty Loveless – context vocals
*Michael McDonald (singer)|Michael McDonald – context vocals
*Steve Nathan – keyboard instrument, keyboards, synthesizer
*Michael Omartian – accordion
*Matt Rollings – keyboard instrument, keyboards, synthesizer
*Milton Sledge – Drum kit|drums, Percussion instrument|percussion
*Michael Rhodes – deep-toned guitar
*Ricky Skaggs – context vocals
*Randy Scruggs – guitar
*Dawn Sears – context vocals
*Steuart Smith – guitar
*Billy Thomas – context vocals
*Carlos Vega – drums, percussion
*Billy Joe Walker, Jr. – guitar
*Pete Wasner – keyboard instrument, keyboards, synthesizer
*Willie Weeks – bass guitar
*Jeff White – context vocals
*Trisha Yearwood – context voices

1982 in music - April - August

*April 13 - David Crosby is apprehended on dope demands for the second time in 3 7-day periods once Dallas police force seize him planning crack behind the scenes beforehand a show.
*April 15 – Billy Joel is gravely hurt in a bike mishap in Long Island, New York. Joel

uses up over a month in the infirmary experiencing material treatment for his hand.
*April 17 - Johnny Cash holds Saturday Night Live with Cash and Elton John and his timeless group as the melodic visitors. Cash sings I Walk The Line, Folsom Prison Blues, Ring of Fire and Sunday Morning Coming Down. John sings Empty Garden (Hey Hey Johnny) and Ball and Chain. The last one ought to not emerge on the NBC show once more till 2011.
*April 24 – Germany in the Eurovision Song Contest|Germany gains the 27th yearly Eurovision Song Contest 1982|Eurovision Song Contest, grasped in the Harrogate International Centre|Harrogate Conference Centre, North Yorkshire, with the tune Ein bißchen Frieden, sung by 17-year-old Nicole (German singer)|Nicole. She as well records the tune in English as A Little Peace, that goes the 500th chart-topping sole in the UK.
*April 26
**Rod Stewart is mugged in Los Angeles. Stewart misses his $50,000 Porsche to the mugger, however is not maim. The automobile is recuperated some days afterward.
**Joe Strummer disappears, making The Clash to defer their U.K. Journey.
*April 30 - Influential rock correspondent Lester Bangs passes away in his New York flat of an obvious accidental o.d. Of prescription narcotics.
*May 14 - The foremost The Prince's Trust|Prince's Trust almsgiving musical performance is grasped at the National Exhibition Centre in Birmingham. With Charles, Prince of Wales|The Prince of Wales within presence, Status Quo (band)|Status Quo, goes the foremost modern group to play to British royalty.
*May 18 - Three 7-day periods following vanishing, Joe Strummer and his sweetheart are noticed exisiting in Paris, 2 days following they ran the Paris Marathon.
*May 26 – The Rolling Stones open their European journey in Aberdeen, Scotland.
*June 11 – Grease 2, leading Maxwell Caulfield and Michelle Pfeiffer (in her characteristic feature debut), is disseminated.
* June 16 – James Honeyman-Scott passes away of heart letdown triggered by crack dogmatism. He was 25 annums aged.
***June 19 – Amy Grant weds Gary Chapman (musician)|Gary Chapman.**
*July 4 – Ozzy Osbourne weds his administrator Sharon Osbourne|Sharon Arden in Maui, Hawaii.
*July 21 - A second The Prince's Trust|Prince's Trust almsgiving musical performance is grasped at the Dominion Theatre in London. Performers contain Pete Townshend, Robert Plant, Madness (band)|Madness, Phil Collins, Joan Armatrading and Kate Bush.
*August 17 – In Langenhagen nearby Hanover, Germany started the foremost large number manufacture of the firm disc.
*August 18 - Four roads in Liverpool, England|Liverpool are designated following every one of The Beatles.
*August 31 – Ronnie James Dio plays his ultimate show with Black Sabbath (until 1992).

A Christmas Album (Amy Grant album) - Pressings

A Christmas Album was the foremost Amy Grant collection to be disseminated within the Compact Disc setup. The first CD subject had a production fault that triggered a not so large, however obvious leap throughout the change amid traces 3 and 4. The remastered variant does not have this flaw. The collection was as well disseminated like a advertising solely vinyl depiction disc variant in a perish cut cover.

Sharayah

'Sharayah' is a 1985 sole by Contemporary Christian music|Christian tunes vocalist Amy Grant. It was disseminated like the 4th and ultimate sole as of her Unguarded collection. The tune did not attain the normal triumph that the foregoing Unguarded selects had noticed however nevertheless appeared as a chief hit on Contemporary Christian music|Christian broadcast.

Sharayah is an increased tempo, Rock music|rock-styled motivational tune that attributes weighty employ of the synthesiser and galvanic stringed instrument. In the tune, Grant addresses a close pal designated Sharayah, a seemingly fictitious type whoever is undergoing a catastrophes of persuasion. Grant implores her pal to notice redemption in God. However, the words do not especially reference God either Jesus.

Bill Champlin - The Sons of Champlin and solo career

The Opposite Six, Champlin's group as of elevated educational institution, altered their designation to the Sons of Champlin, and finally recorded a numeral of well-reviewed however poorly-selling collections (including Loosen Up Naturally and Circle Filled With Love) by 1977, once the 30 annum aged Champlin repositioned to Los Angeles.During the 1969-1970 time, once Champlin was unsure as to the time to come of the Sons of Champlin, he joined with Jerry Miller of Moby Grape in The Rhythm Dukes, ensuing the retreat of Don Stevenson (musician)|Don Stevenson. The group attained a important level of praise as an beginning play for numerous well-liked artists of that time, and recorded one collection, eventually disseminated within 2005.

In LA he started encompassing Session musician|studio meeting work. He was particularly in request for his crooning, materializing on 100s of recordings all over the 1970s and 1980s. The National Association of Recording Arts and Sciences (NARAS) granted Champlin the Most Valuable Player peer prize for masculine context singers in 1980.

Champlin gained a Grammy Award for Best Rhythm and Blues Song in 1979 for co-writing the hit tune After The Love Has Gone with Jay Graydon and David Foster (which was produced well-liked by Earth, Wind Fire) and a second Grammy Award for Best Rhythm and Blues Song in 1982 for co-writing the tune Turn Your Love Around with Jay Graydon and Steve Lukather (which was produced well-liked by George Benson).

In 1979, Champlin was advanced toward by the then-widely prosperous group REO Speedwagon to append context voices on a few of their tunes, that emerge on the collection Nine Lives (REO Speedwagon album)|Nine Lives; this was the final collection in that REO Speedwagon had a mainly tough rock extremity.

This work permitted Champlin to come to be familiar with different in-demand meeting males such like Jay Graydon, David Foster, Steve Lukather (of Toto (band)|Toto). Among different creators that he operated with remained Al Jarreau, Boz Scaggs, The Tubes, Lee Ritenour, Amy Grant, and Nicky Trebek. He as well emerged on Barry Manilow's 1982 EP, Oh, Julie!.

In 1997, Champlin revitalized the Sons of Champlin, with who he resumes to play live exhibits all over the West Coast of the United States.

Since 2009 Champlin is cooperating as well with the Italian-American melodist, organizer, and maker Manuel De Peppe.

In the fall of 2011, Champlin played the B3 Hammond Organ on the tunes Moon Cry and Mississippi Creek by Curt Campbell and the Eclectic Beast Band.

Also in 2011, Champlin linked up with conductor Lars Erik Gudim and the Norwegian Radio Orchestra (KORK) in Oslo, Norway for a out of the ordinary execution screened December 27, 2011 on NRK TV in Norway.

Sharayah - Background

The head sole as of Unguarded was Find A Way. That tune proceeded No.1 on the Contemporary Christian Music|Christian tunes graphs, however as well gave Grant her foremost hit on Pop music|pop broadcast (as well like the

first-ever Contemporary Christian tunes tune to graph on Pop music|pop radio). The following 2 selects, Everywhere I Go and Wise Up, sustained Grant's newfound normal triumph and remained disseminated to either Christian and normal pop broadcast. Sharayah is alike to the foregoing selects in that it carries a distinctively 1980s Pop music|pop/Rock music|rock sound with motivational words. In 1986, Grant disseminated her foremost compiling collection, The Collection (Amy Grant album)|The Collection. Both Find a Way and Everywhere I Go remained contained, however neither Wise Up nor Sharayah produced the cut. Grant contained Sharayah on her following chief journey following Unguarded, the Lead Me On World Tour, in 1988-89. In the annums eversince, nevertheless, Sharayah has not endured as a pin of Grant's index and is seldom contained within her musical performance set catalogs. To date, the tune has not been contained on whatever of Amy Grant's formal compiling either finest of assemblages.

2002 in music - Awards

*The ensuing creators are inaugurated in to the Rock and Roll Hall of Fame: Isaac Hayes, Brenda Lee, Tom Petty and the Heartbreakers, Gene Pitney, Ramones and the Talking Heads

***Inductees of the Gospel Music Association|GMA Gospel Music Hall of Fame contain Pat Boone, and Amy Grant**

Amy Grant

'Amy Lee Grant' (born November 25, 1960) is an American singer-songwriter, performer, writer, media character and female actor, finest familiar for carrying out modern Christian music|Christian tunes. She has been referenced to like The Queen of Christian Pop. As of 2009, Grant stays the best-selling modern Christian tunes vocalist at any time, experiencing traded over 30 million components international.

Grant produced her first public appearance as a adolescent, and obtained celebrity in Christian tunes throughout the 1980s with such strikes as Father's Eyes, El Shaddai (song)|El Shaddai, and Angels (Amy Grant song)|Angels. In 1986, she netted her foremost Billboard Hot 100|Billboard Hot 100 No.1 tune in a duo with Peter Cetera, The Next Time I Fall. During the 1980s and 1990s, she grew to be one of the foremost Contemporary_Christian_music|CCM creators to Crossover (music)|cross over in to normal pop on the heels of her prosper-

ous collections Unguarded and Heart in Motion, the last one of that contained the No.1 sole Baby Baby (Amy Grant song)|Baby Baby.

Grant has gained 6 Grammy Awards, 25 Gospel Music Association Dove Awards, and had the foremost Christian collection at any time to proceed Platinum album|Platinum. Heart in Motion is her highest-selling collection, with over 5 million duplicates traded in the United States only. She was respected with a star on Hollywood Walk of Fame in 2005 for her donations to the amusement business.

Winter Wonderland - Recorded versions

*A Fine Frenzy as of the collection Oh Blue Christmas
*Abney Park (band)|Abney Park
*Aimee Mann
*Air Supply
*Alexis Stone Lopez
*Al Green
*78violet|Aly AJ
*America (band)|America
***Amy Grant**
*The Andrews Sisters
*Andy Griffith and Dennis Day for the cartoon out of the ordinary Frosty's Winter Wonderland
*Andy Williams
*Anne Murray
*Annie Lennox
*Aretha Franklin
*Arthur Fiedler and the Boston Pops
*Ashanti (entertainer)|Ashanti
*August Burns Red
*Kenneth Babyface Edmonds|Babyface
*Banaroo
*Barbara Mandrell
*Barry Manilow
*Bert Kaempfert
*Bette Midler as of the collection Cool Yule (2006)
*Billy Crash Craddock
*Billy Gilman as of the collection Classic Christmas (Billy Gilman album)|Classic Christmas
*Billy Idol
*Bing Crosby
*Blake Shelton

*Bob Dylan
*Booker T The MGs as of In the Christmas Spirit (Booker T album)|In the Christmas Spirit (1966)
*Boston Pops Orchestra
*Brad Paisley
*Brenda Lee
*Brooks Dunn
*Burl Ives
*Byron Lee the Dragonaires
*The California Raisins
*The Canadian Brass
*Cap'n Jazz
*Carnie Wilson Wendy Wilson
*The Carpenters (as piece of a potpourri with Silver Bells and White Christmas (weather)|White Christmas)
*Cascada as of It's Christmas Time (album)|It's Christmas Time (2012)
*Celtic Thunder
*Charlotte Church (Dream a Dream, 2000)
*Chet Atkins
*Chicago
*Children's Christmas
*Christina Christian
*Clay Aiken
*The Cocteau Twins
*Colbie Caillat as of Christmas In The Sand (2012)
*Collins Bootsy (Winterfunkyland) 2006
*Connie Francis
*Connie Talbot
*Cravin' Melon
*Cyndi Lauper
*Danny Davis (country musician)|The Nashville Brass
*Darius Rucker
*Darlene Love
*Dave Brubeck
*Dave Koz
*Dean Martin as of A Winter Romance (1959)
*The Del Rubio Triplets
*Demi Lovato
*Diamond Rio
*Diana Krall
*Diana Ross
*Dolly Parton (as piece of a potpourri with Sleigh Ride)

*Donny and Marie Osmond
*Doris Day (1964) for The Doris Day Christmas Album
*Galia Durant|Durant
*Eddy Arnold
*Ednita Nazario
*Ella Fitzgerald
*Elvis Presley
*Engelbert Humperdinck (singer)|Engelbert Humperdinck
*Enrico Ruggeri
*Erich Kunzel and the Cincinnati Pops Orchestra
*Etta James
*Eurythmics as of the collection A Very Special Christmas (album)|A Very Special Christmas (1987)
*Fleming and John
*Frank Sinatra
*Faith Hill
*Garth Brooks
*Gary Hoey
*George Strait
*The Golddiggers
*Goldfrapp
*Grandaddy as Alan Parsons in a Winter Wonderland (2000)
*Guy Lombardo
*Harry Connick, Jr. (instrumental on the When Harry Met Sally... (soundtrack)|soundtrack of When Harry Met Sally..., vocal on What a Night! A Christmas Album)
*Hellogoodbye
*Henry Ate
*Herb Alpert|Herb Alpert The Tijuana Brass
*Inge Sonja (Winterwunderland)
*J Rabbit
*Jackie Gleason
*James Taylor
*Jamie Cullum
*Jason Mraz
*Jesse McCartney
*Jewel (singer)|Jewel
*Joey McIntyre on his collection Come Home for Christmas
*Johnny Mathis
*Johnny Mercer
*Jonas Brothers
*Joy Electric
*The Judds

*Kate Havnevik
*Kathy Troccoli
*Keahiwai
*Kenny G
*Kikki Danielsson (as piece of a potpourri with Sleigh Ride) [http://smdb.kb.se/catalog/id/001548791 Kikki Danielsson, Nu ar Det advent] Retrieved November 29, 2011
*Kim Wilde and Rick Astley
*Kiri Te Kanawa
*Larry Carlton
*Larry Groce on the collection Disney's Christmas Favourites
*Leon Redbone
*Leona Lewis as of the collection Christmas, With Love
*Lionel Richie
*Liz Phair
*Louis Armstrong
*Lou Rawls
*Macy Gray
*Madison Park (musical duo)|Madison Park
*Mandy Moore
*The Manhattan Transfer as of the collection An Acapella Christmas
*Mannheim Steamroller
*Mantovani
*Martina McBride as of the collection White Christmas (Martina McBride album)|White Christmas
*MercyMe
*Michael Bolton
*Michael Bublé
*Miley Cyrus
*Mireille Mathieu (in German)
*Mitch Miller

*Mormon Tabernacle Choir
*Neil Diamond
*Neil Sedaka
*Newsboys
*Olivia Holt
*Ozzy Osbourne Jessica Simpson
*The Partridge Family
*Pat Boone
*Pat Green
*Paul Anka
*Paul Carrack

*Peggy Lee
*Percy Faith
*Perry Como
*Peter Alexander (Austrian performer and singer)|Peter Alexander (in German: Winterwunderland)
*Peter Nero
*Phantom Planet
*Pink Army
*The Platters
*Point of Grace
*Postmarks
*Radiohead
*Randy Travis
*Rankin Bass
*Ray Charles
*Ray Conniff
*Rene De Haan (Kerstfeest In Ons Mooie Nederland)
*Rene Marie
*Reparata and the Delrons
*Ricky Van Shelton
*Ringo Starr
*Robert Goulet
*The Roches
*Rockapella
*Rod Stewart
*The Ronettes
*Rosemary Clooney
*Royce Campbell
*Sammy Kershaw
*The Saturdays
*Selena Gomez The Scene
*Scott Weiland
*Shirley Horn
*Sin City Sinners
*Smokey Robinson The Miracles as of Christmas with The Miracles (1963)
*Steve Goodman
*Steve Lawrence Eydie Gormé
*Steve Lukather
*Steven Curtis Chapman
*Steve Taylor
*Stryper
*Sugarland (band)|Sugarland
*Take 6

*Tanya Tucker
*Tara MacLean
*Taylor Horn
*Ted Weems
*The Three Tenors
*The Toasters
*Till Brönner (feat. Stevie Woods (musician)|Stevie Woods)
*Tina Robin (Winter Wonderland Cha Cha)
*Toby Keith
*Tony Bennett
*Tony Christie
*Travis Tritt
*Tuck Andress
*Vanessa Hudgens
*Vic Damone
*Victoria Justice
*Vince Gill
*Whitney Keyes with Holly Players Orchestra
*Willie Nelson
*Wynonna Judd

In extension, the tune was integrated by Michael Kamen as a tension subject in to his result for the 1988 feature Die Hard.

Bill Gaither (gospel singer) - Industry Influence

Gaither has been a dad figure to numerous junior artists within the Contemporary Christian tunes business, when serving to lengthen the professions of these whoever appeared beforehand him. Mark Lowry, Michael W. Smith, Carman (singer)|Carman, Sandi Patty, Steve Green (singer)|Steve Green, Don Francisco (Christian musician)|Don Francisco, Amy Grant, Michael English (singer)|Michael English, Jonathan Pierce, Karla Worley, and Cynthia Clawson are altogether CCM creators whoever whichever received their commence either grew to be well-liked when touring with the Gaithers.

He has preserved the Gaither Vocal Band with a diversity of singers via the annums, containing Gary McSpadden, Steve Green (singer)|Steve Green, Lee Young, Jon Mohr, Larnelle Harris, Michael English (singer)|Michael English, Lemuel Miller, Jim Murray, Mark Lowry, Terry Franklin, Buddy Mullins, Jonathan Pierce, Guy Penrod, David Phelps, Russ Taff, Marshall Hall (singer)|Marshall Hall and Wes Hampton. Guy Penrod and Mark Lowry remained the participants of the Gaither Vocal

Band with the lengthiest term beyond Bill Gaither him self. Guy Penrod was with the cluster as of 1995–2008 and Mark Lowry as of 1988-2001. It was proclaimed in January 2009 that Mark Lowry, Michael English (singer)|Michael English and David Phelps remained rejoining the group; at the similar time the statement was produced that Guy Penrod and Marshall Hall (singer)|Marshall Hall remained leaving in line to follow a unaccompanied vocation.

Gaither's Homecoming visits, that commenced in 1991, accompanied alltogether chief stars of the southern canon and CCM business, sparking a resurgence of the categories. The visits have traded further compared to 1.1 million passes athwart the planet, and have contained such noteworthy sites as the Kennedy Center and Carnegie Hall. Pollstar recorded the journey as vending further passes in 2004 compared to Elton John, Fleetwood Mac either Rod Stewart. Lynda Randle, The Isaacs, Russ Taff, the Hoppers, Jessy Dixon and numerous further have accomplished on the visits.

Amy Grant discography - Digital only releases

***ITunes Originals - Amy Grant, disseminated 2005**
*Songs as of Mosaic, disseminated October 23, 2007 on iTunes
*Christmas: The Complete Collection, disseminated November 18, 2008 on iTunes
*She Colors My Day EP, disseminated May 5, 2009
*Top 5: Hits EP, disseminated January 4, 2013

Jesus movement - Belmont Avenue Church of Christ

Don Finto was named to Belmont Avenue Church of Christ (now plainly [http://www.belmont.org Belmont Church]), an ailing aged internal town kirk in Nashville, Tennessee on Music Row amid the common lodging and some colleges – Peabody, Vanderbilt University|Vanderbilt and Belmont College etcetera. By the summertime of 1971, the associateship spin had let go to regarding 75 aging participants. The kirk had normal origins in the Churches of Christ, however was changed and resolutely put in the Jesus motion by an inflow of countercultural Christians.

Seating ran out, with folks sitting on the pane sills either on the stage. It was not unusual to notice them strolling the nastiest bits of Lower Broadway attesting to prostitute|hookers and addicts. Within a annum either 2 the companionship matured to 100s and the well known Koinonia Coffee House was unlocked, being run by Bill and Sherry Duguid at 1004 16th Avenue South, as it was familiar additionally, and a annum either thus afterward was guided by Bob and Peggy Hughey. The second Koinonia constructing following entrance at 1000 16th Avenue S. (16th and Grand) had been an aged Five and

Dime store on Music Square that had shut down. The musical performances grasped there on Saturday and Sunday aided East shore Christian tunes to mature in reputation. The home group was Dogwood, and numerous well known performers frequently hit the stage, containing Dogwood, Amy Grant, Brown Bannister, Chris Christian, Don Francisco (Christian musician)|Don Francisco, Fireworks, Annie and Steve Chapman, Clay In The Potter's Hand and numerous other ones.

Contemporary Christian

'Contemporary Christian music' (or 'CCM'—and sometimes 'inspirational music') is a category of contemporary well-liked tunes that is lyrically concentrated on interests worried with the Christianity|Christian persuasion. Today, the expression is characteristically applied to allude to pop music|pop, Rock music|rock, either Contemporary reverence music|praise reverence methods. Artists depicting the category include

MercyMe, Casting Crowns, Jeremy Camp, Third Day, Matthew West, tobyMac, Chris Tomlin, Brandon Heath and Aaron Shust. Historically, Amy Grant, Jars of Clay, DC Talk, Steven Curtis Chapman, Newsboys and Michael W. Smith have as well belonged to this category.

The business is constituted by the Billboard (magazine)|Billboard Christian Albums, Hot Christian Songs Hot Christian AC (Adult Contemporary), Christian CHR, Soft AC/Inspirational, and Christian Digital Songs graphs. On the iTunes Store, the category is constituted like piece of the Christian and canon category.In the US iTunes store, the part is allowed Christian Gospel. In the UK iTunes store, it's Gospel. Canada's and Australia's iTunes part is allowed Inspirational.

Other sub-genres such like Christian punk, Christian diehard, Christian alloy and Christian hip jump, though not usually contemplated CCM, may as well come under the genre's parasol. Contemporary reverence tunes is as well integrated in contemporary CCM. Contemporary reverence is either recorded and accomplished throughout kirk facilities.

Several normal creators, such like The Byrds, Bob Dylan, Van Morrison, Elvis Presley, Creed (band)|Creed, Lifehouse (band)|Lifehouse and U2, have dealt with Christian subjects in their tunes, up till now are not piece of the CCM business.

In Concert Volume Two (Amy Grant album) - Personnel

***Amy Grant: Vocals.**
*Dana Key: Guitars, Vocals.
*Billy Sprague: Guitars, Vocals.
*Mike Brignardello: Bass.
*Greg Morrow: Drums.
*Eddie DeGarmo: Keyboards.
*Gerry Peters: Oberheim.
*David Durham: Background voices.
*Theresa Ellis: Background voices.
*Jan Harris: Background voices.
*Gary Pigg: Background voices.

Gordon Kennedy (musician) - Contemporary Christian music

In 1984, simply a pair annums out of school, Kennedy joined the modern Christian cluster WhiteHeart once his elevated educational institution pal, at the moment famous maker Dann Huff, left the cluster and suggested him to fill the mark. Kennedy visited for 6 annums with WhiteHeart, throughout that time the group disseminated one of his best-loved collaborations to date, the 1989 collection Freedom. He left WhiteHeart in 1990 to get off the way and follow meeting work.

The annums that right away pursued remained essential in forming Kennedy's existence and vocation. He consumed a limited annums scraping by and founding him self as a meeting guitar player, firstly for modern Christian creators like Amy Grant, Twila Paris, Susan Ashton, PFR and Steven Curtis Chapman. At the similar time, home existence radically altered for him and his spouse with the acquisition of their foremost home and the birthing of their 2 kids.

Michael Card - Other works featuring Michael Card

*Christmas (1988) Michael Card sings What Child Is This?. Not accessible somewhere else.
*Coram Deo (1992) Michael Card sings 2 Duets with Charlie Peacock: Amen! Praise and Glory! and Lord of Love.

*Steve Green (singer)|Steve Green People Need the Lord (1994) Duet on Embrace the Cross.
*Promise Keepers- A Life That Shows (1994) Song Bearers of the Light, afterward accessible on Poiema, debuts here.
*Wedding collection (1995) Michael Card's Earthly Perfect Harmony and Lord of Love, a duo with Charlie Peacock emerge.
*Wes King A Room Full of Stories (1997) Wrote Who But God?
*Songs 4 Life: Feel the Power (1998) Love Crucified Arose
*Songs 4 life: Renew your heart! (1998) Joy In The Journey
*John Michael Talbot Cave Of The Heart (1999) Backing voices.
*30 Years of Award-Winning Music (1999) El Shaddai
***Songs From The Book (1999) The Book shows. Michael Card as well plays auditory stringed instrument on El Shaddai sung by Winans Phase 2 Amy Grant.**
*John Michael Talbot Wisdom (2001) Backing voices.
*I Will Be Here: 10 Contemporary Wedding Songs contains The Wedding
*Giving You the Rest of My Life: 13 Contemporary Classics for Memorable Weddings Michael Card Charlie Peacock's Amen! Praise and Glory is contained, however Charlie Peacock is not recognized as crooning.
*Let Us Pray: The National Day of Prayer Album Heal Our Land
*My Cry Ascends: New Parish Psalms (2010) (various creators, Gregory Wilbur, composer)http://www.ligonier.org/store/my-cry-ascends-new-parish-psalms-cd/

List of guitarists - G

*Steve Gaines (Lynyrd Skynyrd)
*Declan Galbraith
*Eric Gale
*Noel Gallagher (Oasis (band)|Oasis)
*Rory Gallagher
*Shane Gallagher (+44 (band)|+44)
*Cliff Gallup
*Frank Gambale
*Tim Gane (Stereolab)
*Sunil Ganguly
*Charly García (Sui Generis, Porsuigieco, La Máquina de Hacer Pájaros, Serú Girán)
*Enrik Garcia (Dark Moor)
*Jerry Garcia (Grateful Dead)
*Ricardo Garcia (musician)|Ricardo Garcia
*Chuck Garvey (moe.)
*Kyle Gass (Tenacious D)

*Synyster Gates (Avenged Sevenfold, Pinkly Smooth)
*Danny Gatton
*Dick Gaughan
*Björn Gelotte (In Flames)
*Vicki Genfan
*Antony Genn (The Mescaleros, The Hours (band)|The Hours)
*Dave Genn (Matthew Good Band)
*Lowell George (Little Feat)
*Rocky George (Suicidal Tendencies)
*Janick Gers (Iron Maiden)
*Per Gessle (Gyllene Tider, Roxette)
*Andy Gibb
*Barry Gibb (Bee Gees)
*Ben Gibbard (Death Cab for Cutie, The Postal Service, ¡All-Time Quarterback!)
*Billy Gibbons (ZZ Top)
*Paul Gilbert (Mr. Big (band)|Mr. Big, Racer X (band)|Racer X)
*João Gilberto
*Daniel Gildenlöw (Pain of Salvation)
*Nick Gilder (Sweeney Todd (band)|Sweeney Todd)
*Brad Gillis (Night Ranger)
*David Gilmour (Pink Floyd)
*Vince Gill (Pure Prairie League)
*Gordon Giltrap
*Greg Ginn (Black Flag (band)|Black Flag)
*Chad I Ginsburg (CKY (band)|CKY)
*Mauro Giuliani
*George Gobel
*Nicolas Godin (Air (French band)|Air)
*Mircea Gogoncea
*Lynval Golding (The Specials)
*Sander Gommans (After Forever)
*Pier Gonella (Mastercastle-Necrodeath)
*Adam Gontier (Three Days Grace)
*Dave Gonzalez (guitarist)|Dave Gonzalez (The Paladins, Hacienda Brothers)
*José González (singer)|José González
*Pedro Javier González
*Myles Goodwyn (April Wine)
*Nina Gordon (Veruca Salt)
*Martin Gore (Depeche Mode)
*Scott Gorham (Thin Lizzy)
*Grisha Goryachev
*Chris Goss (Masters of Reality)
*Stone Gossard (Green River (band)|Green River, Mother Love Bone, Temple of the

Dog, Pearl Jam)
*Manuel Göttsching (Ash Ra Tempel)
*Johnny Goudie (Goudie (band)|Goudie)
*Ellie Goulding
*Guthrie Govan
*Laura Jane Grace (Against Me!)
*Gerhard Graf-Martinez
*Davey Graham
***Amy Grant**
*James Grant (musician)|James Grant (Love and Money (band)|Love and Money)
*Rocky Gray (Soul Embraced)
*Jay Graydon
*Doug Grean
*Boris Grebenshchikov (Aquarium (band)|Aquarium)
*Dallas Green (musician)|Dallas Green (Alexisonfire, City and Colour)
*Freddie Green (Count Basie)
*Gary Green (musician)|Gary Green (Gentle Giant)
*Grant Green
*Peter Green (musician)|Peter Green (Fleetwood Mac)
*Norman Greenbaum
*Alex Greenwald (Phantom Planet)
*Brian Greenway (April Wine, Mashmakhan)
*Jonny Greenwood (Radiohead)
*Dave Gregory (musician)|Dave Gregory (XTC)
*David Grier
*Ryan Griffiths (guitarist)|Ryan Griffiths (The Vines (band)|The Vines)
*Steve Grimes (The Farm (band)|The Farm)
*Carl Johan Grimmark (Narnia (band)|Narnia, Rob Rock, Saviour Machine, Beautiful Sin)
*Dave Grohl (Foo Fighters, Nirvana (band)|Nirvana)
*Luther Grosvenor (Spooky Tooth)
*Todd Grubbs
*Lalo Guerrero
*Guinga
*Michael Gulezian
*Trey Gunn (King Crimson), (David Sylvian)
*Tracii Guns (L.A. Guns, Guns N' Roses, Brides of Destruction)
*Brett Gurewitz (Bad Religion, Error (band)|Error)
*James Gurley (Big Brother and the Holding Company)
*Michael Gurley (Dada)
*Gus G (Firewind)
*Buddy Guy

Adult contemporary music - 1980s—Adult contemporary succeeds as radio format

On April 7, 1979, the Easy Listening graph formally grew to be familiar like Adult Contemporary, and these 2 terms have stayed coherent in the designation of the graph at any time subsequently. Adult modern tunes grew to be one of the most well-liked broadcast setups of the 1980s. The development of AC was a normal effect of the propagation that foremost paid attention to the further specific tunes of the mid-late 1970s increasing aged and not being engrossed in the weighty alloy music|heavy alloy and hip jump music|rap/hip-hop tunes that a spic-and-span propagation aided to control the Top 40 graphs.

Mainstream AC its normal self has developed in a alike style over the years; customary AC creators like Barbra Streisand, the The Carpenters|Carpenters, Dionne Warwick, Barry Manilow, John Denver, and Olivia Newton-John noticed it tougher to have chief Top 40 strikes as the 1980s sported on, and expected to the impact of MTV, creators whoever remained pins of the Contemporary Hit Radio setup, such like Richard Marx, Michael Jackson, Bonnie Tyler, George Michael and the belated Laura Branigan started crossing over to the AC graphs with considerable incidence. However, with the amalgamation of MTV and AC broadcast, grown-up modern emerged tougher to describe as whichever, recognized soft-rock creators of the bygones (who remained nevertheless graphing pop hits), either the normal broadcast fare as of recently developed creators at the time.

The quantity of crossing amid the AC graph and the Hot 100 has diverse founded on in what way a lot the passing pop tunes tendencies of the periods pleaded to grown-up ones listening. Not numerous discotheque either New Wave music|new Wave tunes remained especially prosperous on the AC graph throughout the belated 1970s and first 1980s, and a lot of the hip-hop and tougher rock tunes highlighted onto Contemporary hit radio|CHR setups afterward in the period of 10 years ought to have been intolerable on AC broadcast.

Although dance-oriented, microelectronic pop and rock controlled the 1980s, malleable rock/AC tunes relished a gentle triumph cheers to creators like Amy Grant, Lionel Richie, Christopher Cross, Dan Hill, Leo Sayer, Billy Ocean, Julio Iglesias, Bertie Higgins and Tommy Page. No tune consumed further compared to 6 7-day periods at #1 on this graph throughout the 1980s, with 9 tunes achieving that achievement. Two of those remained by Lionel Richie, You Are (Lionel Richie song)|You Are in 1983 and Hello (Lionel Richie song)|Hello in 1984, that as well extended #1 on the Hot 100.

In 1989, Linda Ronstadt disseminated Cry Like a Rainstorm, Howl Like the Wind, depicted by reviewers as the foremost genuine Adult Contemporary collection of the period of 10 years, presenting American psyche vocalist Aaron Neville on some of the 12 traces. The collection was endorsed Triple Platinum in the United States only and grew to be a chief triumph all over the sphere. The Grammy Award-winning selects, Don't Know Much and All My Life (Linda Ronstadt song)|All My Life, remained either long-running #1 Adult Contemporary strikes. Several extra selects as of the disc produced the AC Top 10 as well. The collection gained over numerous reviewers in the demand to describe AC, and emerged to shift the acceptance and receipt of AC tunes in to normal day to day broadcast play.

48th Grammy Awards - Gospel

Awards for Gospel music:
*Grammy Award for Best Gospel Performance|Best Gospel Performance
:CeCe Winans for Pray
*Grammy Award for Best Gospel Song|Best Gospel Song
:Yolanda Adams, James Harris III, Terry Lewis James 'big Jim' Wright, songwriters for Be Blessed, accomplished by Yolanda Adams
*Grammy Award for Best Pop/Contemporary Gospel Album|Best Pop/Contemporary Gospel Album
:Casting Crowns for Lifesong
*Grammy Award for Best Rock Gospel Album|Best Rock Gospel Album
:Audio Adrenaline for Until My Heart Caves In
*Grammy Award for Best Southern, Country either Bluegrass Gospel Album|Best Southern, Country either Bluegrass Gospel Album
:Amy Grant for Rock of Ages...Hymns Faith
*Grammy Award for Best Traditional Soul Gospel Album|Best Traditional Soul Gospel Album
:Donnie McClurkin for Psalms, Hymns Spiritual Songs
*Grammy Award for Best Contemporary Soul Gospel Album|Best Contemporary Soul Gospel Album
:CeCe Winans for Purified
*Grammy Award for Best Gospel Choir either Chorus Album|Best Gospel Choir either Chorus Album
:Gladys Knight, chorus director Saints Unified Voices for One Voice

Michael Card - Musician

Card not ever designed to be a non-amateur performer. He received his commence once his university teacher and adviser, William L. Lane, questioned Card to record a few tunes to escort once a week talks at their kirk. His pal, performer Randy Scruggs, additionally questioned him to record a demonstration tape thus

Scruggs might acquire a assignment like a maker. The record label decided to employ Scruggs as long like his foremost program was to make an collection presenting Card. Since then Card has disseminated 19 first collections and at minimum 6 compiling collections. Another collection, Starkindler, is devised of Card's explanations of customary Celtic music|Celtic hymns. The collections frequently contain one either 2 spic-and-span tunes alongside with formerly disseminated matter. With the anomaly of Starkindler, Card records the huge major part of the tunes he records (although occasionally with collaborators).

Many of Card's collections are organized about a uniting subject. For instance, the tunes as of The Beginning are altogether founded on the Pentateuch. The single tunes have topics such like Genesis (Hebrew Bible)|Genesis, Leviticus, Abraham, Isaac and Moses. Card is especially adept at connected hard either unclear notions as of the Old Testament to further comprehensible subjects as of the New Testament. For instance, the tune Jubilee chats about the time of respite and the discharge as of arrears and bondage commanded in the Jubilee (Biblical)|Jubilee annum like depicted in Leviticus 25, however as well divulges in what way the thought climaxed in the respite and liberty as of censure presented via Jesus.

Card's nearly all well known tune is El Shaddai (song)|El Shaddai, that was recorded by Amy Grant as well like by Card him self. Grant's transcriptioning was designated No. 326 on the Recording Industry Association of America|RIAA's catalog of 365 Songs of the Century in 2001. Other well-liked Card tunes contain Immanuel, Joy in the Journey, and Heal Our Land. Heal Our Land was ordered as the 1993 National Day of Prayer's subject tune.

Despite his triumph in tunes, Card has on every relevant occasion preserved that his tunes vocation is subordinate to his naming as a Bible educator. He has at periods distanced him self as of the CCM business by disapproving the encouragement of characters over melodic content[http://www.webcitation.org/query?url=http://www.geocities.com/Athens/Forum/3505/cardconv.htmldate=2009-10-25+05:59:59 Conversations/Michael Card, CCM 12/95] and the moving prominence off as of God in line to vend further collections.

One present tunes program is his authoring and mentoring of performers under the [http://ByFor.org ByFor.org] Project.

Joni Mitchell - Influence on other artists

Mitchell's work has had an impact on numerous different creators, containing Mikael Åkerfeldt, Marillion, their erstwhile singer and songwriter Fish (singer)|Fish, Paul

Carrack, and Taylor Swift. Madonna (entertainer)|Madonna has as well quoted Mitchell as the foremost feminine creator that actually talked to her as a teenager; I was actually, actually in to Joni Mitchell. I realized any expression to Court and Spark; I worshipped her once I was in High School. Blue (Joni Mitchell album)|Blue is astonishing. I ought to have to utter of altogether the females I've perceived, she had the most heartfelt result on myself as of a poetic point of view.

A numeral of creators have had triumph cover version|covering Mitchell's tunes. Judy Collins's 1967 transcriptioning of Both Sides Now extended No. 8 on Billboard graphs and was a success in the vocation of either creators (Mitchell's own transcriptioning did not perceive discharge till 2 annums afterward, on her second collection Clouds (Joni Mitchell album)|Clouds). This is Mitchell's most-covered tune by long, with 587 adaptations recorded at newest reckon. Hole (band)|Hole as well veiled Both Sides Now in 1991 on their first public appearance collection, Pretty on the Inside, retitling it Clouds, with the words changed by frontwoman Courtney Love. Pop cluster Neighborhood (band)|Neighborhood in 1970 and Amy Grant in 1995 netted strikes with covers of Big Yellow Taxi, the second nearly all veiled tune in Mitchell's repertory (with 223 covers). Recent deliverances of this tune have been by Counting Crows in 2002 and Nena in 2007. Janet Jackson applied a tester of the chorus of Big Yellow Taxi as the bottom line of her 1997 hit sole Got 'Til It's Gone, that as well attributes rapper Q-Tip (rapper)|Q-Tip indicating Joni Mitchell not ever reposes. Rap creators Kanye West and Mac Dre have as well sampled Mitchell's voices in their tunes. In extension, Annie Lennox has veiled Ladies of the Canyon for the B-side of her 1995 hit No More I Love You's. Mandy Moore veiled Help Me in 2003. In 2004 vocalist George Michael veiled her tune Edith and the Kingpin for a broadcast show. River has been one of the most well-liked tunes veiled in new annums, with adaptations by Dianne Reeves (1999), James Taylor (recorded for TV in 2000, and aimed at CD discharge in 2004), Allison Crowe (2004), Rachael Yamagata (2004), Aimee Mann (2005), and Sarah McLachlan (2006). McLachlan as well did a variant of Blue in 1996, and Cat Power recorded a cover of Blue in 2008. Other Mitchell covers contain the well known Woodstock (song)|Woodstock by either Crosby, Stills Nash (and Young)|Crosby, Stills, Nash and Young and Matthews Southern Comfort, This Flight Tonight by Nazareth (band)|Nazareth, and popular adaptations of Woodstock by Eva Cassidy and A Case of You by Tori Amos, Michelle Branch, Jane Monheit, Prince (musician)|Prince, Diana Krall, James Blake (musician)|James Blake, and Ana Moura. A 40th day of remembrance variant of Woodstock was disseminated within 2009 by Nick Vernier Band presenting Ian Matthews (formerly of Matthews Southern Comfort).

Prince's variant of A Case of U emerged on A Tribute to Joni Mitchell, a 2007 compiling disseminated by Nonesuch Records, that as well highlighted Björk (The Boho

Dance), Caetano Veloso (Dreamland), Emmylou Harris (The Magdalene Laundries), Sufjan Stevens (Free Man in Paris) and Cassandra Wilson (For the Roses), amid other ones. Some of the recordings remained produced in the belated 1990s once a program allowed A Case of Joni was elaborated however left deficient. Among these whoever recorded traces for the foremost accolade collection, that stay unreleased, remained Janet Jackson, Steely Dan, and Sheryl Crow. Chaka Khan recorded Ladies Man as of Mitchell's LP Wild Things Run Fast on her 2007 CD named Funk This.

Several additional tunes mention Joni Mitchell. The tune Our House (Crosby, Stills, Nash Young song)|Our House by Graham Nash alludes to Nash's two-year matter with Mitchell at the time that Crosby, Stills Nash and Young recorded the Déjà Vu (Crosby, Stills, Nash Young album)|Déjà Vu collection. Led Zeppelin's Going to California was indicated to be authored about Robert Plant and Jimmy Page's Limerence|infatuation with Mitchell, a assert that appears to be borne out by the reality that, in live executions, Plant frequently speaks Joni following the line To notice a monarch short of a ruler, they utter she plays stringed instrument and bawls and sings. Jimmy Page utilizes a duple let go D stringed instrument adjusting alike to the alternate tunings Mitchell utilizes. The Sonic Youth tune Hey Joni is designated for Mitchell. Alanis Morissette as well references Mitchell in one of her tunes, Your House. British people vocalist Frank Turner references Mitchell in his tune Sunshine State. The Prince (musician)|Prince tune The Ballad of Dorothy Parker holds the words – 'Oh, my best-loved song' she indicated – and it was Joni crooning 'Help myself I consider I'm falling' . Lavender (Marillion song)|Lavender by Marillion was somewhat affected by going via parks paying attention to Joni Mitchell, depending to singer and songwriter Fish (singer)|Fish.

In 2003, playwright Bryden MacDonald started When All the Slaves Are Free, a melodic variety show founded on Mitchell's tunes.Gabrielle H. Cody and Evert Sprinchorn, The Columbia cyclopaedia of contemporary drama: M-Z, Volume 2 (p. 843). Columbia University Press, 2007. ISBN 9780231144247.

To commemorate Mitchell's 70th anniversary, the 2013 Luminato Festival in Toronto grasped a set of accolade musical performances allowed Joni: A Portrait in Song – A Birthday Happening Live at Massey Hall on June 18 19. Performers contained Rufus Wainwright, Herbie Hancock, Esperanza Spalding, and scarce executions by Mitchell herself.

Hawk Nelson - Smile, It's the End of the World (2006–2007)

On April 4, 2006 Hawk Nelson disseminated Connect Sets EP with 6 auditory traces including: Bring Em' Out, Thing We Go Through, and California.

In October 2005, the group re-released Letters to the President, with spic-and-span matter containing their cover of The Who's My Generation, 3 auditory adaptations of a few of their strikes, and a restricted issue cover. Hawk Nelson plays the party group for the feature Yours, Mine and Ours (2005 film)|Yours, Mine and Ours (2005). Their tunes The Show and Something on my Mind remained highlighted in the game Thrillville in 2006.

On March 27, 2007, Hawk Nelson disseminated a Double Take that contains selections as of Letters to the President and Smile It's the End of the World. They additionally disseminated a holiday-themed EP named Holiday Trio on November 20, 2007.

The group disseminated their second workshop collection, Smile, It's the End of the World, on April 4, 2006. The collection was as well co-written by Trevor McNevan of Thousand Foot Krutch. The collection gained a GMA Canada Covenant Awards|Covenant Award for Modern Rock/Alternative Album of the Year in 2006. The album's foremost sole, Everything You Ever Wanted, proceeded on to strike No.1 for 9 7-day periods on the RR (magazine)|RR Christian CHR graph, and was the 4th most-played tune of 2006. The group consumed the mid of 2006 touring the chief Christian tunes fetes, and as well took part in Jeremy Camp's Beyond Measure journey. Hawk Nelson disseminated a three-track Christmas Extended play|EP named Gloria EP|Gloria on November 21, 2006, and then visited with TobyMac's Winter Wonder Slam journey alongside with The Afters, Family Force 5, and Ayiesha Woods.

Bulletproof Records and maker Ralph Sall have constructed the compiling Charlotte's Web: Music Inspired By The Motion Picture presenting tunes by Christian creators containing Hawk Nelson, Amy Grant, and Billy Ray Cyrus, that was disseminated December 12, 2006. In extension, Bob Carlisle, Leigh Nash (Sixpence None The Richer), and The Send have altogether donated unique traces.

Hawk Nelson accomplished in 2006 on the Fringe Stage at Creation Festival Northwest, additionally once more on the principal stage at Creation in 2007. They accomplished at some time amid July 25–28, 2007, at Creation Festival Northwest on the Main Stage, and they played once more on the Fringe Stage at Creation Festival Northeast at some time amid June 27–30, 2007. In 2007, (and once more in 2009), Hawk Nelson accomplished at Winter Jam with a diversity of different Christian groups, containing Newsong, Jeremy Camp, Steven Curtis Chapman, Sanctus Real, and Britt Nicole. Hawk Nelson as well visited with MxPx, Run Kid Run, Project

86, The Fold, and The Classic Crime on the Tooth and Nail Tour.

In 2007, Aaron Tosti left the group to follow additional melodic undertakings and was substituted by Justin Benner.

Mosaic: Pieces of My Life So Far - Heirlooms

Named following her prosperous sole, Heirlooms, as of 1983's A Christmas Album (Amy Grant album)|A Christmas Album, the second themed part in Mosaic bothers Grant's kin, either the one she matured up with and the one she strained as an grown-up via 2 weddings. The narratives in this part characteristically disclose an encounter that had a heartfelt influence on the author's existence either the existence of her kids.

The tune words held inside the Heirlooms part are: Heirlooms, Say Once More, How Can We See That Far?, Saved by Love, Baby Baby (Amy Grant song)|Baby Baby, Mimi's House, I Will Remember You (Amy Grant song)|I Will Remember You, Missing You (Amy Grant song)|Missing You, Oh Tennessee, and True Love (Amy Grant song)|True Love. The final 2 tunes are noteworthy since, as of the book's issue within 2007, neither had been recorded by Grant either anybody other. Mosaic pronounced the first public appearance of either tunes, that have been unverified reported to be prospective traces on a time to come workshop collection.

Independent record label - History

Independent tags have a prolonged past of directing elaborations in well-liked tunes, expanding back to the post-war time in the United States.Rogan, Johnny (1992) Introduction in The Guinness Who's Who of Indie and New Wave Music, Guinness Publishing, ISBN 0-85112-579-4 Disputes with chief tags about issuing guided to a rapid increase of tags concentrating in Country Music|country, jazz, and Blues. Sun Records played an essential piece in the creation of Rock 'n' spin as well like region, with creators such like Elvis Presley, Carl Perkins, Johnny Cash, Jerry Lee Lewis, Roy Orbison, and Charlie Rich. The autonomous tags normally directed their deliverances at a not so large however dedicated public, not depending on large number selling for triumph, assigning creators a lot further range for trialling and creative liberty.

In the United Kingdom throughout the 1950s and 1960s, the chief record businesses EMI, Philips Records|Philips, and Decca Records|Decca had thus a lot power that autonomous tags fought to come to be recognized. Several British creators started autonomous tags as outlet vents for their work containing Joe

Meek (Triumph), Andrew Oldham (Immediate), and Larry Page (British vocalist and manager)|Larry Page (Page One). Chrysalis Records, started by Chris Wright and Terry Ellis, was maybe the most prosperous as of that age, and sustained to enlarge. Several chief rock stars set up their personal autonomous tags - The Beatles with Apple Records, The Rolling Stones with Rolling Stones Records, and Elton John with The Rocket Record Company, however they normally disappointed as profit-oriented undertakings either remained swallowed up by the majors.

No past of autonomous tags may be perfect short of mention to the most prosperous autonomous record label of altogether time, AM Records. Founded in 1962 by cornetist Herb Alpert (the A) and record agent Jerry Moss (the M), AM was originally the label and distributer for Alpert's own Tijuana Brass hit recordings, however the label swiftly started autographing additional creators. Over its 37-year run, AM traded records as of such creators as Sergio Mendes Brazil '66, The Carpenters, Phil Ochs, Carole King (AM dispersed her label, Ode_Records|Ode), Joe Cocker, Free (band)|Free, Cat Stevens, Procol Harum, Humble Pie (band)|Humble Pie, Peter Frampton, The Police and Sting (musician)|Sting as a unaccompanied creator, Styx (band)|Styx, Bryan Adams, Amy Grant, Suzanne Vega and Sheryl Crow. AM was as well the opening distributer of Windham Hill Records and George Harrison's Dark Horse Records. Alpert and Moss traded AM Records to Polygram in 1989 with the caveat that Alpert and Moss ought to resume to run it separately. Polygram was afterward purchased by Universal Music Group in 1998 and AM as a label and a brand passed away the following annum. There is itty-bitty argumentation that AM's 37-year run and index of either monetarily prosperous and seriously admired recordings qualifies it like the most prosperous autonomous record label in past.

The punk rock age accompanied about a revolving point for autonomous tags, the do-it-yourself ethos of the time identifying the appearance of a excess of autonomous tags. In the US, autonomous tags such like Beserkley as well noticed triumph with creators such like The Modern Lovers. Many of the UK tags finished ended up autographing dispersion transacts with chief tags to stay feasible, however other ones kept their self-determination (e.g. Industrial Records, Factory Records, Warp_(record_label)|Warp, Ninja Tune, Wax On, BlancoMusic) and the reason that appeared to describe autonomous tags was dispersion, that had to be autonomous of the majors for records to be contained within the UK Indie Chart, that was foremost assembled in 1980.Lazell, Barry (1997) Indie Hits 1980-1989, Cherry Red Books, ISBN 0-9517206-9-4 The expression 'indie' and the graph its normal self was unconnected to a concrete category of tunes, and the graph highlighted a varied span of tunes, as of punk to reggae, to Middle of the way (music)|MOR and normal Pop music|pop, containing some strikes as of the likes of Kylie Minogue and Jason Donovan on the PWL label. The belated 1970s had noticed the formation of autonomous dispersion businesses such like Pinnacle and Spartan, assigning autonomous tags an effectual intents of dispersion short of including the majors. The state of affairs ameliorated additional with the formation of 'The Cartel', an alliance of businesses such like Rough Trade Records, Backs Records, and Red Rhino, whoever aided to take deliverances as of not so large tags and get them in to the markets countrywide. The 'Indie Chart' grew to be a chief origin of subjection for creators on indie tags, with the top 10 selects frequently screened on the national TV show The Chart Show. By the belated 1980s, the chief tags had recognized an occasion to split spic-and-span acts by way of the indie graph, and started positioning up subordinate tags that remained funded by the majors however dispersed by way of the autonomous net-work, thus being entitled for the graph. With the chief tags successfully thrusting the bona fide indie tags out of the trade, the autonomous graph grew to be fewer important in the first 1990s, with 'alternative' progressively being applied to report creators, and 'indie' frequently applied to report a broad span of guitar-based rock and pop. The Offspring's 1994 collection Smash (The Offspring album)|Smash is the biggest vending autonomous record of altogether time.Sputnikmusic. [http://www.sputnikmusic.com/review/11903/The-Offspring-Smash/], April 28, 2007. Retrieved 2012-01-26. The collection was endorsed 6 periods platinum in the U.S and traded further compared to 12 million duplicates international.

Faithless Heart - Background

The foremost 2 selects as of Lead Me On (Amy Grant album)|Lead Me On broken the normal pop graphs in extension to topping the U.S. Christian graphs. The album's 4 still existing selects, nevertheless, charted solely on Christian broadcast. The discharge of Faithless Heart appeared at a time once Grant was at what appeared to be the stature of her vocation, experiencing not long ago come to be the foremost Contemporary Christian tunes creator to attain triumph on pop broadcast (though she ought to afterward attain long considerable triumph in the 1990s). It as well appeared at a time once Grant and her spouse at the time, Gary Chapman (musician)|Gary Chapman, remained positioned so as to face continuing Marital difficulties. Chapman had fought dope dependence in the 1980s however it was Faithless Heart that foremost Clued the common in to the difficulties that Grant fronted at home. Grant and Chapman separated 10 annums afterward.

The Lead Me On (Amy Grant album)|Lead Me On collection is extensively contemplated one of the largest and nearly all prosperous Christian collections at any time recorded and was designated the largest of altogether time by CCM Magazine.

List of artists who reached number one on the U.S.

Adult Contemporary chart - G

* Art Garfunkel
* Gale Garnett
* John Gary
* Genesis (band)|Genesis
* Stan Getz / Astrud Gilberto
* Barry Gibb
* Bobby Goldsboro
* Gotye
* Goo Goo Dolls
* **Amy Grant**
* Lorne Greene
* Josh Groban

Sparrow Records - Current Artists

* Above the Golden State
* Bellarive
* City Harbor
* Crowder (musician)|Crowder
* Danyew
* Colton Dixon (with 19 Recordings)
* Jon Foreman
* Peter Furler
* **Amy Grant**
* Matt Hammitt

* Adam Hayworth
* Hillsong Live
* Hillsong United (band)|Hillsong United
* Hillsong Young Free
* Kari Jobe
* Luminate
* Mandisa
* Shawn McDonald
* Newsboys
* Britt Nicole (with Capitol Records)
* Christy Nockels
* Nichole Nordeman
* Passion

* Matt Redman
* Sarah Reeves
* Rony Renfrow
* Samestate
* Sanctus Real
* Soulfire Revolution
* Michael W. Smith (with Capitol Records)
* Kristian Stanfill
* Switchfoot
* TobyMac
* Chris Tomlin
* Matthew West
* Josh Wilson (musician)|Josh Wilson

Better Than a Hallelujah - Track listing

#Better Than a Hallelujah - 3:44

Although there was an Ambient Mix (3:34) produced of the tune, it was not accessible on the sole however was afterward disseminated within 2011 as a trail on the extended issue of the collection Somewhere Down The Road (Amy Grant album)|Somewhere Down the Road.

Simple Things (Amy Grant album)

'Simple Things' is the 19th collection by Contemporary Christian music|Christian tunes and pop tunes singer-songwriter Amy Grant, disseminated within 2003 in music|2003.

Grant's foremost nonreligious collection (while holding Christian themes) eversince 1997's Behind the Eyes (Amy Grant album)|Behind the Eyes, Simple Things did not perceive the normal triumph alike to Grant's collections as of the 1990s. While the collection exceeded Billboard (magazine)|Billboard's Christian collection graph and the name trail grew to be a Top Ten Christian sole, Simple Things reached its highest point simply external the Top 20 on the Billboard 200, at #23. The name trail reached its highest point at the similar placing on the Adult Contemporary graph.

Jimmy Webb

'James Layne Jimmy Webb' (born August 15, 1946) is an American composer, melodist, and vocalist. He has authored countless gold record|platinum-selling epitomes, containing Up, Up and Away (song)|Up, Up and Away, By the Time I Get to Phoenix, Wichita Lineman, Galveston (song)|Galveston, The Worst That Could Happen, All I Know, and MacArthur Park (song)|MacArthur Park. His tunes have been accomplished by numerous well-liked modern creators, containing The 5th Dimension, Glen Campbell, The Supremes, Richard Harris, Johnny Maestro, Frank Sinatra, Thelma Houston, The Temptations, Barbra Streisand, Art Garfunkel, Joe Cocker, Judy Collins, Donna Summer, Linda Ronstadt, America (band)|America, Amy Grant, John Denver, Michael Feinstein, Rosemary Clooney, R.E.M., and Carly Simon.

Webb was inaugurated in to the Songwriters Hall of Fame in 1986 and the Nashville Songwriters Hall of Fame in 1990. He experienced the National Academy of Songwriters Lifetime Achievement Award in 1993, the Songwriters Hall of Fame Johnny Mercer Award in 2003, the ASCAP Voice of Music Award in 2006, and the Ivor Novello Awards|Ivor Novello Special International Award in 2012. According to Broadcast Music Incorporated|BMI, his tune By the Time I Get to Phoenix was the 3rd nearly all accomplished tune in the fifty annums amid 1940 and 1990. Webb is the solely creator at any time to have experienced Grammy Awards for tunes, words, and arrangement.

Chevelle - Christianity controversy

Chevelle has triggered disagreement amid Christian groupings, since at one point they remained on a Christian rock label, and consequently the group has wrongly been tagged Christian rock. Keith Miller of EvangelSociety.org has been serious of Chevelle expected to the group touring on Ozzfest with groups such like Cradle of Filth, whoever he asserts integrate forceful diabolical and anti-Christian subjects in to their words. Sam Loeffler indicated, It's somewhat that is undoubtedly going to come after us about incessantly and that is great. It's appealing straightforward. We initially signed with a record corporation that was sponsored by Word Records|Word (a Christian label lodging John Tesh and Amy Grant), thus the record [Point #1] was in Christian book stores. It was actually an accidental object.

Chevelle has attempted to space themself as of being tagged as a Christian group. Sam teasingly declared in an conference, We're recuperating Catholics. Sam as well informed the Chicago Tribune, Our persuasion is nevertheless very essential to us, however it's as well real private. None of us perceives being a rock group on stage ought to be a stand for preaching.

Pete Loeffler as well indicated in a 2009 interview: To us, it was and is, not that great of a transact. Our foremost label was possessed by a distributorship that dispersed to Christian book stores and items like that. And it does not trouble us at all to be named a Christian group. Although we have produced a concrete point to hold our faith out of our group and out of our exhibits since we trust it is everybody's option to proceed and undertake whatsoever they desire. And although we do have our single faiths and altogether these items, it is not somewhat that we will sermonize to the folks out there. So there remained not ever whatever misapprehensions for us either for our label in that considers. It actually was what everyone other was placing out there.

Faithless Heart

'Faithless Heart' is a 1988 sole by Contemporary Christian music|Christian tunes vocalist Amy Grant. It was disseminated like the 6th and ultimate sole as of Grant's real prosperous Lead Me On (Amy Grant album)|Lead Me On collection. Unlike a few of Grant's foregoing selects, this tune produced a selling and airplay influence on Christian broadcast however not on Pop music|pop either normal broadcast.

Faithless Heart is a down-tempo tune that triggered eyebrows to rise once it was disseminated within the belated 1980s. The tunes embraces a haunting sound with Hammond organ tunes, Whispering, and ominous context voices. The real private words particular Grant's hesitations about her wedding with then-husband Gary Chapman (musician)|Gary Chapman. In the tune, she deliberates her enticement to stroll out on her spouse however her intransigent option to withstand enticement and pick the individual that waits for myself with a heart that is genuine. Such communications of distrust had been a principal subject of Grant's tunes up to the point and subsequently, however the words that a few detected as hinting at annulment either polygamy produced a few in the Christian group anxious. Nevertheless, the tune was prosperous on Christian broadcast.

The tune has experienced general serious commend and is this day frequently signalled as a courageous masterwork. In a 2002 Lifetime (TV network)|Lifetime docudrama on Grant's vocation, the artist's administrators singled out Faithless Heart as a timeless tune that produced them real pleased of Grant's vocation, notwithstanding the disagreement they fronted once the tune disseminated to broadcast.

Adult contemporary music - Contemporary Christian music

Contemporary Christian tunes (CCM) has some sub-genres, one being Christian AC. Radio Records, for example, catalogs Christian AC amid its setup graphs. There has been crossing to normal and very warm AC setups by numerous of the central part creators of the Christian AC category, especially Amy Grant, Michael W. Smith, Kathy Troccoli, Steven Curtis Chapman, Plumb (band)|Plumb, and further not long ago, MercyMe.

Big Yellow Taxi - Lyrics variations

There are different slight changes of the words as of dissimilar adaptations. Joni Mitchell's first variant runs
while in Amy Grant's variant, the folks are charged twenty-five bucks, and in Joni Mitchell's 2007 re-recording the folks are charged an arm and a leg.

Bob Dylan in lieu of crooning about the great yellow cab that took off my aged individual sings A great yellow dozer took off the home and terra firma. Similarly, in Mitchell's live variant of the tune disseminated on Miles of Aisles in 1974, she sings about a great yellow Tractor that thrusted about my home, thrusted about my terra firma. She additionally replicates the similar poetry, however with the first words. **While Amy Grant keeps the cab, her ultimate repeat of the line about paved paradise peruses vapor spinned paradise.**

The Christmas Collection (Amy Grant album)

'The Christmas Collection' is a Christmas music|Christmas compiling collection disseminated by United States|American Pop music|pop and Contemporary Christian music|Christian vocalist Amy Grant in 2008. It is her second Christmas compiling collection, following 2005's My Best Christmas.

According to Amy Grant's formal internet site,

1980 in music - Release Date Unknown

* A-Z (album)|A-Z – Colin Newman

* Acnalbasac Noom – Slapp Happy
* Alone Together (Clare Fischer album)|Alone Together – Clare Fischer
* Andy Gibb's Greatest Hits – Andy Gibb
* Another String of Hits – The Shadows
* Army Life – The Exploited
* Authority Stealing – Fela Kuti
* Autumn (George Winston album)|Autumn – George Winston
* Baby's Got a Gun – The Only Ones
* The Barbara Dickson Album – Barbara Dickson
* The Beginning – Midnight Star
* Between a Hard Place and the Ground – Mike Bloomfield
* Bird Noises – Midnight Oil
* Blue Angel (Blue Angel album)|Blue Angel – Blue Angel (band)|Blue Angel
* The Brains (The Brains album)|The Brains – The Brains
* Breaking Glass – Hazel O'Connor – Soundtrack
* Brother Ray is at it Again – Ray Charles
* Bunny Wailer Sings the Wailers – Bunny Wailer
* Butcher Baby (EP) – Plasmatics
* Camellia III and Camellia IV – Ebiet G. Ade
* Carnaval (Spyro Gyra album)|Carnaval – Spyro Gyra
* Caught You – Steel Pulse
* Change of Address (album)|Change of Address – The Shadows
* Cognac Bologna – Doug and the Slugs
* The Correct Use of Soap – Magazine (band)|Magazine
* A Decade of Rock and Roll 1970 to 1980 – REO Speedwagon – Compilation
* Dome 1 – Dome (band)|Dome
* Drastic Measures – 7 Seconds (band)|7 Seconds – cassette
* Dub Disco – Bunny Wailer
* East – Cold Chisel
* 80/81 – Pat Metheny
* Eje Nlogba – King Sunny Ade
* Star Wars Episode V: The Empire Strikes Back (soundtrack)|Empire Strikes Back Soundtrack – John Williams – Soundtrack
* Exploited Barmy Army – The Exploited
* The First, the Best and the Last – Sham 69
* Framed – Asleep at the Wheel
* Frost and Fire (album)|Frost and Fire – Cirith Ungol (band)|Cirith Ungol
* Gamma 2 – Gamma (band)|Gamma
* Gap Band III – The Gap Band
* The Game (Sham 69 album)|The Game – Sham 69
* Glass House Rock – Greg Kihn
* God Save the Queen/Under Heavy Manners – Robert Fripp
* Good News – Sweet Honey in the Rock

* Gravity (Fred Frith album)|Gravity – Fred Frith
* Greatest Hits (Rita Coolidge album)|Greatest Hits – Rita Coolidge
* Group Sex – Circle Jerks
* Gyrate – Pylon (band)|Pylon
* Hail H.I.M. – Burning Spear
* Half Mute – Tuxedomoon
* Hanx – Stiff Little Fingers
* Happy Woman Blues – Lucinda Williams
* Hideaway – David Sanborn
* Hold On – Carolyne Mas
* Humans (Bruce Cockburn album)|Humans – Bruce Cockburn
* I Am What I Am (George Jones album)|I Am What I Am – George Jones
* I Believe – The Buzzcocks
* Ikite Itemo Iidesuka – Miyuki Nakajima
* Immer nur träumen – Die Flippers
* In Concert, Zürich October 28, 1979 – Chick Corea and Gary Burton
* Inside Job – Dion DiMucci
* Inside My Brain – Angry Samoans
* The Inside Story – Robben Ford
* Iron Curtain Innocence – Bobb Trimble
* Is This Real? – Wipers
* It's What's Inside That Counts – Critical Mass (rock band)|Critical Mass
* Jack Rabbit! – Doug Dillard
* Jane as of Occupied Europe – Swell Maps
* Jazziz- John Serry, Jr.
* The Jealous Kind – Delbert McClinton
* Jeopardy (album)|Jeopardy – The Sound (band)|The Sound
* Joan Jett (album)|Joan Jett – Joan Jett
* Joy and Pain – Maze presenting Frankie Beverly
* Just Like That – Toots the Maytals
* Just Testing – Wishbone Ash
* Kano – Kano (band)|Kano
* Keeping Our Love Warm – Captain Tennille
* Lady T (Teena Marie album)|Lady T – Teena Marie
* Ladies Man (April Wine album)|Ladies Man – April Wine – Live EP
* Little Stevie Orbit – Steve Forbert
* ...Live... – Klaus Schulze – Live
* Live at Last – Good Rats
* Live at the North Sea Jazz Festival, 1980 (Oscar Peterson album)|Live at the North Sea Jazz Festival, 1980 – Oscar Peterson
* Live in der Balver Höhle – Piirpauke
* Live In Vienna – Cluster (band)|Cluster Farnbauer
* Live Seventy Nine – Hawkwind

* Living Dub – Burning Spear
* LKJ in Dub – Linton Kwesi Johnson
* The Long Riders – Ry Cooder
* Lookin' For Trouble – Toronto (band)|Toronto
* Looking at Bird – Archie Shepp
* Loonee Tunes! – Bad Manners
* The Lord Will Make a Way – Al Green

* Lose It Tonight – Commander Cody and His Lost Planet Airmen
* Love Crimes – Harlequin (band)|Harlequin
* Love in Exile – Eddy Grant
* Love Lives Forever – Minnie Riperton
* Love Zombies – The Monochrome Set
* Loverboy (Loverboy album)|Loverboy – Loverboy
* Maestra Vida: Primera Parte – Ruben Blades
* Me Myself I – Joan Armatrading
* Mekons – The Mekons
* Memento Z banalnym tryptykiem – SBB (band)|SBB
* Michael Franks with Crossfire Live – Michael Franks (musician)|Michael Franks
* Merzbild Schwet – Nurse With Wound
* Ming (album)|Ming – David Murray (jazz musician)|David Murray Octet
* Monster (Herbie Hancock album)|Monster – Herbie Hancock
* Music of Many Colors – Fela Kuti with Roy Ayers
* A Musical Affair – Ashford and Simpson
* My Babe – Roy Buchanan
* **Never Alone – Amy Grant**
* New Hope for the Wretched – Plasmatics
* Night Passage (Weather Report album)|Night Passage – Weather Report
* 1980 – Gil Scott Heron
* Now We May Begin – Randy Crawford
* Nurds – The Roches
* Off the Coast of Me – Kid Creole and the Coconuts
* The Official Secrets Act (album)|Official Secrets Act – M (band)|M
* On the Edge (The Babys album)|On the Edge – The Babys
* One Bad Habit – Michael Franks (musician)|Michael Franks
* 100 M.P.H. – Vardis
* Operation Radication – Yellowman
* Ori Mi Ja Fun Mi – King Sunny Ade
* Paranoid Time (EP) – Minutemen (band)|Minutemen
* Party 'Til You're Broke – Rufus (band)|Rufus
* Paul Davis – Paul Davis (singer)|Paul Davis
* Penguin Eggs – Nic Jones
* People – James Brown

* The Personal Touch – Oscar Peterson
* Play – Magazine (band)|Magazine
* Play Me either Trade Me – Parlet
* Rastakraut Pasta – Moebius Plank
* Real Eyes – Gil Scott Heron
* Red Exposure – Chrome (band)|Chrome
* Reflections (Chet Atkins and Doc Watson album)|Reflections – Chet Atkins
* Répression – Trust (band)|Trust
* Roberta Flack Featuring Donny Hathaway – Roberta Flack and Donny Hathaway
* Roky Erickson and the Aliens – Roky Erickson|Roky Erickson and the Aliens
* Running for My Life – Judy Collins
* Sails of Silver – Steeleye Span
* San Antonio Blues – Willie Nelson with Ray Price (musician)|Ray Price
* Selbstportrait - Vol. II – Hans-Joachim Roedelius
* Selbstportrait Vol. III Reise durch Arcadien – Hans-Joachim Roedelius
* Silent Knight (album)|Silent Knight – Saga (band)|Saga
* Something Better Change – D.O.A. (band)|D.O.A.
* Snap Crackle and Bop – John Cooper Clarke
* Sneak Me In – Lucifer's Friend
* Snockgrass – Michael Hurley (musician)|Michael Hurley
* Social Studies – Carla Bley
* Something Better Change – D.O.A. (band)|D.O.A.
* Songs the Lord Taught Us – The Cramps
* S.O.S. (S.O.S. Band album)|S.O.S. – The S.O.S. Band
* Soul Syndrome – James Brown
* Spellbound – Dennis Brown
* Stone Jam – Slave (band)|Slave
* Storm Windows – John Prine
* Strange Boutique (album)|Strange Boutique – The Monochrome Set
* Sunrise in Different Dimensions – Sun Ra
* Sweat Band – Sweat Band
* Take It Easy Baby – Buckwheat Zydeco
* Tears and Laughter – Johnny Mathis
* Tennis (album)|Tennis – Chris Rea
* This Time (Al Jarreau album)|This Time – Al Jarreau
* To the Quiet Men as of a Tiny Girl – Nurse With Wound
* Touch – Touch (band)|Touch
* Trilogy: Past Present Future – Frank Sinatra
* Truth Decay (album)|Truth Decay – T-Bone Burnett
* Two (GQ album)|Two – GQ (band)|GQ
* Two Bit Monsters – John Hiatt
* Two Miles as of Heaven – Mott the Hoople – Compilation
* Ultra Wave – Bootsy Collins

* The Unknown Soldier (album)|The Unknown Soldier - Roy Harper
* Up-Front (EP)|Up-Front – The Fleshtones
* The Voice of America (album)|The Voice of America – Cabaret Voltaire (band)|Cabaret Voltaire
* Wanna Be A Star – Chilliwack (band)|Chilliwack
* Waters Edge – Sweet (band)|Sweet
* We Are...Every One of Us – Sweet Honey in the Rock
* When Two Worlds Collide – Jerry Lee Lewis
* Who's Been Talking – Robert Cray|The Robert Cray Band
* Yellow EP|Untitled (Yellow EP) – Gang of Four (band)|Gang of Four
* Young And Restless – Prism (band)|Prism
* Your Cassette Pet – Bow Wow Wow
* Zydeco Gris Gris – BeauSoleil

Big Yellow Taxi - Cover versions

Many different creators have veiled the tune.

*A sole variant by the crooning cluster The Neighborhood extended the Billboard Top 40 graph (No. 29) in the summertime of 1970.
*Joe Dassin Le Grand Parking (French Cover) in 1970 as of the collection La Fleur AUX Dents.
*Bob Dylan's cover of Joni Mitchell's Big Yellow Taxi was recorded in 1970 and disseminated within 1973.Dylan (1973 album)
*BB Gabor re-interpreted it on his BB_Gabor_(album)|1980 eponymous collection.
*Pinhead Gunpowder cover the tune on their 1994 collection Jump Salty.
***In 1995, Amy Grant disseminated a cover of Big Yellow Taxi to pop and Adult Contemporary broadcast in the United States and United Kingdom. The tune was the 4th pop broadcast sole as of her House of Love (Amy Grant album)|House of Love collection (the 3rd in the U.S.). Grant's variant highlighted somewhat changed words, that she altered at Joni Mitchell's appeal. The sole reached its highest point at No. 67 on The Billboard Hot 100, No. 18 on the Adult Contemporary graph, and at No. 20 in the U.K. Grant as well disseminated a tunes audiovisual for the sole, that was screened in the U.S. And U.K. And disseminated to home audiovisual on Grant's Greatest Videos 1986-2004 DVD. Grant as well accomplished the tune for her 2006 musical performance collection, Time Again... Amy Grant Live.**
*In 1996 a Big Yellow Taxi (Traffic Jam Mix) reached its highest point on the Hot Dance Club Play|U.S. Sway graphs at No. 39 and was piece of the Friends discography|Friends: Music as of the TV Series sound recording collection (see Joni_Mitchell_discography#Singles|Joni Mitchell's Singles and #External links|External links).

*The tune is sampled in Janet Jackson and Q-Tip (rapper)|Q-Tip's sole Got 'Til It's Gone, as of Jackson's 1997 collection The Velvet Rope.
*CKBE-FM David Tyler (radio personality)|David Tyler.
*Counting Crows presenting Vanessa Carlton (on back-up vocals) cover of the tune is highlighted onto the sound recording to the feature Two Weeks Notice and is the most prosperous variant to date (U.S. Billboard Adult Top 40). Originally the tune was a concealed trail on the band's 2002 collection Hard Candy (Counting Crows album)|Hard Candy and did not contain Vanessa Carlton till it was to be highlighted in the feature. New deliverances of the collection contained it like a trail with her appended, as with her in the audiovisual, though Counting Crows and Vanessa Carlton did not emerge in the audiovisual alltogether either record alltogether. This tune grew to be the band's solely Top 20 sole in the UK, peaking at No. 13. This variant somewhat altered Mitchell's first words to report once the eponymous cab took my female child off, in lieu of Mitchell's my aged individual.
*This tune is sampled by Labrinth in the tune Sundown as of his first public appearance 2012 collection Electronic Earth.http://www.bbc.co.uk/music/reviews/vmwx
* Kelly Rowland tests this tune in the trail Gone, on her 2013 collection, Talk a Good Game.
* Australian vocal cluster The Idea of North recorded a cover on their 2013 collection Smile.

Thomas Schlamme - Production

Schlamme repositioned as of his innate Houston to New York in 1973. After servicing in some low layer stances for manufacture businesses, he set up his personal corporation, Schlamme Productions, in 1980. From there, he created crusades for a numeral of musicals, containing Cats (musical)|Cats. He directed the foremost I Want My MTV! marketing drive in 1981 for maker Buzz Potamkin, and singer/songwriter Amy Grant's 1985 tunes audiovisual Find A Way for creators Fred Seibert and Alan Goodman. Throughout the 1980s, he created a numeral of specials on different performers containing Whoopi Goldberg and Rowan Atkinson.

Starting in the belated 1990s, he serviced like maker for exhibits such like Tracey Takes On... And has managed exhibits such like Ally McBeal, Boston Public, Friends, ER (TV series)|ER and Shaun Cassidy's movement best-loved discipline stories TV show Invasion (TV series)|Invasion.

Jim Brickman - Brickhouse Direct

Brickman set up Brickhouse Direct (BHD) in 2003, a corporation that delivers planned promoting and e-commerce results for customers in a diversity of

businesses. Brickhouse Direct has completed work for a ample span of customers over the annums containing Universal Music, Concord Music Group, Carly Simon, Michael W. Smith, Amy Grant, Sandi Patty, Casey Kasem, Dave Koz, Chris Sligh, Lenz Entertainment, Anita Renfroe and numerous other ones.

Christian music industry - History

The Christian tunes business has origins in the belated 1960s and first 1970s Jesus Movement and its Jesus Music creators. The Encyclopedia of Contemporary Christian Music details out 3 rationales that the Christian tunes business elaborated as a collateral construction to the common tunes business. First, the Jesus motion created a great numeral of groups in a real small time, that the common trade was incapable either-or reluctant to attract. This was in piece expected to a absence of gratitude for the beliefs communicated by such creators. Finally, Jesus tunes creators inclined towards distrust of nonreligious organizations. According to one other commentator, the business in this time was described by 4 characteristics: absence of public receipt for methods, lesser manufacture, ineffective dispersion, and absence of ample broadcast subjection. Petra (band)|Petra, for example, fought to notice an public for their tough rock sound, partly expected to restricted dispersion to Christian book stores.

Even thus, the 1970s saw great organizations come to be included in the Christian tunes trade. Word Records, set up in 1951, was purchased in 1976 by ABC Records|ABC. Other tunes business behemoths as well received included, Columbia Records|CBS commenced a brief Christian label, Priority Records, and MCA Records|MCA as well fielded a label for a time.

While the Jesus motion had finished by the 1980s, the Christian tunes business was developing and changing in to a multi-million buck organization. The first 1980s saw an rise Christian booksellers seizing article, and an rise in selling pursued, notwithstanding Domestic plan of the Reagan administration#Reaganomics and the economy|the slump. As a fraction of gross selling, Christian tunes rose as of 9% in 1976 to 23% in 1985. By Age to Age|her 1982 discharge Amy Grant had inundated the Christian market and produced important advances in to the common trade. Sandi Patti and Michael W. Smith as well obtained impact inside Christian tunes, every one performing important parts within the creation of the business.

Harder forms of Christian tunes, such like alloy music|heavy alloy, as well started to obtain receipt. This is mostly recognized to Stryper, whoever had started creating advances in to the common trade by 1985. Still, rock and Christian alternate rock|alternative acts fronted a lengthier combat for receipt compared to Contemporary Christian music|contemporary acts, as the shape was against by important devout directors such like Jimmy Swaggart and other ones on the Christian right. While in 1981 whole canon tunes business earnings remained about $180 million, solely 10 annums afterward they ought to whole $680 million, depending to CCM Magazine.

According to RIAA information, trade share for selling of Christian tunes collections further compared to doubled amid 1993 and 1997. In the 1990s the Christian tunes business grew to be the quickest increasing section of the tunes business. This was expected to some circumstances, containing integration of record labels, and autonomous Christian book stores in to chains.

The Christian tunes business started embracing SoundScan in 1995, though effectuation was aperiodic even in to the millenary. Even thus, the acceptance triggered the clarity of Christian creators to rise notably, and accompanied trustworthiness to the business as Christian collections grew to be amalgamated in to altogether Billboard charts|Billboard graphs.

In 1985, 90% of Christian tunes selling derived at Christian book stores. By 1995, that numeral had let go to 64%, with common retail traders seizing 21%, and the residue responsible via additional techniques, such like straight post. At that similar time, the business was approximated to gross $750 million, with $381 million in collection selling. In the belated 1990s, common trade retail traders, particularly great container stores such like Best Buy, Wal-Mart, Target Corporation|Target, and Blockbuster Inc.|Blockbuster started bearing a broader choice of Christian tunes articles. By 2000 these stores had excelled Christian trade in specifications of the numeral of Christian collections traded, depending to Soundscan numerals. This occurrence was partly accountable for crossing triumphs. P.O.D., for instance, traded 1.4 million collections in 2001, though selling at Christian trade outlet vents considered for solely 10%.

The spic-and-span millenary has accompanied 2000s in tunes industry|challenges for the record business as a entire, and those have influenced the Christian tunes business as well. Contemporary reverence tunes, a prolonged time pin of the business, started to obtain important trade share in regarding the annum 2000. By concentrating on promoting reverence tunes to teens intellectual/artistic awareness, this category grew to be a development driver notwithstanding the downswing in the common tunes business.

Growth sustained till about 2003, however has normally pursued the tendencies of the greater tunes business eversince that point. In 2009 a The New York Times op-ed put the whole tunes business on a deathwatch, signalling out that spic-and-span forms of media, pirating, and spic-and-span costing choices are powering gross selling down. In one other illustration of correspondence, the Christian tunes business has accomplished mostly the similar occurrence. In the Christian market, tunes use has risen by as a lot like 30% eversince 2005, however altogether collection selling have let go to regarding fifty per cent of their 1999 degrees. However, a few reviewers point out that the present downswing might have prolonged period optimistic results for the business. John J. Thompson informed Christianity Today that The absence of financial help has filtered out a few of the folks whoever ought to not have been undertaking this in the foremost place. If the folks whoever are in it for the cash are moved, it departs further ground for these whoever had somewhat a itty-bitty bit loftier in mind.

House of Love (Amy Grant album) - UK version

 # Lucky One (Amy Grant, Keith Thomas) – 4:11
 # Say You'll Be Mine (Amy Grant, Wayne Kirkpatrick, Keith Thomas) – 4:04
 # Whatever It Takes (Amy Grant, Gary Chapman, Keith Thomas) – 4:10
House of Love (duet with Vince Gill) (Greg Barnhill, Kenny Greenberg, Wally Wilson) – 4:38
The Power (Tommy Sims, Judson Spence) – 3:54
Oh How the Years Go By (Simon Climie, Will Jennings) – 5:12
Big Yellow Taxi (Joni Mitchell) – 3:01
 # Helping Hand (Amy Grant, Tommy Sims, Beverly Darnall) – 4:39
 # Politics of Kissing (Amy Grant, Clif Magness, Wayne Kirkpatrick) – 4:17
 # Love Has a Hold On Me (Amy Grant, Keith Thomas) – 3:55
 # Our Love (Amy Grant, Tom Hemby) – 5:08
 # Children of the World (Amy Grant, Wayne Kirkpatrick, Tommy Sims) – 5:16
 # Say You'll Be Mine (Radio Mix) (Amy Grant, Wayne Kirkpatrick, Keith Thomas) – 3:57

31st Annual Grammy Awards - Gospel

*Grammy Award for Best Gospel Vocal Performance, Female|Best Gospel Performance, Female
****Amy Grant for Lead Me On**
*Grammy Award for Best Gospel Vocal Performance, Male|Best Gospel Performance, Male
**Larnelle Harris for Christmas

*Grammy Award for Best Gospel Vocal Performance by a Duo either Group, Choir either Chorus|Best Gospel Performance by a Duo either Group, Choir either Chorus
**The Winans for The Winans Live at Carnegie Hall
*Grammy Award for Best Soul Gospel Performance, Female|Best Soul Gospel Performance, Female
**Aretha Franklin for One Lord, One Faith, One Baptism
*Grammy Award for Best Soul Gospel Performance, Male|Best Soul Gospel Performance, Male
**BeBe Winans for Abundant Life
*Grammy Award for Best Soul Gospel Performance by a Duo either Group, Choir either Chorus|Best Soul Gospel Performance by a Duo either Group, Choir either Chorus
**Take 6 for Take 6

Wayne Kirkpatrick

'Wayne Kirkpatrick' (born C. 1961) is an United States|American composer and performer born in Baton Rouge, Louisiana however at the moment lives in Nashville, Tennessee|Nashville, Tennessee. He graduated as of Baton Rouge Magnet High School in 1979.

Kirkpatrick has consumed nearly all of his vocation in the context, frequently delivering context voices, performing stringed instrument, performing keyboards either authoring tunes for different creators. Writing in Contemporary Christian, Country, and Pop methods, his tunes have been recorded by Little Big Town, Faith Hill, Garth Brooks, Kenneth Babyface Edmonds|Babyface, Amy Grant, Joe Cocker, Kathy Mattea, Martina McBride, Wynonna Judd, Trisha Yearwood, Bonnie Raitt, Susan Ashton, Michael W. Smith, Jill Phillips, Michael Crawford, Peter Frampton, Casting Crowns and Eric Clapton, whose variant of Kirkpatrick's Change the World gained the Grammy Award for Song of the Year.

At the 24th GMA Dove Awards, Kirkpatrick experienced the prize for Producer of the Year.

In 2005, Kirkpatrick commenced to make Little Big Town next to the cluster beginning with their second collection The Road to Here and as well the following 2 A Place to Land (Little Big Town album) The Reason Why. He as well co-wrote nearly all of the tunes on altogether 3 collections with the cluster.

Also in 2005, The Road to Here appeared out for Little Big Town. Kirkpatrick has authoring debt on 12 of the 13 tunes. He has unaccompanied authoring acclaims on one tune, Looking For The Reason, with the respite authored with him and part/all of the cluster either with different songwriters. He co-wrote with cluster participants on their biggest graphing tune Bring It on Home, that produced it to No.4 on Hot Country 100 tunes graph. Kirkpatrick as well authored Little Big Town's 'signature' tune, Boondocks, that they employ like the ending tune at any display.

In 2007, Little Big Town and Kirkpatrick proceeded back in to the workshop to create a spic-and-span record, A Place to Land (Little Big Town album)|A Place to Land. He co-wrote 12 of the 16 traces on the Deluxe Edition, containing the real foremost tune that Little Big Town chanted alltogether named Love Profound.

In 2010, the latest record as of Little Big Town, The Reason Why, was disseminated that Kirkpatrick co-produced. The record launched at No.1, a foremost for Little Big Town. He co-wrote 7 of the 12 tunes with the cluster, containing the hit Little White Church.

Kirkpatrick has indicated that Karen Fairchild, Jimi Westbrook, Kimberly Schlapman and Philip Sweet have produced him sense like the 5th associate of the group.

In 2000, Kirkpatrick disseminated a unaccompanied program allowed The Maple Room that contained Wrapped Up in You, a tune that ought to afterward come to be a hit for Garth Brooks, and My Armageddon, that was initially planned for Brooks' Garth Brooks in ... The Life of Chris Gaines program. Kirkpatrick serviced like a main composer on that collection, alongside with Gordon Kennedy (musician)|Gordon Kennedy and Tommy Sims.

Later in 2000, he linked up with Kennedy and some different songwriters (Phil Madeira and Billy Sprague) to record Coming From Somewhere Else, that was a CD of their personal tunes that had formerly been recorded by different creators, containing Change the World.

Gary Chapman (musician) - Early life and music career

Born in Waurika, Oklahoma, Chapman is the boy of an Assemblies of God minister, Terry Chapman. He matured up in De Leon, Texas|De Leon, Texas.

Chapman accomplished in groups all over elevated educational institution and school. After going to Bible school at what is at the moment Southwestern Assemblies of God University in Waxahachie, Texas, he repositioned to Nashville, Tennessee and was employed as stringed instrument participant

for The Rambos. In 1979, his tune Father's Eyes was recorded as the name trail to Amy Grant's Grammy-nominated second collection My Father's Eyes (album)|My Father's Eyes. In 1982, his tune Finally recorded by T. G. Sheppard extended No. 1 on the region tunes graphs. He as well experienced a GMA Dove Awards|Dove Award like Songwriter of the Year as of the Gospel Music Association in 1981.

During the respite of the 1980s and the first 1990s, Chapman sustained to record, record, and make tunes, when touring as an beginning play for different creators. He chanted Brave Hearts in 1987 for the Touchstone Pictures feature Ernest Goes to Camp.

He was proposed for a Grammy Award for Best Pop/Contemporary Gospel Album in 1994. The Light Inside as well followed in a Dove Award recommendation for Male Vocalist of the Year. It as well remitted a modern Christian tunes graph No. 1 tune, Sweet Glow of Mercy. He gained a second Dove Award in 1994 for co-producing the collection, Songs as of the Loft, presenting different creators.

In April 1996, Chapman gained Male Vocalist of the Year at the GMA Dove Awards. His 1996 collection, Shelter, provided one other No.1, One of Two, with Man After Your Own Heart ensuing in a Dove Award for Inspirational Recorded Song of the Year and presenting on the Dove prize conquering Special Event Album of the Year, My Utmost for His Highest (album)|My Utmost for His Highest. Shelter as well experienced a 1997 Grammy recommendation for Best Pop/Contemporary Gospel Album. At the 1998 Dove Awards, his collection as well presenting additional creators, Hymns From The Ryman, gained Country Album of the Year.

Christmas Spirit (Donna Summer album)

'Christmas Spirit' is a Christmas-themed collection by Donna Summer, disseminated within 1994 in music|1994. Summer's Gospel tunes context is real obvious on this collection that comprises of customary and popular Christmas tunes and Christmas carols|carols, as well like spic-and-span first tunes and a cover of Amy Grant's Breath of Heaven (Mary's Song).

Christmas Spirit was created by Michael Omartian, whoever had co-operated with Summer on the collections She Works Hard for the Money and Cats Without Claws in the first 1980s, either as a maker and melodist. On this collection Omartian as well co-wrote the traces Christmas Is Here and Lamb of God with Summer, and the name trail next to Summer and her spouse Bruce Sudano. Traditional carols O Come All Ye Faithful, What Child Is This, Do You Hear What I Hear?, Joy To The World and O Holy Night are highlighted next to White Christmas (song)|White Christmas, The Christmas Song and I'll Be Home for Christmas, altogether of that are well known Christmas tunes.

Christmas Spirit was re-issued by Universal Music on the Mercury label in 2005 under the name '20th Century Masters: The Best of Donna Summer: The Christmas Collection'.

Breath of Heaven (Mary's Song)

'Home for Christmas' is the 13th collection by Contemporary Christian music|Christian tunes and pop tunes vocalist Amy Grant, disseminated within 1992 in music|1992.

Home for Christmas is Amy Grant's second break collection, the foremost being 1983's A Christmas Album (Amy Grant album)|A Christmas Album. coming off of the heels of Grant's hugely prosperous 1991 collection Heart in Motion, Home for Christmas accomplished even stronger compared to Heart in Motion on the Billboard magazine|Billboard graphs, arriving at No.2 on the Billboard 200|Billboard 200 and No.1 on the Christian collection graph. It was afterward reissued in 2003 as '20th Century Masters - The Christmas Collection: The Best of Amy Grant'. It has traded 2,542,000 duplicates as of December 2012.

Béla Fleck - Grammy nominations

Béla Fleck has been proposed in further classes compared to whatever different performer in Grammy past.
*2009
**Best Contemporary World Music Album Throw Down Your Heart
**Best Pop Instrumental Performance Throw Down Your Heart
**Best Classical Crossover Album The Melody Of Rhythm
*2008
**Pop Instrumental Album Jingle All The Way
**Country Instrumental Performance Sleigh Ride (from Jingle All The Way)
*2006
**Pop Instrumental Subterfuge (from The Hidden Land)

*2005
**Country Instrumental Who's Your Uncle (from Best Kept Secret by Jerry Douglas)
**Contemporary Jazz Album Soulgrass by Bill Evans (saxophonist)|Bill Evans
*2002
**Country Instrumental Performance Bear Mountain Hop (from The Country Bears Soundtrack)
*2000
**Pop Instrumental Zona Mona (from Outbound (Béla Fleck and the Flecktones album)|Outbound)
*1999
**Bluegrass Bluegrass Sessions
*1998
**Pop Instrumental Big Country (from Left Of Cool)
**Country Instrumental The Ride (from Restless On the Farm by Jerry Douglas)
*1996
**World Music Tabula Rasa
*1995
**Country Instrumental Cheeseballs In Cowtown (from The Bluegrass Sessions: Tales as of the Acoustic Planet, Vol. 2)
*1994
****Spoken Word For Children The Creation by Amy Grant**
*1992
**Jazz Instrumental Magic Fingers (from UFO Tofu)
*1991
**Jazz Album Flight of the Cosmic Hippo
**Jazz Instrumental Blu-Bop
*1990
**Jazz Album Béla Fleck The Flecktones
**Jazz Instrumental
*1989
**Country Instrumental Bigfoot (from Friday Night In America by New Grass Revival
*1988
**Bluegrass collection Drive
*1987
**Country Instrumental Metric Lips (from Hold to a Dream by New Grass Revival)
*1986
**Country Instrumental Seven By Seven (from New Grass Revival by New Grass Revival)

Soundstage (TV series) - Season 2: 2004

* Fleetwood Mac at the TD Banknorth Garden|FleetCenter in West End Boston,

June 2004 [http://www.fleetwoodmac-uk.com/articles/presskits/pr_liveinboston.html Press Release], Sep. 10, 2005
* Sheryl Crow, June 2004
* Ronald Isley and Burt Bacharach, July 2004
* Alanis Morissette, July 2004
* Lisa Marie Presley and Peter Wolf, July 2004
* Cyndi Lauper, August 2004
* Joan Baez, Gillian Welch, and Nickel Creek, August 2004
* Counting Crows and Shelby Lynne, August 2004
* Dan Fogelberg, September 2004
* Steve Winwood, September 2004
* 30 Odd Foot of Grunts and Kris Kristofferson, September 2004
* Yes (band)|Yes at Tsongas Arena, Lowell, MA, September 2004
* Chris Isaak Christmas collection Special, with visitors Michael Bublé, Brian McKnight and Stevie Nicks, September 2004
* **George Jones 50 Years Special, with visitors Alan Jackson, Kenny Chesney, Wynonna, Martina McBride, Aaron Neville, Harry Connick Jr., Randy Travis, Lorrie Morgan, Vince Gill, Trick Pony, Amy Grant, Sammy Kershaw, Trace Adkins, Uncle Kracker, Connie Smith, Emmylou Harris, Joe Diffie, Kris Kristofferson, Shelby Lynne and Tanya Tucker, November 2004**

Ocean Way Recording

'Ocean Way Recording' is the designation of a serials of transcriptioning studios in Hollywood, California and Nashville, Tennessee. Ocean Way Studios is well familiar in the transcriptioning business expected to the award-winning collections that remained created there.http://www.oceanwayrecording.com/about-awards.php

The first United Western studios, created within 1952, was the home of numerous chief transcriptioning meetings in the 1960s and 1970s, containing Ray Charles' variant of I Can't Stop Loving You, The Beach Boys' Good Vibrations, Frank Sinatra's It Was a Very Good Year, and The Mamas the Papas' California Dreamin'. Bill Putnam, the first possessor, traded it to Allen Sides in 1985, whoever rebranded it Ocean Way Recording. In 1999, the first Ocean Way/Western Recorders provision at 6000 Sunset Blvd. Was traded to Cello Recording Studios (now EastWest Studios), and Sides kept the constructing following entrance at 6050 Sunset Blvd. http://www.oceanwayrecording.com/about-history.php

Two extra studios remained afterward appended to the Ocean Way Family; Record One studios in Sherman Oaks, Los Angeles, California|Sherman Oaks in 1988, and Ocean Way/Nashville unlocked on famed Music Row in 1997. The Ocean Way

Nashville provision was afterward traded to Belmont University. Ocean Way transcriptioning at the moment supports on trade at 2 places - Hollywood and Sherman Oaks. Additionally, Ocean Way Audio produces and markets Allen Sides' extremely considered screen speaker setups. Ocean Way Drums, in cooperation with maker Steven Miller, is generating melodic tool plug-ins.

Some elevated outline creators to have applied the studios include: Brad Mehldau, Paula Abdul, AC/DC, Steve Perry (musician) | Steve Perry, Whiskeytown, Deborah Allen, Bob Seger, Tori Amos, B.B. King, Biffy Clyro, Bon Jovi, B'z, Eric Clapton, Joe Cocker, Michael Jackson, Paul McCartney, No Doubt, Counting Crows, Dr. Dre, Bob Dylan, John Mayer, Fishbone, Amy Grant, Green Day, Elton John, Miles Davis, Waylon Jennings, Weezer, R. Kelly, K.d. Lang, Luis Miguel Gallego Basteri|Luis Miguel, Maná, Eminem, Meshell Ndegeocello, Willie Nelson, Aaron Neville, Tom Petty, Radiohead, Red Hot Chili Peppers, R.E.M. (band)|R.E.M., Richard Marx, Rolling Stones, Rush (band)|Rush, Joe Sample, Rod Stewart, Barbra Streisand, Tool (band)|Tool, Travis (band)|Travis, The Wallflowers|Wallflowers, XTC, Namie Amuro, Avril Lavigne, The Mars Volta, Toto (band)|Toto, and Billy Thermal (Record One), Australia's You Am I.

CPSIA information can be obtained at www.ICGtesting.com
Printed in the USA
BVOW10s1821240615

406017BV00006B/59/P

9 781488 557873